The
Path *of* Self-
Transformation

CLIMB THE HIGHEST MOUNTAIN SERIES

The
Path of Self-
Transformation

Mark L. Prophet · Elizabeth Clare Prophet

SUMMIT UNIVERSITY  PRESS®

Corwin Springs, Montana

THE PATH OF SELF-TRANSFORMATION
by Mark L. Prophet and Elizabeth Clare Prophet.
Copyright © 2000 by Summit University Press.
All rights reserved.

Library of Congress Catalog Card Number: 99-68543
ISBN: 0-922729-54-9

SUMMIT UNIVERSITY ✆ PRESS®

Summit University Press and ✆ are registered trademarks.
Printed in the United States of America

Cover: *Pearl of Searching,* a painting by Nicholas Roerich

05 04 03 02 01 00   6 5 4 3 2 1

*To sons and daughters of God
returning to their own Edenic consciousness*

Contents

THE THIRD RAY:
The Love of Twin Flames in the Hallowed Circle of God   143

2 · Reembodiment 241

Appendix:

Figures

Note: Because gender-neutral language can be cumbersome and at times confusing, we have used the pronouns *he* and *him* to refer to God or to the individual and *man* or *mankind* to refer to people in general. We have used these terms for readability and consistency, and they are not intended to exclude women or the feminine aspect of the Godhead. God is both masculine and feminine. We do, however, use the pronouns *she* and *her* to refer to the soul because each soul, whether housed in a male or a female body, is the feminine counterpart of the masculine Spirit.

Editor's Preface

T HE PATH OF SELF-TRANSFORMATION is the spiritual blossoming of the soul. To walk this path is to emerge from the effects of karmic sowings into an ever-new world, a world of infinite possibilities for growth and for renewal. This book is like a spiritual trailhead. To read it is to set off on a journey where karma is sensed not as something that just happens but as opportunity for spiritual progress.

Most seekers already know about the law of karma: that we reap what we sow. In an extreme case, if I kill a person in one life, that person may end up killing me in a subsequent life. This can lead to a seemingly endless tit-for-tat treadmill existence in the rounds of *samsara,* where souls are imprisoned by their own hatreds, cravings, delusions and other unwholesome momentums.

Indeed, the weavings of personal and planetary karma are complex. For instance, the mercy of karmic law may allow a deserving soul to suffer a relatively minor burn to make amends for causing others great pain through the misuse of fire. And often, group karma draws people together because they are compelled to encounter very specific situations together.

This book offers profound insight into the law of karma. It carries us far beyond the mere understanding of karmic interactions. Meditating on karma as it is presented here can bring us to feel the currents of God growing deep within and seeking resolution. Returning again and again to this book can transport us into realms of higher consciousness, there to learn to master our karma. Then the spiritual path truly becomes the path of self-transformation.

The Messengers did not complete their work on this volume. For instance, the original writing only included sections on the judgments of karma delivered by the Seven Archangels for the first through third rays. However, in order to prepare this volume for publication, at the direction of Mrs. Prophet, the portions from the Archangels of the fourth through the seventh rays were added.

Because portions of what is printed are unfinished, this book includes a few loose ends, apparent contradictions and unevenly developed concepts. Regardless, this book is fresh, insightful, and valuable beyond measure.

The purpose of all spiritual teaching is to bring the soul into consonance with her Higher Self. Thus it is wise to treasure one's communion with the Ascended Masters above any worded expression. For the outer expression can only approximate the Truth within.

In the hope that you may find it useful for your own understanding, I would like to share with you a discussion of one of the apparent contradictions in the text: the teaching on Adam and Eve's compromise of the Christ Flame in their hearkening to the beguiling Serpent.

This book implies, as the Ascended Masters have taught, that Adam and Eve were not the first people on earth. There were many who came before them. Much wickedness already existed in the earth at that time. Eden was a place set apart as a mystery school to provide the most advantageous setting possible for Adam and Eve to demonstrate the path of soul evolution leading to Christhood.

But this book also states that Adam and Eve's fall "was mankind's *first* compromise of the flame of the Christ on Terra."

The Messengers have taught that Genesis, while it does refer to events that happened in earth's history, is not a historical document in the modern sense of the word. Rather, it is an account of archetypal events. Thus these Biblical teachings should be understood in a spiritual context, not limited by time and space. They apply to your soul and mine every bit as much as to the souls of Adam and Eve.

On another level, it is helpful to understand that Adam and Eve represent the masculine and feminine aspects of each of us. The teachings on Adam and Eve are designed to assist the soul to achieve balance: an inner balance of the masculine and feminine poles of being, an outer balance of the soul's karmic relationships with life. To the extent that this balance is missing, the soul suffers. She finds it difficult to enjoy the inherent sparkle of her streaming connection to her Source. And she can more easily find herself mired in karmic relationships.

We are the heirs of the mistakes of our inner Adam and Eve. But we can choose to rectify those mistakes in the joy of our union with the Ascended Masters, who have blazed many homeward trails for us. The light of this volume brightly illumines those trails. I am immensely grateful that the Ascended Masters and their Messengers have extended to us this understanding, so we can quickly transform our karma into God's karma.

LLOYD LEIDERMAN

Chapter 1

Karma: The Law of Integration

*Then I Daniel looked, and, behold, there
stood other two, the one on this side of the
bank of the river, and the other on that side
of the bank of the river.*

*And one said to the man clothed in linen,
which was upon the waters of the river, How
long shall it be to the end of these wonders?*

*And I heard the man clothed in linen,
which was upon the waters of the river, when
he held up his right hand and his left hand
unto heaven, and sware by him that liveth
for ever that it shall be for a time, times, and
an half; and when he shall have accomplished
to scatter the power of the holy people,
all these things shall be finished.*

DANIEL 12:5-7

Karma: The Law of Integration

Let There Be More Light: God's Karma and Man's Karma

K ARMA IS GOD'S ENERGY IN ACTION. Originating in the Mind of God, energy—action-reaction-interaction—is the Trinity of the Logos. The creative forcefield of the Mind of God is the source of karma.

The Sanskrit word *karma* means "deed" or "action." The word has been used both broadly and narrowly through the centuries to define man's ever-evolving concepts of causation, of Cosmic Law and his relationship to that Law.

For the purposes of our study we shall look first to the ancient origins of the word as an energy key governing the flow from Spirit to Matter. *Karma,* according to the Ascended Masters, is taken from the Lemurian root meaning "the *Ca*use of the *Ra*y in *Ma*nifestation"—hence "Ka-Ra-Ma."

"Ka-Ra-Ma" becomes a chant we hear echoing from the priests and priestesses of the Motherland, Mu.[1] They intoned the word in reverence for the energies of the Ka (the will, the desire of the Spirit Creator) sending forth from the Great

Central Sun the impetus of the Ra (the Word or the Logos) for its crystallization as the Ma (the Matter creation).

If the devotee will even now chant in the name of the I AM THAT I AM the energy key "Ka-Ra-Ma," he will tie into the eternal flow of the Father-Mother that manifests as the consciousness of the Son within the heart.

The heart of man is the microcosm of the great macrocosmic heart of God in the Great Central Sun. Each is the source of all life within the system it governs, the replica of the one flame that is God.

Energy Flowing, Energy Growing

In this section we will study the interchange of energy—energy that is God—from man to God, God to man; from Spirit to Matter, Matter to Spirit. We will inquire into the karma that is God's, the karma that is man's, and the application of the law of karma as the law of integration to our present evolution in this system of worlds.

Karma is God—God as Law; God as principle; God as the will, the wisdom and the love of Spirit becoming Matter. The law of karma is the Law of being, being always in the state of becoming—the movement of the Self transcending the Self.

Karma is the law of cycles, the moving out and the moving in through the spheres of God's own cosmic consciousness—the breathing out and the breathing in of the LORD.

Throughout the seven spheres of the Spirit-Matter cosmos, karma is the law of creation, the antahkarana of the creation. It is the integration of energy flow between the Creator and the creation. Karma is causes becoming effects, effects becoming causes—which in turn become effects. Karma is the great chain of hierarchy, link by link transferring the energies of Alpha and Omega, the beginning and the ending of cycles.

"In the beginning God created the heaven and the earth"[2] —and the chain of action-reaction-interaction was begun. God, the First Cause, created the first karma. By his will to be, God willed into being both Creator and creation and thereby set in motion the eternal movement of his energy—karma.

God's Karma

No karma without desire, no desire without the self, no self without God. By God's eternal desiring to be God, the one great Self makes permanent the law of karma in the cycles of the cosmos. God's creation is his karma. Sons and daughters of God are the karma of the living God most high. And the movement of the T'ai Chi, of Father loving Mother, of Mother loving Father, is the eternal rotation of love—love that is the harmony of the spheres, love that is the joy of the Creator in the creation.

Pondering the Father as the great cause of the ray in manifestation in Mother, Lord Maitreya (the coming Buddha) muses upon the cycles of Matter to discover the mystery of the law of energy. To his chelas, would-be initiates of the cycles of the Spirit-Matter cosmos, he says:

"As you trace with your fingers the unfolding petals of the rose, you contact a spiral of life, a geometrization of the God Flame based on the inner Law of the blueprint of life. Hold in your hand an abalone shell or a chambered nautilus. Follow the golden ratio of the movement of life and know that in the geometric designs of creation God is, and where God is there I AM. Behold, the I AM THAT I AM is within you as Law, as geometry, as the science of being.

"Just beyond the veil of Matter and materialization is the matrix of infinity that controls all movement and symmetry in the finite realms of time and space. Just beyond the veils of

Mater, which are the Divine Mother's realization of Spirit's essence, there is the crystal-fire mist, there is the essence of being—immortally brilliant, the Forever Now that lends the quality of permanence to the transient manifestation.

"The rolling of cycles in Matter is like the shifting sands moving in the winds across the desert. Indeed, the rolling of the waves of cosmic energy is the eternal movement of God—the same energy, the same rhythm that controls the tides of the sea, the rotation of the planets, and their evolution on elliptical paths as they make their way round and round the sun-fire sphere—that dot of cosmic consciousness that holds the reins of forces and forcefields in this system of worlds.

> Energy is God.
> How gloriously we find him in all life!
> Organized, systematized,
> Random yet rhythmic motion.
> Energy is God
> Confined yet not confined to Mater.
> Energy is God
> Bound to Mater in the fiery nucleus of life,
> Yet free to bound from atom to atom—
> Free in the flow of the Holy Spirit,
> Hallowing space,
> Crowning time with the majesty of the Mother.
> Each moment in time a cup of her consciousness,
> Each cup filled with the Spirit
> The fulfillment of her love.
> Her habitation is the allness of space.
> Her penetration of the allness
> Is the vapor of etheric consciousness,
> Penetrating as the incense of the Magi,
> The fragrance of violets and lilies of the valley,
> And the distillations of the will of God.

The Cosmic Mother moves
In the currents of God's energy.
Through her blessed hands
Flows the abundance of God's grace.
She is healing, she is joy!
She is the climax of creation.
She is the sun, the moon and the stars!
She is the light reflected in light.
Crystalline fragments of her sunlit hope
Illumine the dark night of the soul
With the laughter of a little child—
Sparkling, dancing eyes and the perfume
Of a baby's skin and angel hair,
Petaled cheeks and dark brown eyes
That span the centuries of the Ancient of Days,
Orbs opening unto the soul's cyclings in infinity."[3]

From out the white fire core of energy that is God—that is life, that is Spirit—came Matter, the ultimate effect of the ultimate cause. And Matter became the playground of Mother. The Father-Mother God is both the force and the forcefield, repulsion and attraction, of Creator and creation, positive and negative, plus and minus. Spirit and Matter—the One, the Whole, the All, yet individed for the evolution of the sons and daughters of God.

Spirit and Matter are one, and yet to understand the allegories and the archetypes of our evolution we must understand life in terms of duality.

"And God said, Let there be light: and there was light. And God saw the light, that it was good: and God divided the light from the darkness. And God called the light Day, and the darkness he called Night. And the evening and the morning were the first day."[4]

The days of the LORD's creation are the days of the LORD's karma, the rituals of his cycles of Spirit becoming Matter. This is the law of integration, the law of harmony in a perpetual polarity of action-reaction-interaction.

The Soul in Polarity with God

Karma presupposes polarity and polarity manifests as duality. Duality presupposes not only Spirit and Matter, good and evil, light and darkness, day and night, male and female, but above all the soul who has separated herself from the center of the Spirit in order that she, too, by free will might become the living Spirit.

That which can be divided in two can be divided again and again until the infinity of God becomes the infinite manifestation of particles of selfhood, each one desiring to be God. "For though there be that are called gods, whether in heaven or in earth (as there be gods many, and lords many), but to us there is but one God, the Father, of whom are all things, and we in him; and one Lord Jesus Christ, by whom are all things, and we by him."[5]

The interpretation of these words of Paul uttered in the Spirit shows his accurate soul understanding of the Holy Spirit's manifestation in atoms of selfhood: Though there be the multiplication of the body and the Spirit and the soul and the Mind of God as the infinite potential of the I AM THAT I AM in every living soul throughout cosmos, yet we know that there is one Law, one LORD, one God, one energy, one karma, one cause, one effect, one Creator, one creation. Though there be numberless souls evolving in the duality of time and space, though every living soul may call on the name of the LORD I AM THAT I AM and appeal in the name of the individual Christ Self to the individualized God Presence I AM—yet in the All, in the One, there is but one soul; one Lord and Saviour;

one Christ, the incarnation of the Word; and one God, the Creator, the Preserver and the Destroyer of all life.

Paul's concept of duality, though necessary and real in the relativity of time and space, did not contradict his concept of the essential unity of God in the Absolute. It is the Holy Spirit, as we shall see, that makes of one Lord and Saviour Lords many and Christs many.

It is the Almighty's love manifest in the Holy Spirit (the third person or third aspect of himself) that multiplies the single Atom (Christ) by the power (the multiplication factor) of the one great Self. Thereby God manifests an infinity of souls— atoms of self-awareness moving in time and space suspended in the planes of Matter.

And we also see in the comforting love of the Holy Spirit the key that resolves all doctrinal disputes concerning the nature of God and man in Christ. It is the Holy Spirit that gives birth to every living soul—that breathes into man's nostrils the breath of life, ignites the one flame on the altar of all hearts and extinguishes the flame in the rounds of rebirth. It is the Holy Spirit that manifests as the I AM Presence and the Christ Self of each soul. It is the Holy Spirit who is the energy, the creativity and the free will that is the foundation of Ka-Ra-Ma.

Only God and God in Man Have Free Will

Without free will there can be no karma, whether in God or in man. Free will, then, is the agency of the Holy Spirit, the cause of the ray in manifestation. Free will is the crux of the law of integration. Only God and man make karma, for only God and God in man have free will. All other creatures— including elemental life, the devic evolution and the angelic evolution—are the instruments of God's will and man's will. Hence they are the instruments of the karma of God and man.

The free will of angels is the free will of God. Angels are required to fulfill God's will, for unlike man, they are not given the liberty to experiment with God's energy. Although angels do make mistakes that produce results which are contrary to God's will, they can later rectify their mistakes and realign that energy with God's will.

Angelic rebellion against God's will is of a different order than the karma-making exercise of free will in man. Free will is central to man's expanding God-identity within the framework of the Great Law. Man is given the liberty to experiment with his free will, for he is a god in the making.

On the other hand, angels, who partake only of the free will of God, remove themselves from their lofty estate if they rebel against the will of God that they are charged to carry out. Thus, if an angel chooses to act against God's will, he must be banished from the angelic realm to the footstool kingdom and embody in the kingdom of man.

Man, who is made a little lower than the angels, is already confined to the lower spheres of relativity. So when he creates negative karma, he simply remains at his own level while he balances it. But an angel who rebels against God's will is removed from his high estate of complete identification with God and is relegated to the lower spheres of man's habitation to balance the energy of God that he has misqualified.

The Soul's Karma: Her Free Will to Unite with the Christ

As Christ is the unity of the Word made flesh, so the Holy Spirit is the plurality of the Spirit manifest in the monads of consciousness suspended in Matter. These we call souls, lifestreams or cells of consciousness.

The Christ is permanent; the soul is nonpermanent. By free will the soul, in imitation of the Spirit's will, may elect to become the Ka-Ra-Ma of the Christ. By free will, that which is a nonpermanent aspect of God may elect to become a permanent aspect of God.

The choice to be or not to be in God is the soul's karma. The negative karma (the negative energy spirals) of the soul who chooses not to be in God is canceled out in the second death, according to the cycles of the manvantaras of Spirit and Matter, by the great positive spiral of the Causal Body of the LORD. This is the law of integration whereby God may rescind a soul's free will, balance her karma and in the process cancel out her individuality.

Karma is the law that governs all manifestation in Spirit and in Matter. It presents the Creator as the thesis of being, the creation as the antithesis, and the crystallization of God Self-awareness as the synthesis of both Creator and creation. Is the son or daughter of God the Creator? No. The creation? No. He is neither, he is both. He is the Creator in the creation, the creation in the Creator.

Karma is a law that, though observed in duality, is not of duality. Karma is the law of the Trinity. It is the law of the Father as the thesis, who becomes the Mother as the antithesis of the Self. And the synthesis, the Christ and the Holy Spirit, is at once the end of the beginning and the beginning of the end— like the ancient symbol of the serpent swallowing its tail.

The Christ as the Real Self of every man and woman self-identified in the duality of time and space is the end of that life which is the beginning, which is Spirit. And it is the beginning of that life which is the ending—Matter. The Holy Spirit is the energizer of the soul as she evolves her karma, to be or not to be in God.

God Multiplies Selfhood

The Word, the synthesis of Creator and creation, is in the beginning of all cycles with God. "Without him [the Word] was not any thing made that was made."[6] In the allegory of the Creator and the creation that we read in the first book of Genesis, God the One polarizes and manifests as duality in order to create a backdrop for the expansion of his own Self-awareness.

The soul that went forth from the center to once again become the center beholds herself in relation to the whole, and the relative position of the soul vis-à-vis the whole provides the definition of individuality.

Thus God, in the desire to become more of God, created the karma of duality. Out of the One, heaven and earth; out of the light, the day and the night. And the firmament dividing the waters of Spirit from the waters of Matter; and out of the waters of Matter the earth and the seas; and out of the earth, plant life and the mineral kingdom. And lights in the firmament for the cycles of the day and the night, for signs and seasons, for days and years. And the lights in the firmament as spirals of consciousness, spirals governing the day and the night, the sun, the moon and the stars. And every moving creature that hath life made in the image of the lesser light, and man made in the image of the greater light, having dominion over every living thing that moveth upon the earth.

Thus male and female, representing the One, were created as the dual aspects of the one consciousness—to be fruitful, to multiply and to replenish the earth[7] by the law of karma. Man and woman are the microcosm of God's karma suspended in the Macrocosm of his karma. They contain within the self the entire cosmos of God's karma in manifestation. All of this, the Creator and the creation of God, was and is the karma of God.

God's Karma: The Karma of Perfection

God's karma is the karma of perfection—perfection being the flow of harmony from Spirit to Matter and from Matter to Spirit. This karma is neither good karma nor bad karma in the relative sense. It is the karma of absolute reality that is beyond measure.

God's karma, fulfilling the law of his energy in motion, can be understood as the movement of his will in an endless succession of primary forces producing secondary forces and tertiary forces and so on ad infinitum, from the center of his being to the circumference and from the circumference to the center.

Drop a stone in the center of a pond. This is an act of will creating an active force that moves in concentric rings until the rings reach the boundaries of the pond. The passive resistance of the border is the secondary force that sends the rings of the originating force back toward the center whence they came.

The returning rings will meet some of the original rings and the impact will initiate a new force, the synthesis of the thesis and the antithesis of the original ritual of cause and effect in the eternal chain of karmic cycles. God's karma is the synchronization of such cosmic forces interplaying through cosmic forcefields, extending to the bounds of his habitation in Spirit and in Matter.

In order to understand man's karma, we must understand God's karma. Whatsoever God soweth, that he also reaps. The LORD has affirmed the principle of his karma in his statement "So shall my word be that goeth forth out of my mouth: it shall not return unto me void, but it shall accomplish that which I please, and it shall prosper in the thing whereto I sent it."[8]

Is this not the same Word without which was not anything made that was made? The science of the Word as the science of the Christ—and as the release of the energies of the Word through the spoken Word of God and man—is the key to Ka-Ra-Ma, hence the key to creation in Spirit and in Matter.

If man would make his karma God's karma and thereby elect to dwell forevermore in the spirit of God consciousness, he must become an imitator of the Word incarnate and use the science of the spoken Word as the science of being.[9]

Centers of Self-Awareness

The science of God's karma is released through seven key vibrations of his consciousness. These key vibrations being sent forth through the Seven Elohim are anchored in man and woman as the seven centers of flow, centers of self-awareness, called chakras.

Through these centers the outbreath and the inbreath of God are continually and simultaneously acting, reacting and interacting to produce the warp and woof of Creator and creation. This is the law of integration; this is the law of harmony; this is the law of karma.

To understand God in manifestation, the realm of soul evolution, we shall diagram levels of our awareness of the individualized God Flame. This will help us to understand the science of energy flow by illustrating the law of integration in the Macrocosm and the microcosm and the flow that links the two worlds of God and man. It will also show how the chakras integrate the energies of the Word in man and woman, spiritually and materially.

Let us first take the sphere as the wholeness of being, as the white fire core whence we came and to which we shall return (figure 1). All that unfolds in the *Climb the Highest Mountain* series is an attempt to assist the soul in establishing a conscious contact in time and space with absolute reality, the Source, the origin behind the beginning and the ending of cycles—the Alpha and Omega of her evolution as symbolized by the circle of oneness.

When relativity is understood as illusory and the forces and forcefields of the soul's self-contained karma have been brought into balance with the wholeness of God, then and only then will relativity be dissolved. Thesis and antithesis will have been dissolved in synthesis, and that which came out of the One will return to the One. Then the teacher and the teaching will no longer be necessary, as they are applicable only to the soul's relative position in a relative world.

Karma as Movement

Taking a cross section of the sphere that is life, we see that the two halves of the whole of cosmic consciousness represent Father and Mother in the white fire core of being. The plus and the minus factors of the polarity create the internal movement

FIGURE 1: The circle of oneness.
The beginning and the ending of the soul's evolution.

of God that is karma in obedience to the law of harmony, the law of integration.

The law of harmony governs the soul's coming out and going within to the white fire core of her being. Only in harmony can she garner the energies of Spirit and grow in the grace of God. And through this growth she continually synthesizes new, more expansive elements of God consciousness. She integrates herself into greater and greater spheres of the One. Thus the law of integration is a corollary to the law of harmony.

Out of God, polarity; out of polarity, movement; out of movement, the cycles of Creator-creation. God's energy in motion is the action-reaction-interaction of Father-Mother at one in the center of life (figure 2).

The sphere of God begins to infold itself in a clockwise/counterclockwise motion (figure 3). This is God desiring to be God, God pursuing God, God the one Self polarized in an expanding Self-awareness that is both Creator and creation within the whole.

Yet God is more than Creator and creation—for the Word, the energy, the movement is the integrating factor of Father-Mother flow. Although the whirling within the white fire core of being creates the plus-minus polarity of Father and Mother, within each half of the whole once again oneness is born, for neither half can continue to exist as half.

Because the Word is inherent within Creator and creation, each half of the whole takes on an additional polarity so that the plus and the minus factors each become plus and minus self-contained. The eye in the center of each of the serpents' heads in the T'ai Chi becomes the center of a new circle of infinity (figure 4).

And lo, a God is born. Out of God's own self-awareness of the One, the multiplication of the One is seen again and again throughout infinity. The two spheres within the whole

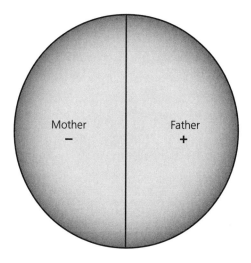

FIGURE 2: The Father-Mother polarity of the white fire core of being.
The plus and minus factors of the polarity create the internal
movement of God that is karma.

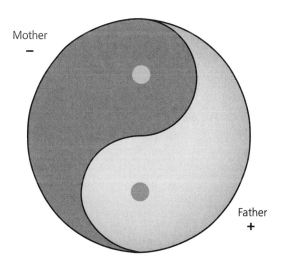

FIGURE 3: The T'ai Chi.
God the one Self polarized in an expanding Self-awareness.

continuously interact as the action-reaction of the Father-Mother God. Spirit and Matter are one and inseparable within the Cosmic Whole (figure 5). As the individing of the whole continues within each sphere, numberless finite numbers reach

FIGURE 4: The individing of the whole.
Numberless finite numbers reaching for infinity.

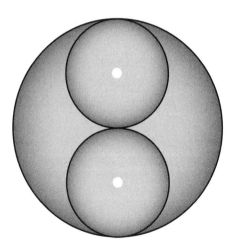

FIGURE 5: Spirit and Matter—
one and inseparable within the Cosmic Whole.

for infinity, yet never attain the goal of unbounded being in God until the moment of the return to the One.

In figure 6 we see the creation of the Spirit and Matter spheres out of the spherical consciousness of the One.

The Personalities of God

Now let us return to the diagram of the One and consider the two halves that have become two wholes. Saint Germain describes these in terms of the plus-minus polarity that each assumes.

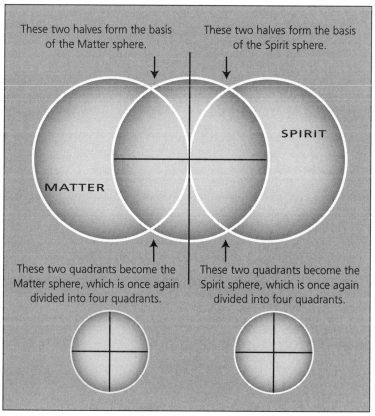

These two halves form the basis of the Matter sphere.

These two halves form the basis of the Spirit sphere.

SPIRIT

MATTER

These two quadrants become the Matter sphere, which is once again divided into four quadrants.

These two quadrants become the Spirit sphere, which is once again divided into four quadrants.

FIGURE 6: The creation of the Spirit and Matter spheres out of the sphere of the One.

The positive polarity of the positive half he designates as the Impersonal Impersonality. This force and forcefield figures on the north side of the sphere. It is designated by two plus signs—one signifying that it is the positive polarity of the original whole, and the other signifying that it is the positive polarity of the new whole that is formed out of the half (figure 7).

The negative polarity of the negative half figures on the south side of the sphere. It is called the Personal Personality and is indicated with two minus signs—one signifying that it is the negative polarity of the first whole, the other that it is the negative polarity of the second whole.

On the east side of the sphere Saint Germain designates the new polarity as the Impersonal Personality. Called the plus-minus, it is the minus of the original half that is the positive

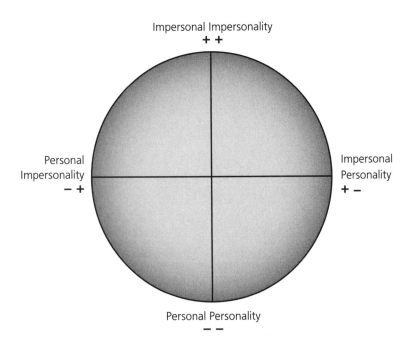

FIGURE 7: The personalities of God.

polarity. On the west side of the sphere the Master designates the new polarity as the Personal Impersonality. This is the plus half of the original half that is the negative polarity of the whole, hence it is a minus-plus.

Now we diagram this polarization of forces and forcefields within God as a sphere (figure 8). Here we show how the sphere of God, through the polarization of Father and Mother, cut in two, results in four quadrants on each half of the sphere. Each half of the whole retains its original designation as the positive or the negative sphere, but within that whole are the four polarizations that are the foundations of Spirit and of Matter.

Diagramming these two halves of the whole, we see that the energy flow between the two is over the figure eight (figure 9).

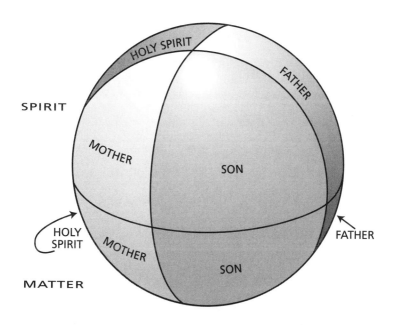

FIGURE 8: The personalities of the Father-Mother God—
as Above, so below.

These two spheres and the interchange of energy "as Above, so below" illustrate God's karma in Spirit and in Matter. When man wills to be one with God by making his karma the karma of God, he moves with God as God's energy in motion—flowing over the figure-eight spirals that are in every part of the creation governing the flow of energy, light, love, wisdom and power from Creator to creation, from the fiery core of Spirit to its densification in Matter.

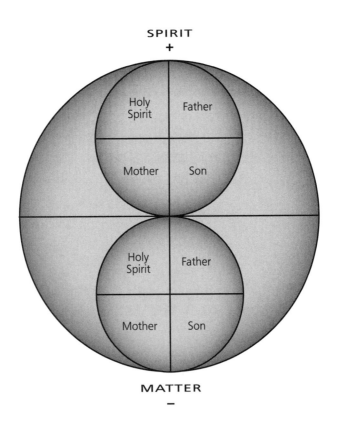

FIGURE 9: The personalities of God
in a figure-eight flow through Spirit and Matter.

The Seven Steps of Precipitation

Examining more closely each sphere of the Father-Mother God, we observe the interplay of cosmic forces that is repeated over and over again throughout the Creator and the creation. Like the force of energy from the stone that is dropped into the center of the pond, we see the action-reaction-interaction repeated in the seven steps of precipitation (figure 10):

1. The force of God is thrust from the center of the sphere to the side on the north. Here the first thesis of God is manifest as the Father consciousness. (In the case of the soul, she goes forth from the white fire core of being and realizes herself in and as the Father consciousness, the Impersonal Impersonality.)

2. Encountering the boundary of the north, the original thrust manifests the plus-plus that creates the antithesis, the antithrust that sends the energy to the south boundary of the sphere where it manifests as the minus-minus. Here Father, the thesis, manifests his antithesis, Mother. (Here the soul realizes herself in and as the Mother consciousness, the Personal Personality.)

3. The thrust from north to south produces the antithrust from south back to north. (The soul returns to the wholeness of the white fire core.)

4. When the antithrust reaches the center, it meets the oncoming thrust from the north. And the interaction of the original action-reaction, turning at right angles to itself, becomes a new thrust from the center to the side of the east. Upon reaching the boundary of the east, the extremity of the new thrust of the synthesis of Father and Mother is manifest as the Son consciousness, the plus-minus. (The soul synthesizes herself in and as the Son consciousness, the Impersonal Personality.)

5. Here the new thrust of the synthesis of Father-Mother

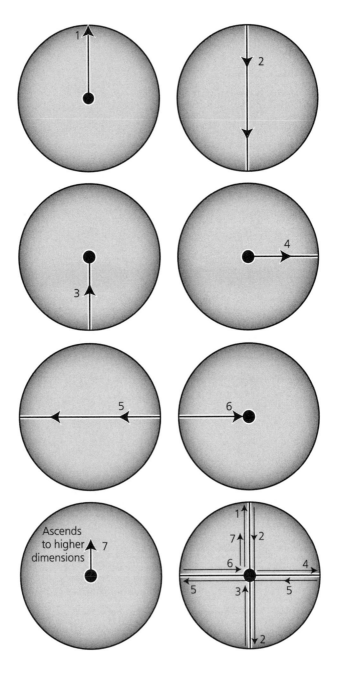

FIGURE 10: The seven steps of precipitation.

becomes its own thesis in the thrust that travels from east to west. Upon reaching the side of the west, the new thesis finds its own antithesis in the Holy Spirit, the minus-plus. (The soul becomes endued with the geometry and the grace of the Holy Spirit consciousness, the Personal Impersonality, as an atom of self-awareness in time [grace] and space [geometry].)

6. The resistance of the boundary of the sphere on the side of the west creates the antithrust that is the synthesis of Son and Holy Spirit, which in terms of initiation is the grace-filled atom, the anointed son or daughter. This energy (a new thrust) travels back to the east, receives its antithrust and goes to the center for the fulfillment of its synthesis. (The soul imbues the self that is son or daughter with the anointing of the Word whereby "in flesh" [in the planes of Matter] she sees and synthesizes the four aspects of God and knows this God as the Christ Self.)

7. The energy returns to the white fire core in the ritual of the ascension of the energy of the current cycle. (The soul returns to the white fire core of being a God Self-realized atom in the Alpha-to-Omega ritual of the ascension of the energy employed in that cycle of precipitation.)

Thus through the seven steps of precipitation, God wills the expansion of his own Self-awareness. Man becomes the instrument, self-willed, of God's own expanding Self-awareness. The going out and the coming in of the energy spiral that eventuates in Self-conscious being always results in a net gain, an increase in the dimension and the mass of the white fire core (its impelling force) and a corresponding increase in the dimension of the sphere (the forcefield).

As the soul exercises her free will to qualify this energy as God intends, she expands her consciousness and God is glorified in the earth. When she misqualifies God's energy, that energy does not return to Spirit and the victory of that cycle is delayed until its energy is requalified to fulfill God's intent.

Saint Germain teaches that this law not only governs the activities of the electron but is the cause behind the effect we observe as the expanding universe. The inner movement of energies within the sphere of life perpetually creates the infinite individualizations of the four aspects of the whole throughout the hierarchies of cosmos.

The Failure Syndrome

The seven steps of precipitation are followed over many incarnations of the soul's evolution outward from God and inward to God. Over and over again the seven rituals are traversed by the soul. The cycles do not wait for man, but man must wait upon the law of cycles.

Each of the seven steps of precipitation marks a single incarnation wherein the soul chooses to be or not to be in God. By her choices made day by day, hour by hour, the soul creates positive and negative spirals of karma. The positive energy spirals ascend to the Causal Body, forging her permanent individuality in God; the negative energy spirals descend into the electronic belt, forging the patterns of the not-self, the synthetic self.

Each positive spiral is a reinforcement for the victory on each succeeding step of precipitation of the God Flame. Each negative spiral is a deterrent, a test that was taken and failed and that must be retaken before the soul can proceed to new levels of cosmic consciousness.

When the soul has created more negative spirals than positive spirals, as is the case with so many among mankind, each succeeding embodiment becomes a greater and greater burden. The task of undoing the negative spirals and redoing positive spirals becomes so overwhelming that the soul sinks back into a sense of futility (the failure syndrome) and says, "I can't."

She rebels against the laws governing the cycles of God's karma and man's karma. She evolves her own religion, her own philosophy of existence, which is a philosophy of death (not life). She resigns herself to oblivion. She contents herself through habit and through the programming of the mass media to a life of pleasure in the not-self, waiting for the day of liberation through the second death when all of her misery will be canceled out—not by self-effort in creating positive spirals but by the great positive spiral of God's karma.

In this frame of mind the soul accepts a religion of vicarious atonement, of a saviour coming in the form of a master, a political or economic system, science, humanism, the welfare state—so many systems, so many "isms" taking the place of the Saviour of mankind, when the eternal Saviour is the Lord, the Law, the self-existent One, the Real Self in the white fire core of one's own being.

The Ascended Masters have come in this hour of the turning of the cycles of Pisces and Aquarius, in this moment of the Kali Yuga, to show mankind—cemented in the concrete of the negative spirals of their own karma—the way out of the dense dilemma of degeneration.

For by their misuse of the law of integration, mankind have followed the seven steps in a ritual of miscreation. Within the negative spirals of their consciousness the counterfeit creation (mechanical man in his own miasma of matter) has taken the trinity of action-reaction-interaction of God's energy flow to perpetuate his unreal existence outside the realm of God. This existence, being on the negative, downward spiral of energy borrowed from the LORD, leads to degeneration and death from its inception.

If they refuse to accept the regeneration of the LORD's Spirit in these last days, mankind will one day find themselves at the bottom of the roller coaster, all impetus of the Alpha thrust spent through the total perversion of the Omega return. Those who are on this collision course with their own karma do not see the end from the beginning. They know not where they have come from, nor where they are going. What's more, they have no point of perspective of the self in relation to the Greater Self.

They are on the death spiral, but they know it not. Their course is one of self-annihilation. Unless they heed the word and the prophecy of the Gurus of the age—the ascended and unascended masters—they will not awaken to real selfhood within the time-space allotment allowed by God for the soul's evolution from the nonpermanent to the permanent atom of being, from the nonpermanent atom of self-awareness to the permanent atom of God Self-awareness.

The Creation of the Spirit Sphere

In this chapter we shall examine mankind's karma in the light of the misuses of the seven aspects of the Christ as these unfold in the first seven chapters of the Book of Genesis and according to the admonishments of the Seven Archangels and their Archeiai (their feminine complements). Each chapter presents the choice to qualify or to misqualify God's energy on one of the seven rays.

The Word of God, which went forth from the white fire core as the fiat of creation, was transmitted by the Seven Elohim through the action-reaction-interaction of the seven rays. The story of the seven cycles (seven days) of creation is recounted in the first thirty-six verses of the Bible (Genesis 1:1–31; 2:1–5). Each thrust, antithrust and new thrust establishes the lines of duality—dual energies—of positive and negative forces.

In these thirty-six keys, which unlock successive stages

of God's consciousness, the energies of Elohim are released through the twelve hierarchies of the sun by the power of the Trinity—three times the cycle of twelve. But here the Trinity is still two halves of the whole. The Word is yet "with God," not externalized in the Matter sphere.

The creation of the Spirit sphere can be studied as the action of four times nine, preparing for the precipitation of the Matter sphere. The events recorded in each set of nine verses mark the spiritual blueprint that is recorded in the four quadrants of the Spirit sphere (figures 11 and 12).

The midpoint of the creation, the fourth day (Genesis

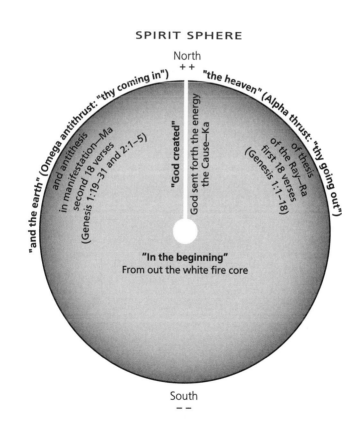

FIGURE 11: Ka-Ra-Ma in the Spirit sphere.

1:19), falls precisely on the south side of the sphere. All that precedes this point is the etheric-mental matrix; all that follows is the emotional-physical matrix. The thirty-third verse (Genesis 2:2) marks the completion of the work of God on the seventh day. Herein is fulfilled the ritual of alchemy on the seventh ray through the thirty-three steps of initiation, which mark the attainment of the Christ and the Buddha in the LORD's house of reality.

Thus these thirty-six verses mark the Alpha-to-Omega thrust and antithrust, the two halves of the first whole—Spirit. They define the initiations of the Father and the Mother in the

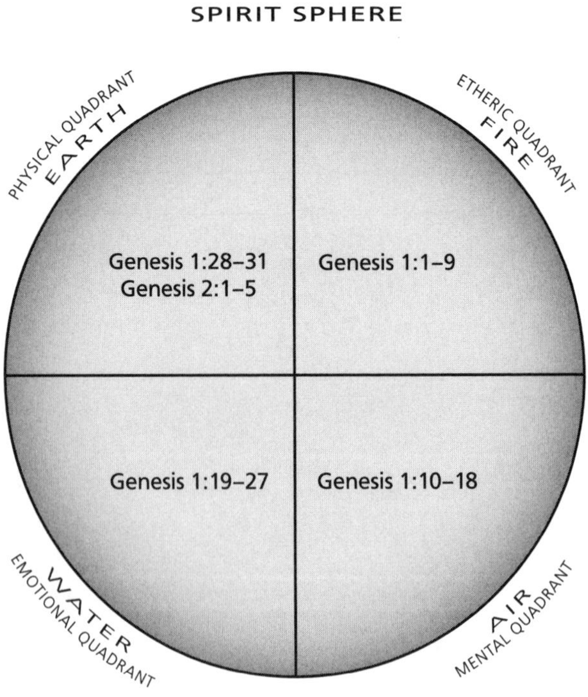

SPIRIT SPHERE

FIGURE 12: The verses of Genesis corresponding to the four quadrants of the Spirit sphere.

Spirit sphere. Here the first heaven and the first earth are complete. "These are the generations of [the cycles of] the heavens and of the earth when they were created, in the day that the LORD God made the earth [– –] and the heavens [+ +]" (Genesis 2:4).

In the thirty-sixth verse (Genesis 2:5), we find the key of the Spirit sphere—the creation of the plants of the field and the herbs of the field before they were in the earth (before they were in the quadrants of Matter) and before they grew (before the Matter sphere separated out of the Spirit sphere). In the same verse it is written that there was no "rain upon the earth," signifying that the water element had not been formed in Matter. God had already created man in Spirit in his image, after his likeness—"male and female created he them" (Genesis 1:27)— yet "there was not a man to till the ground." Man had been created—the living soul suspended in the etheric sheath, provided with mental consciousness—yet he did not exist in Matter.

The Creation of the Matter Sphere

Having shown how the Spirit sphere was created, we note that this process takes place within the Alpha half of the Spirit-Matter whole. From this broader perspective the Spirit-Matter whole comprises four quadrants: the etheric (+ +) and mental (+ –), in which the Spirit sphere is created; and the emotional (– –) and physical (– +), in which the Matter sphere is created.

The Matter sphere represents the Omega half of the Spirit-Matter whole. Its creation and its separation from the Spirit sphere and the interaction of the two within the whole of the Spirit-Matter cosmos over the figure-eight pattern begins with Genesis 2:6. (See figures 13 and 14.)

The separation of the Matter sphere from the Spirit sphere occurs on the south side of the Spirit-Matter whole. The

MATTER SPHERE

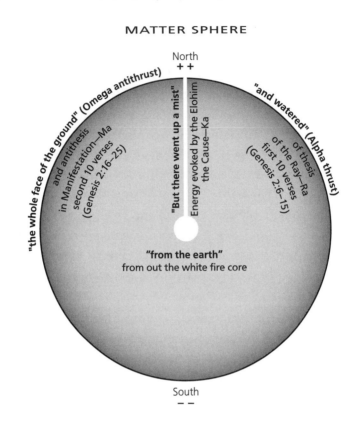

FIGURE 13: Ka-Ra-Ma in the Matter sphere.

precipitation of Matter is two times the cycle of ten—ten for the Alpha thrust, ten for the Omega antithrust.

Just as the number nine is the power of the three-times-three for creativity in Spirit, so the number ten is the creativity of the Mother and the mark of her children's initiation in Matter. The test of the ten is the test of sacrifice, surrender, selflessness and service—the effacing of the lesser self in order that the Greater Self might appear.

The tests of the seven days of creation by the power of the three-times-three signify the mastery of the Father and the Son in the Spirit sphere. In the Matter sphere, man and woman will face the testing of their souls in the ten perfections of the Law as taught by Lord Buddha, signifying the mastery of the Mother and the Holy Spirit. These ten perfections are for the mastery of the self by the action-reaction-interaction of the five secret rays.

Thus, beginning on the north side of the Matter sphere, there are five acts of creation that take place in each of the four quadrants of Matter, presaging the tests of the five secret rays that man and woman will be given as they evolve the consciousness of God as Father, as Mother, as Son, as Holy Spirit. Each of the seven steps of precipitation is inherent within each of the twenty steps described in Genesis 2:6–25.

In the first five verses of the creation of the Matter sphere,

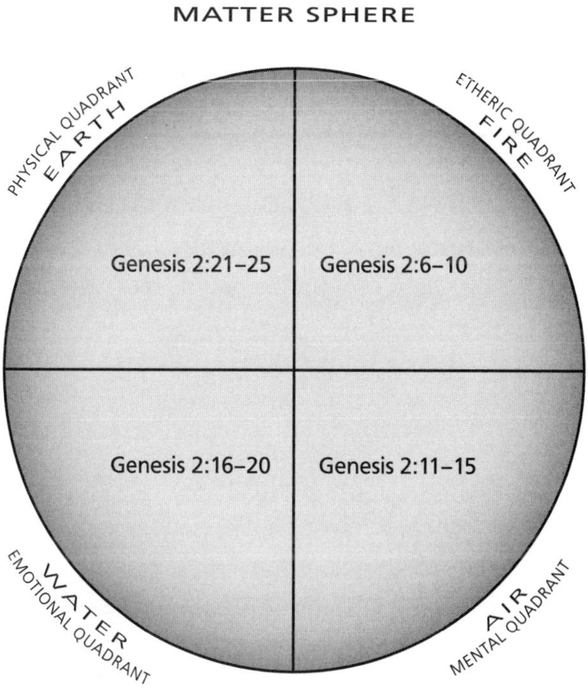

MATTER SPHERE

FIGURE 14: The verses of Genesis corresponding to the four quadrants of the Matter sphere.

we find unveiled the mystery of the creation of the individual-ized God Flame.

"And there went up a mist from the earth, and watered the whole face of the ground" (Genesis 2:6). This mist is the thrust of energy evoked by Elohim out of the white fire core. Here in the first quadrant of the Matter sphere, the Impersonal Impersonality of the Godhead sets forth the etheric blueprint for the soul's individualization in Matter. "The Lord God formed man of the dust of the ground [the Matter aspect of Spirit], and breathed into his nostrils the breath of life; and man became [in Matter] a living soul" within his own individualized Causal Body, the garden that is planted eastward in Eden (Genesis 2:7–8).

Three Types of Trees, Three Types of Initiation

And out of the Great Causal Body the Lord God brings forth "every *tree*," every aspect of the Trinity (Genesis 2:9). The *t* stands for the cross of life: the descending bar is Alpha, the horizontal bar is Omega. The *r* stands for the ray, and the double *e* refers to the electron sustaining the energy of Spirit in Matter, showing that the three types of trees that are created in Spirit extend to the Matter sphere. The three types of trees represent three types of initiation in the Trinity of Father, Son and Holy Spirit.

The "tree that is pleasant to the sight, and good for food" is the tree that presents the testing of the Law in the Holy Spirit, testing man's perceptions of God in the five material senses and the five spiritual senses, providing body, mind and soul with sustenance. There are twelve of these trees, providing man and woman with their initiations in the twelve virtues of the Holy Spirit.

The "Tree of Life" is the I AM Presence "in the midst of the garden" (the Causal Body). Through it come the tests of the will of the Father.

The "tree of knowledge of good and evil" is the Christ Self, the discriminator of Absolute Good and relative good and evil, who stands at the nexus of the flow of the figure-eight interchange of the energies of Spirit and Matter.

The river that goes out of Eden to water the garden (Genesis 2:10) is the great crystal cord that descends from the Causal Body to water the garden that is the counterpart of the Causal Body in the planes of Matter. In Matter, the river is parted and becomes "four heads"—the four quadrants of Matter. Thus the four planes of Matter are created, and the entire blueprint of the creation of the Matter sphere is seen in the first five verses.

The four rivers (Genesis 2:11–14), which are described in the mental quadrant, are the four lower bodies of man.

And God placed man in the garden "to dress it and to keep it" (Genesis 2:15). Man is to be the instrument of the flow of the energies of Alpha and Omega—of action-reaction-interaction.

In verses 16 through 20, God sets the limits of the desire body, the emotional quadrant. He teaches man the correct use of desire—as God's desiring to be God within him. God explains to man the path of initiation that he may not eat of the fruit of the tree of the knowledge of good and evil (Genesis 2:17), for he has not yet passed the initiations of the twelve trees pleasant to the sight and good for food. He must first master his spiritual and material senses and the energies that flow through the seven chakras and the eighth (the secret chamber of the heart) for the nourishment of the soul and the four lower bodies.

Lord Maitreya, the personification of God in the Garden of Eden, tells man the consequences of disobedience and of the misuse of the desire body: the death of man's God Self-awareness, the end of the path of initiation. Maitreya explains that the choice to partake of the fruit of the tree of the knowledge of good and evil before man's Christ Self extends it to him would release an action of the light of the threefold flame that man's four lower bodies are not yet able to contain.

These energies prematurely released as the lightning and the thunder of the gods would mean the death of soul awareness, of the senses of the soul, of man's sensitivity to the inner calling of the soul and the soul's perception of the Spirit. (Have we not seen the consequences of this disobedience in the fact that men and women dwelling wholly outside of the Edenic consciousness have no spiritual awareness and no sensitivity to the God within?)

The Creation of Woman

Having defined the path of initiation as the joyous way to God Self-realization, Maitreya deals with another aspect of God's desiring to be more of God. Just as Matter was formed out of Spirit and Mother came forth out of Father's first longing to be more than Self and to have an objectified Self-awareness, so the Great Initiator saw that it was not good that man should be alone in the Matter creation. Man would have a helpmeet, and the original pattern of the creation of male and female in the image of God in the Spirit sphere would be reproduced in the Matter sphere.

But before the helpmeet appears, all aspects of Adam's consciousness—the beasts of the field, the fowl of the air, and every living creature—are given emotional/physical bodies. Therefore Adam named the living creatures according to the virtues and qualities of the Deity that formed his self-awareness. But the helpmeet is not yet found for Adam (Genesis 2:20).

The creation of woman occurs in the fourth quadrant (the physical quadrant) of the Matter sphere. The soul of Adam returns to the white fire core for the creation of that soul which is the twin-flame counterpart of himself—the ribs symbolic of the Gemini twins, male and female. Out of the positive polarity, man (who contains the plus-minus wholeness of Father-Mother), comes forth the negative polarity, woman.

Adam exalts the physical manifestation of the Matter sphere: "bone of my bones [the spiritual skeletal blueprint] and flesh of my flesh [the Matter substance of the creation]." The calling of the helpmeet "woman, because she was taken out of man" (Genesis 2:23) is the celebration in the four planes of Matter of the fulfillment of the Matter sphere taken out of the Spirit sphere.

And the marriage of twin flames, as in Spirit so in Matter, is pronounced: "Therefore shall a man leave his father and his mother, and shall cleave unto his wife: and they shall be one flesh" (Genesis 2:24). Man and woman are the inseparable whole of the Creator-creation.

The final test, on the fifth secret ray in the physical quadrant, underscores the fact that the victory in the test of the ten (the test of obedience through sacrifice, surrender, selflessness and service) is manifest through the innocence of the man and his wife.

The Path of Initiation

Once God has fulfilled the cycles of himself in Spirit and in Matter, he has completed the manifestation of his karma in the two spheres of wholeness. Now man and woman—clothed etherically, mentally, emotionally and physically—can enter the spheres of God's consciousness. It is their opportunity by free will to make their karma God's karma, and their choices will be made one by one according to the original cycles of God's creation.

Out of the divine mind came forth the etheric blueprint, the mental matrix, the emotional spiral and the physical precipitation of Creator-creation in order that the perfection of God's karma might be manifest as Above, so below.

Out of the carnal mind comes forth the counterfeit creator-creation called the Serpent to present the choices of anti-Spirit and anti-Matter that will manifest as the counterfeit spiritual/material cosmos.

At the conclusion of Genesis 2, the curtain falls on the divinely ordained marriage ritual of man and woman. God has set them as jewels in the perfect setting of his Edenic consciousness with all that will be required for them to enter the path of initiation and to attain solar (soul) awareness, Christ awareness and God awareness.

At this step on the ladder of attainment, all that is required is obedience to the Guru Maitreya. He is referred to as the LORD God, walking and talking with man and woman in the garden. If they will manifest obedience both to the Law and to the Lawgiver—the impersonal and personal aspects of God in Spirit and in Matter—step by step they will be given the initiations of the sacred mysteries. These initiations are for the mastery of soul awareness leading to Christ Self-awareness through the fruit of the tree of the knowledge of good and evil, and to God Self-awareness through the fruit of the Tree of Life.

To partake of these fruits before the initiation is given by the LORD, who has the attainment of all three states of cosmic consciousness, is to deify the will, the ego and the intellect of man and woman. It is to endow these aspects of the uninitiated self with the power, the wisdom and the love of the Real Self *before* the soul, who has separated from Spirit, has proven herself capable of correctly exercising the gift of free will.

Says Maitreya, "Were I to place the rod of initiation upon the brow of those who kneel before the altar of the Cosmic Christ prior to their initiation in the cycles of life, I would but lend the momentum of my authority in life as a reinforcement of death as the supreme denial of the Real Self that is God.

"The light that flows 'heart, head and hand' from the consciousness of the Cosmic Christ is the light that makes permanent all that is real and good and beautiful and joyous within you. This is the light that can endow the soul with everlasting life, and this is the light that the LORD God has held back from mortals until they are willing to put on immortality.

"Thus it is written as the edict of the Law that 'this corruptible must put on incorruption, and this mortal must put on immortality.'"[10]

What, then, will be the karma of man and woman? The choice is to be or not to be within the Spirit-Matter cosmos of God, to be in or out of the matrix of spiritual-material perfection—the four quadrants of self-awareness in Spirit and in Matter. The choice is to be or not to be within the figure-eight spiral of the Father-Mother flow of that karma, which is the perfect movement of energy according to the law of harmony and the law of integration.

Choose to Make Your Karma God's Karma

Chapter 3 of Genesis opens with the figure of the not-self, presenting the choices of two existences. For the Law requires man and woman to choose. This is the requirement for the enjoyment of reality as existence, knowledge, bliss.

The test is one of supreme faith in the Law and in the Guru and in the action of the Law through the Guru; supreme hope of the salvation of the soul through the wisdom of the Law and of the Guru; and supreme love of the Law and of the Guru as the interpreter, integrator and initiator of the Law.

What, then, will be the choice of man and woman? Will they choose to make their karma God's karma? Will they choose to put on—line upon line, precept upon precept—the spirals of God's Spirit-Matter consciousness?

Will they accept in the person of the Guru the Mediator of their own soul's perfection in Christ and in God? Will they be patient and diligent, humble and long-suffering, as their souls are God-taught in the way of the putting on of the garment of the LORD's consciousness?

Or will they be tempted by the shortcut method presented by the not-self, the Serpent? The choice is made by man and woman in the moment of the soul's birth in time and space and in each succeeding embodiment and day, each cycle of being. This choice determines the karma of man and woman, individually and collectively.

The Fall of Man and Woman in the Garden of Eden

The choice not to be in God and not to enjoy his existence, his knowledge and his bliss came about as the result of the abandonment of the flame of love and the logic of the heart. Thus the Fall of man and woman, through selfishness and self-love, was a compromise of the energies of the Holy Spirit on the third ray. Love and the fire of love as holy purity are the very life (the Spirit, the essence) of all of the seven rays.

Through the Fall of man and woman recorded in the third chapter of Genesis, maya became the foundation of existence in Matter. And the mayic overlay of the spiritual-material creation deprives man and woman of the vision of God the Father and of the cradle of their evolution in the Garden of Eden: God the Mother.

Expelled from the God-realization of the Self as both Father and Mother, man and woman go forth from the karma of perfection to the karma of imperfection. Their karma is no longer God's karma, their thoughts are no longer God's thoughts,[11] their feelings are no longer God's feelings. And the matrix and the measure of the manifestation, man and woman, is but the shadowed self, the synthetic self, the not-self.

Karma on the Seven Rays As Depicted in Genesis

The Archeia of the seventh ray, Holy Amethyst, describes the first seven chapters of the Book of Genesis as "a poetic overview of the uses and misuses of the sacred fire in the seven rays. In the first chapter of the creation is the recording of the fiat of the LORD God and its implementation by the Elohim in the creation of the cosmos and of the early root races—man and woman created in the image and likeness of God, sent forth to be cocreators, to take dominion in the planes of Mater.

"Interspersed with this accounting is the record of the creation of animal life and of all of the living creatures—an allegorical presentation of the creation of elemental life tainted by the fact that the authors of the Book of Genesis spoke from a point of reference in relativity; for the book was written after the Fall of man and woman, after the descent of consciousness from the plane of Absolute Good to the plane of relative good and evil. Therefore the record of the misuses of the first ray on the mental and astral planes is also included in the account. But 'God saw every thing that he had made, and, behold, it was very good.'[12] This is the etheric blueprint of the cosmos, the power of the first ray that undergirds the all of the creation.

"In the second chapter of Genesis, there is the sealing of the creation in the Mind of God through the second ray of illumined action. And immediately the factor of Antichrist, as the mist that went up from the earth and watered the whole face of the ground, compromised the light of the Logos in man and woman. Now the counterpart, the material creation of the male and female formed of the dust of the ground, is given.

"Here evolution has reached the physical plane watered by the energies of Spirit; and out of the cloven tongues of the fire of wisdom, the counterpart of man is set before him as woman. Simultaneously the tree of the knowledge of good and evil is placed in the midst of the garden, that man and woman might exercise free will to obey or not to obey, to believe or not to believe, the Word of the LORD.

"Thus the Divine Us, as twin flames in the white fire core who were created in the beginning, realize their oneness in Matter as a duality of expression. While they remain in the light of the Christ, their innocence is sealed. But the record in the third chapter of Genesis deals with the uses and misuses of the flame of love; and this is where the carnal mind, personified in the Serpent who typifies the Fallen One tempting the members of the fourth root race on Lemuria, presents its carnal logic. Temptation is always presented as the lie that goes against the intuition of the heart and its natural inclination toward devotion to God.

"The Fall of man and woman came about as the result of their abandonment of the flame of love and the logic of the heart. The misuses of the sacred fire of love were grave indeed upon Lemuria, and they spread to every corner of the earth. The mechanization of creation caused man and woman to forfeit the holy communion of love shared in the Holy Spirit. The judgment of the men and women of the fourth root race was also the judgment of love. Outside the paradise of God's consciousness, Adam and Eve are required to master the fourth ray—no longer by the alchemy of the sacred fire, but in sorrow and in shame.[13]

"The white light of the Mother in the fourth ray is so intense that it arouses anger and jealousy in Cain, eventuating in the desecration of the Mother. Unto Cain and Abel it was given to keep the flame of Alpha and Omega in the white chakra, and to that end they offered burnt offerings unto the LORD. The killing of righteous Abel by Cain[14] was the beginning of the profanation of the flame of the Mother by the children of the Mother. And so the fires of the Mother were used for the multiplication of the consciousness of Cain in a degenerate humanity.

"But with the coming of Seth, the LORD's replacement for

the seed of Abel, men and women began once again to call upon the name of the LORD. Through the application of the law of Truth in the science of the fifth ray, the generations of Adam through Seth brought forth great lights in the history of the earth—Enos and Cainan and Mahalaleel and Jared and Enoch and Methuselah and Lamech and Noah.[15] These men had the mastery of the fifth ray and therefore lived hundreds of years through its application in the science of Mater.

"But the children of the fallen ones and the generations of Cain brought about the misuse of the light of the Christ in the sixth ray. Instead of service to that light and the mastery of the emotions, it is recorded in the sixth chapter of the Book of Genesis that every imagination of the thoughts of man's heart was only evil continually. And in the antediluvian society there was a mingling of light and darkness, and the rebellious ones contaminated the whole earth with their laggard consciousness. But the generations of Noah were perfect in the sight of God; and therefore he instructed Noah and his sons—Shem, Ham and Japheth—to build the ark to prepare for the coming of the judgment.[16] The sixth ray is the mastery of water, and Noah and his house kept that mastery. Therefore unto them the judgment was a blessing and the preparing of the way for a new order.

"And thus the flood came as the action of the seventh ray—of the violet flame of transmutation, the ritual of the undoing of the perverted rituals of fallen man and fallen woman. And in that period of purification, of forty days, the four planes of Mater were washed by the waters of the living Word even as Jesus reenacted the period of purification during forty days of fasting in the wilderness.[17] While the fallen ones experienced the judgment and the trial by fire as the great purging even unto the death of their four lower bodies, Noah and his family entered into the ritual of the ark whereby the energies of Spirit and Mater arc and there is that perfect communion and that perfect flow between the heart of God and the heart of son and daughter incarnate as the living Word."

Karma Yoga: The Return to God

Holy Amethyst counsels us to "meditate upon these seven chapters in the presence of the Holy Spirit" so that we may understand "that in every century mankind have taken the seven rays of the Logos and qualified them according to their level of attainment in the Christ consciousness."

It is necessary that each individual on the path of initiation consider himself within the sphere of his own karma—how he has qualified or misqualified the seven rays and the seven steps to precipitation. Holy Amethyst says: "Those who would keep the flame of life in the day of judgment that is at hand, those who would return to the center of God consciousness and be allowed to pass by the flaming sword and the cherubim who keep the way of the Tree of Life, must traverse the cycles of their own uses and misuses of the seven rays.

"Step by step, line by line, karma must be balanced to the right and to the left. Each individual who reads my words must know that the responsibility to balance the energies of life is the meaning of the judgment. When you determine to get back to Eden, to return to the house of the Father-Mother God, you must be willing to retrace every footstep you have taken since the descent of your soul into the planes of Mater.

"The road of return has two aspects: the sorrowful way and the glorious way. It all depends upon your perspective; for the bliss of the divine reunion is experienced within—even in the moment of agony, through the dark night of the soul, and on the cross.[18]

"The sixty-ninth Psalm of David contains three cycles of twelve. In thirty-six verses David reveals the experiences of one who passed through the dark night of the soul to the full realization of the Christ consciousness. You who have determined to pass through the dark night of both the soul and the spirit would do well to ponder the meditations of David and then to apply yourself diligently to the invocations of the sacred fire, especially to the violet flame that is the concentrated energy of the Holy Spirit in the forgiveness of sin, the righting of all wrong, and the bringing of the four lower bodies into alignment with the original blueprint of creation."[19]

Man's Karma: The Web of Circumstance

Karma is God's energy in action in man. Man and woman as cocreators with God become the cause of the ray in manifestation. By free will they determine whether causes set in motion in time and space will be the causes that the LORD God originally set in motion (the blueprint, the matrix, the energy spirals, the crystallization) that originate in the Causal Body of man and woman—or whether they shall be of the generations of Adam and Eve, the causes and effects that come forth from the collective subconscious of mankind as well as from the individual's electronic belt.

By his failure to accept the law of God's karma as the law of his own life, upon his expulsion from Eden man became a law unto himself. The law of his own karma became the law of the cause-effect sequences outside of the realm of God's karma. From the time of Adam and Eve to the present, dwelling in the planes of relative good and relative evil, most men have lived by the law of the carnal mind. Verily are they condemned by the laws of mortality, self-made and self-imposed. Thus they suffer disease, decay, degeneration and death. (See figure 15.)

Although death is not real, man experiences death because he has placed himself in bondage to the laws of mortality. Yet

Paul exclaimed: "O death, where is thy sting? O grave, where is thy victory? The sting of death is sin; and the strength of sin is the law. But thanks be to God, which giveth us the victory through our Lord Jesus Christ."[20]

SPIRIT

God's karma: the web of consciousness

MATTER

Man's karma: the web of circumstance

FIGURE 15: Meditation for Adam and Eve:
"I AM Alpha and Omega in the white fire core of being."
The flow of God's energy to the creation comes forth and returns
to the white fire core in the center of being. Energy not returned
to the center feeds the carnal mind.

The Karma of Man on the Seven Rays

NOW WE SHALL EXAMINE MANKIND'S karma in the light of the misuses of the seven aspects of the Christ consciousness, as the judgment of this karma has been delivered by the Seven Archangels.

The year 1975 began the final quarter of the century, marking the fruition in man and woman of the works of the Holy Spirit. At that time it was given unto the Seven Archangels to deliver "the coils of mankind's karma—not alone on this planet or this system of worlds, but on planets in numberless systems where the fruit of the tree of the knowledge of good and evil has been partaken of by the man and the woman whom the LORD God hath made."

From the Temple of the Tabernacle of the Testimony they come, servants of God and man bearing the golden vials of the seven last plagues filled with the wrath of God.[21] As Archangel Michael explains, "the wrath of God is the wrath of man that the LORD God himself does turn against the idolatrous generation."

Coming by the authority of Alpha to announce this judgment, Archangel Michael says, "Now behold how the Lords of Karma and the Four and Twenty Elders[22] stand back with heads bowed as the seven plagues of mankind's misuse of the sacred fire are turned upon them by the LORD God of hosts, by the Law that is infallible and irrevocable.

"[This is] the same Law that does govern the cycles of a cosmos and the inbreath and the outbreath of the seven Spirits of the Seven Elohim, the same Law that governs the harmony of the spheres and the rolling chords of cosmic consciousness. This is the Law that declares unto man ascended and man unascended, 'Till heaven and earth pass, one jot or one tittle shall in no wise pass from the law, till all be fulfilled.'[23]. . .

"Judgment is the alignment of energies to the right and to the left of the flame. Judgment is the All-Seeing Eye focusing right and wrong to the consciousness and to souls of light and souls of darkness. Judgment is the opportunity to see every infraction of the Law within and without. Judgment is the measuring of the measure of man and woman by the rod of the Law and by the scepter of his authority. . . .

"In this hour of the Dark Cycle's turning[24] when mankind reap the karma of their abuses of the feminine ray and of the energies of the white fire core anchored in the base-of-the-spine chakra, the Law does require the children of the light to pursue the transmutation of the misuse of these sacred energies in the seven rays that converge in the white flame of the Mother."[25]

God's Will Enacted through the Blueprint of Creation

T HE FIRST RAY IS THE BLUE RAY, THE ray of the will of God. It is the ray of the power of the Creator with which he infused the creation. It is the ray of the action of the Elohim ("And there was light") as they responded to the fiat of the LORD ("Let there be light").[26] The blue ray carries the blueprint of the creation, and it is the energy of God released in perpetual joy through the matrix of the blueprint.

The first chapter of Genesis records the creation of the spiritual blueprint for a microcosmic Spirit-Matter cosmos according to the will of God, with all that would be contained therein—energy fields, elemental life, man and woman made in the image and likeness of Elohim.

Challenging God's Plan

Through the Fallen One, Lucifer, came the perversion of the first ray and of the science of the sacred fire within that ray as it is released through the throat chakra of God and man in the power of the spoken Word.

Before his fall from grace, Lucifer (the light-bearer, the "son of the morning"[27]) had attained to the level of Archangel. He was well tutored in the cycles of the cause of the ray in manifestation. The seven steps of precipitation had been the building blocks of his cocreations with the LORD.

He knew the cycles of thesis, antithesis and synthesis and the laws of the integration of the caduceus of Alpha and Omega. The LORD had not kept his secrets from his son. Alas, the folly of the fallen Archangel was his familiarity with the LORD. Lucifer was not content to make himself equal with God (which equality God shares with his sons and daughters, for he made them cocreators). But Lucifer placed himself above the LORD God and boasted before the hosts of the LORD that he, Lucifer, could bring forth a creation better than the LORD's. He could do anything that the LORD could do, or so he thought.

In fact, Lucifer could not do everything, but he could do many things—enough to impress one-third of the angels serving in this galaxy, as well as the evolutions of mankind on a number of planets in this and other solar systems. His pride in the power originally derived from the LORD, his ambition to answer the LORD's creation with his own creation, was accepted by thousands among the angelic hosts and eventually by man and woman through the same pride of power in the ego, now separated from the Ego of God.

From the hour of his fall from grace, Lucifer was cut off from the LORD God and from the energies of the Source. He was cast out of heaven into the earth—out of the Spirit sphere into the Matter sphere. But he had at his command the energies of his own momentum of attainment in God as well as the energies of the angels who descended with him and were cast down into the earth, into the Matter sphere, there to abort the cycles of the Mother and her children for thousands and thousands of years.

This was the karma of man and woman when they elected to depart from the state of grace that they enjoyed in the Edenic consciousness. The consent of woman to compromise the tree of the Christ consciousness and to believe the lie of the Serpent placed upon her the fiat of the LORD: and they believed the lie and their damnation was just.[28]

The Tares Sown among the Wheat

Through the same ambition that is the aggrandizement of the self, the works of Lucifer and the fallen angels who were with him also resulted in the counterfeit creation of a counterfeit world—a world peopled with mechanical men and women, the offspring of Lucifer, the children of the devil who are without a threefold flame or a living soul. The Ascended Master known as the Great Divine Director describes this mechanical creation:

"You will recall that Jesus, in his parable of the wheat and tares, announced that an enemy had sown tares among the wheat.[29] These tares are the counterfeit man. Jesus said they were the children of the Wicked One, which exist apart from the original creation of God. And yet, inasmuch as nothing cannot create something, that which was created must have been created by some one who at some time some where drew forth the necessary information to so create.

"In many cases in the New Testament it is recorded in the life of Jesus that he referred to certain individuals as a 'generation of vipers,' as 'hypocrites,' and as sons of Satan, addressing them in these words: 'Ye are of your father the devil, and the lusts of your father ye will do.'[30] This reference obviously does make a distinction between all men and some men.

"Let me hasten to assure you, then, that there do exist

upon the planet creatures who did not come forth from God—who are the counterfeit of the real manifestation. Many of these are consciously in league with the insipid and insidious purposes of the powers of darkness. They seek through conspiracy and plot to ravish the world of its good, to set brother against brother, to confuse, disturb and destroy harmonies wherever they exist. These function on the physical plane, utilizing and directing their energies in a concerted effort against the light. They are, however, the pawns of 'spiritual wickedness in high places.'[31] And the league of the spiritually negative forces with these embodied wicked individuals has resulted in the slaughter of many noble souls down through the ages.

"I am not so interested in identifying and describing these individuals as I am in calling to your attention that they do exist. John the Baptist, as he preached the coming of the Christ, foretold the end of this race of mechanical men when he said, 'O generation of vipers, who hath warned you to flee from the wrath to come?' Again referring to the barrenness of this counterfeit creation he said, 'Every tree therefore which bringeth not forth good fruit is hewn down, and cast into the fire.' He prophesied the coming of one who would baptize with the Holy Ghost and with fire (with the sacred fire and the purifying power of the violet transmuting flame), 'whose fan is in his hand, and he will throughly purge his floor, and will gather the wheat into his garner; but the chaff he will burn with fire unquenchable.'[32]

"Needless to say, these human automatons are the chaff, and their final end can come through only one process: transmutation. For this is the only approved method whereby the wicked shall be removed from the face of the earth.

"In the Bible these soulless beings are referred to throughout as 'the wicked,' for they have seen to it that all more specific descriptions of their race have been removed—lest mankind discover them and rise in righteous indignation against their overlords. And thus the death of John the Baptist and that of Jesus the Christ were brought about by the counterfeit race who for thousands of years have set brother against brother, race against race, and have caused the children of God to blame one another for the murders of the saints.

"Today, as always, they occupy positions of authority and financial power. They have gained control of the destiny of empires, and they seek ever to thwart the pure purposes of God. The injudicious use of taxation exerted by their direction has placed an unconscionable yoke upon the neck of humanity.

"Their control of entertainment media and the trends of youth toward dissonant art forms and discordant music has perverted noble attitudes and spawned a race of delinquent rebels whose code, or lack of it, has gnawed at the vital future of America and the people of many nations. Modern means of communication and distribution of the printed word, the spoken word and the dramatic word through television and motion pictures have caused ideas to span continents and the world almost with the speed of light. Like a prairie fire, the dry grass consumes itself to the roots of the hopes of mankind, which are blighted, then, by the searing infamy of wasted energy and emotion."[33]

Elemental life, meant to ensoul the virtues of man as his counterpart in the nature kingdom, was imprisoned by the archdeceivers of mankind in grotesque animal forms. The threefold flame, the spark of the Christ consciousness and the focus of the Trinity, was subverted through the human will, the human ego and the human intellect. And the mechanical creation, programmed to these three counterfeits of Father, Son and Holy Spirit, began to implement that programming among the generations of mankind, who in turn imparted it to the children of God. It is the power of the Trinity that Lucifer and the fallen angels subverted through their mechanical creations.

The Generations of Cain

The term "mankind" or "kind of man" can be taken to refer to the descendants of Cain (the Cainites), of whom Jesus said, "Ye are of your father the devil, and the lusts of your father ye will do. He was a murderer from the beginning, and abode not in the truth, because there is no truth in him. When he speaketh a lie, he speaketh of his own: for he is a liar, and the father of it."[34] Cain, though born of the seed of Adam, was conceived through the uniting of Eve's consciousness with that of the Serpent, the liar who told her that her soul awareness in God would not surely die.

Believing this, Eve received the judgment of the LORD, and her own karma returned to her in her firstborn son. In the statement "I have gotten a man from the LORD,"[35] Eve is saying she has gotten a man from the law of her own karma—the law of her own sinful state of consciousness. (See figure 16.)

Thus Cain was born without soul awareness of God or of Christ the Mediator. Sanat Kumara tells us the story of Cain:

"Now the first son of Adam and Eve was the generation of their karma. Called Cain, meaning 'acquisition,' the soul is acquired from outside the circle of their Guru/chela relationship with Lord Maitreya. And if you ponder it, my beloved, you will see that the law of karma is the law of acquisition: 'Whatsoever a man soweth, that shall he also reap.'[36]

"Cain's lifestream—his name also means the 'hollow root' —contained the seeds of his rebellion against the seven covenants of the seven rays that he had outplayed in his prior incarnations on the planet Maldek. His mechanized religion was a ritual of self-will perverting the ray of the LORD's will. He sought to acquire the all-power of God with the anti-power of his sling and his spear. His offering was not respected by Maitreya because his motive was to gain favor from the LORD that he might then subdue the LORD's light to the uses and abuses of his own subterfuge.

"Cain worked hard tilling the ground, not to the glory of God but to gain God's power that he might exercise that power over others."[37] Through the pride and ambition of the Serpent

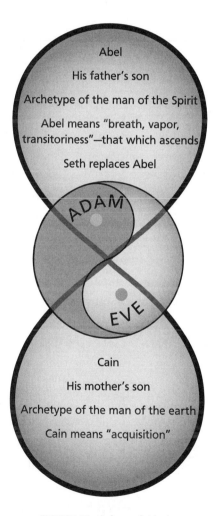

FIGURE 16: Cain and Abel.
Out of the white fire core of Adam and Eve, Cain and Abel are born as archetypes of the Matter and Spirit civilizations that are to evolve on Terra.

who sired his consciousness, willful Cain wanted to please God in his own way, not in God's way. He was angered with the LORD as the teacher, the Initiator.

Cain was not willing to acknowledge the authority of the tester. He was not willing to be tested or to meet the standards of the test. The LORD told him that his offering was unacceptable because he was attached to the fruit of his action. Cain did not perform his work for the sake of being the instrument of the LORD's work or to reenact the ritual of the Creation. He worked for pride of person and to show what his human personality thought it could do apart from the Christ.

When the LORD rejected Cain's offering, Cain became angry with him. "The LORD said unto Cain, Why art thou wroth? and why is thy countenance fallen? If thou doest well, shalt thou not be accepted? and if thou doest not well, sin lieth at the door. And unto thee shall be his desire, and thou shalt rule over him."[38] Cain's ambition was for the fruit of action without the action. He wanted the fruits of the Christ consciousness without putting forth the effort to attain that consciousness by submitting to hierarchy and to the path of initiation (the teacher and the teaching), the steps necessary to the precipitation of the Christ consciousness.

Whether in the seven cycles of the Creation or in the seven steps of precipitation, in order for the soul to become the Christed one and to command within the self the atoms and molecules of God Self-awareness, a process is implied. In order for the soul to move from point A to point B to point C, she must submit to the process prescribed by the LORD God. This process is an energy coil whereby the soul moves from one frequency or plane of God's consciousness to the next. The process of moving over the coil is the step by step testing of the soul on the path of initiation.

But Cain's father, the devil, was a murderer from the

beginning. The Serpent had in effect, for a cycle of time and space, murdered the soul awareness of Eve. By convincing her that she would not surely die,[39] he convinced her to commit spiritual suicide. The dismissal from the sphere of God's consciousness (the Garden of Eden) and from the path of initiation was for Adam and Eve like death itself.

They had lost their opportunity to be initiated according to the process of precipitation of the Christ consciousness. Henceforth the world would be their guru. The world of maya, fashioned out of the mists of their own karma, would teach them the lessons that they refused to learn directly out of the mouth of God (ex cathedra through his vicar Maitreya).

Condemned to the law of their own sin, man and woman went forth from the spirals of God's karma, their habitation in the Electronic Presence of the Most High, to dwell in the spirals of man's karma, the electronic belt of a truly subconscious world—a world where man and woman were no longer conscious of the self in and as God.

And the garment of veiled innocence, sundered by the sin of Adam and Eve, was replaced by Lord Maitreya, who made "coats of skins, and clothed them"[40] in vehicles of consciousness adapted to their descent into the densities of maya.

Pride–Departure from the Path

The generations of the Serpent through Eve (the Cainites) perpetuated the lusts of their father the Serpent. In them the lusts of sensuality and selfishness (the pleasures of the physical senses) replaced the joy in the bliss of God through the senses of the soul. As murder is the lust of anger, so are all of the sins of this unrighteous generation the lusts of the unbridled will. They rebelled against the commandments of the LORD given to Moses—ten rules of living to guard them from the lustful consciousness of the Serpent. The serpentine mind overshadowed Eve in her conception of Cain, and that serpentine mind was the seed of the carnal mind that remains today as the element of conflict with the Christ in all mankind.

Cain was the first of the descendants of the initiates of Lord Maitreya to murder the representative of the Christ consciousness. He was the first of the generations of Adam to respond to the spirals of Antichrist under this dispensation of hierarchy. And so Cain and his descendants received the judgment to be wanderers on the face of the earth: "A fugitive and a vagabond shalt thou be in the earth."[41]

Not only was Cain the first murderer, but he was the false prophet who initiated the spiral of the path that the fallen angels espouse, as well as their philosophy that the ends justify the means. The Luciferians, who had rebelled against God and his laws, would not submit to the path of initiation. Instead, they created an alternate path, the "way that seemeth right unto a man, but the end thereof are the ways of death."[42] The way that seemeth right is the way of Cain. In his violation of God's karma and man's karma to be God, Cain passed on to the generations of mankind the denial of the ritual of the Law, the denial of the teacher and the teaching, and the denial of the opportunity of atoms of self-awareness suspended in the Holy Spirit to return to Christ and to become one with God.

Cain's sin, then, was threefold. It was the denial of the Law of God as Father, the denial of the Son in the person of Abel, and the denial of the Holy Spirit in the action of Abel and in the action of the seven steps of precipitation. It was for his denial of the Holy Spirit that he was denied the obedient service of the servants of God in nature. No longer would elemental life be obedient to his call.

Now we see that, after the manner of Cain's prideful ways, man has manipulated elemental life and has thereby amalgamated that misqualified energy into the beast of the Fallen One. This is the beast that rises up out of the sea, who received his power from the dragon and the beast that cometh up out of the earth. This beast imposes upon mankind his returning karma, which manifests as the mark of the beast, the name of the beast, and the number of his name.[43]

All of this is the usurpation of the energies of the first ray of the will of God. Because mankind and certain of the children of God and the sons and daughters of God followed in the way of the worship of the Antichrist, both the Antichrist and his creation have become a part of the world karma that must be transmuted on the first ray.

The Judgment of Lucifer and the Luciferians

Archangel Michael and his divine complement, the Archeia Faith, present to us an outline of mankind's karma on the first ray and provide us with vital keys for the balancing of that karma. To those who would stand, face and conquer the imbalance of karma in the four lower bodies that is the perversion of the will of God in the Divine Mother and in her children, Archangel Michael says:

"Let those who march with the Divine Mother carrying the banner of Maitreya, the Cosmic Christ, call forth the sacred fire from their own Causal Bodies of light, from the I AM THAT I AM, to consume the cause and core of the disintegration and the death that is the record of the murder of the Divine Mother and the slaughter of the holy innocents that has been enacted again and again on Lemuria, on Atlantis, and in every civilization ancient and modern where the fallen angels have moved in with their darkness and their deviltry, their degradation of the image of the Woman and their degeneration of the energies of the children of the light."

Archangel Michael discusses the judgment of the fallen angels for their misuses of the light of the will of God and the binding of the fallen Archangel, Lucifer, on April 16, 1975:

"The invocations of the two witnesses made simultaneously Above and below in the octaves of Spirit and Matter for the binding of that Lucifer were fulfilled by the Seven Archangels and the hosts of the Lord Christ. And so the duty and the dharma fell to us to bind that one and to remand him to the Court of the Sacred Fire convoked on the God Star Sirius, where the Four and Twenty Elders tried and sentenced the archdeceiver of mankind to the second death. 'Now is come salvation and strength and the kingdom of our God and the power of his Christ: for the accuser of our brethren is cast down, which accused them before our God day and night.'"[44]

Archangel Michael explains that "with the Fallen One, many who followed him in the Great Rebellion were also brought to trial. And these trials are continuing as day by day the end of the cycle of opportunity for repentance comes to those who for thousands of years have refused to bend the knee and bow before the Lord Christ and to acknowledge the supremacy of the flaming Word incarnate in the sons and daughters of God. Thus while judgment is passed by the Four and Twenty Elders, judgment comes also to those in incarnation on numbers of planets where the end of cycles is also come."

In order to balance this karma, the creation of the fallen angels that remains even after their judgment at the Court of the Sacred Fire, Archangel Michael explains to the children of the One that "in this hour of salvation, it is your duty and your dharma to challenge the carnal mind in the name of the Christ; and it is your privilege in the name of the living God to challenge the Antichrist and to call forth the legions of Victory to give mankind the flaming consciousness of victory over the beast and over his image and over his mark and over the number of his name. So let it be done in the name of the living God, and let it be fulfilled—heart, head and hand—through the children of the light!"

From Archangel Michael we learn that the LORD God will reenact the judgment of the fallen angels through us as we "give voice in the power of the spoken Word to the fiats of the LORD." Therefore he admonishes: "Take then the decrees and invocations vouchsafed to you by the two witnesses, and let your voices be the rising of the smoke of incense that is pleasing unto the LORD. And let your voices rise in invocation in affirmation of the judgment twenty-four hours a day."[45]

The LORD God Has Not Left Us Comfortless

Of mankind's karma released by Archangel Michael, the Archeia Faith says: "This plague is a dark energy that covers the sky at noonday as though the hand of God had scattered the dust of the centuries, distributing to the four winds mankind's willful pollution of the elements of being."

Yet in the hour of the judgment we are assured by Archeia Faith that the LORD God has not left us comfortless. The sword of Kali, which cuts the children of the Mother free, is a comfort to all who adore the Mother Flame. Therefore Faith calls us to sing the song of Moses, to sing the name of God I AM THAT I AM, and to chant the AUM into the night and into the day.

Archeia Faith tells us to sing the song of the Lamb, the mantra that was given to John the Revelator, that we might use the sacred Word to implement the victory by the sword of the Spirit. This is the mantra that will counteract mankind's misuses of the energies of the Law and the Lawgiver on the first ray:

"Great and marvelous are thy works, LORD God Almighty; just and true are thy ways, thou King of saints. Who shall not fear thee, O LORD, and glorify thy name? for thou only art holy: for all nations shall come and worship before thee; for thy judgments are made manifest."[46]

The children of Zion will gain their salvation from all self-imposed karma when they come to the sun of the I AM THAT I AM and fall down and worship with the Lord Christ. Those who are one with the Christ and with the I AM THAT I AM will not be judged with the fallen angels and with the Antichrist. The legions of Faith will come and stand before the children of God:

"Now my legions come forth! And they stand before the altar of the Divine Mother and before her representative on earth. They stand before the children of God to bind the powers of darkness, of doubt and fear, of the spirals of disintegration and death. For in the flaming presence of faith is the transmutative action of the Law.

Face Squarely the Enemy Within and Without

"This is the hour for the reaping of the sowings of doubt and fear and death. Therefore the angels are come to take from you the harvest of your wrong sowings in the will of God. Prepare yourselves; and let them come to separate the tares and the wheat of your consciousness, and let them gather the tares that they might be burned in the sacred fire of the will of God."

The Archeia Faith counsels us to enter the fray, to enjoin the hosts of the LORD and to "put on the whole armor of God that ye may be able to stand against the wiles of the lieutenants of Lucifer. These are the *devils* who have _d_eified _evil_, who have worshiped the golden calf and raised up the carnal mind to pervert the serpentine energies of the caduceus, which Moses raised up in the wilderness as the sign of Christ's healing wholeness unto the children of Israel."[47]

There is only one way to overcome the Antichrist who has

perverted the will of God, says Faith, and that is to "face squarely the enemy within and without and receive the admonishment of Alpha," who says:

" 'Now let all evolutions and lifewaves know: The challenge of the hour is the consuming by the sacred fire of the cause, effect, record and memory of all that has been impressed upon the body of the Mother—that body the entire cosmos— by the fallen ones. Now let us behold how the Fallen One has left seeds of rebellion even in the four lower bodies of the children of God. And so the Evil One came and sowed the tares among the wheat.

" 'Now let the sons of light go forth! Let them go into the fields white with the harvest. Let them, as the reapers with the angelic hosts, separate the tares from the wheat. And let it be done by the fiat of Alpha and Omega! Let it be done by the action of the flow of sacred fire from the I AM Presence of each one!

" 'More dangerous even than the Fallen One are the seeds of rebellion that remain to be consumed, for the seed contains within itself the pattern of the whole. And therefore I release the light of the fiery core of the flow of our oneness for the canceling-out of the seed of the Fallen One. I release this energy to the level of the etheric plane, the plane of fire. Farther it cannot go without the assent of your free will and your invocation, for the sacred fire will burn and consume the wheat with the tares unless it first be assimilated in the consciousness of the lightbearers.

" 'Let the sacred fire, then, in the increment that can be borne by each one, be sealed in the third eye and the crown and in the heart as a trinity of action that can be called forth and released in the plane of the mind and the mental belt of a cosmos. It is the Mind of Christ that the fallen ones have determined to seize, to misuse. They have no power from Alpha and Omega; yet the fiery core of life within the children of the sun has been used to affirm that power, to acquiesce to it and to reinforce it.

"'I say then, withdraw by the authority of your free will all affirmation, all consent that you have given unto the fallen ones, unto their rebellion, unto the seed, and unto the carnal mind of your own creation. Only thus will the mental belt be cleansed of the remnant of the Fallen One.

"'Now let the beast that occupies the bottomless pit of the subconscious and the desire body be exposed also! And let it be seen that this creation instigated by the fallen ones has also received the seal of your approval. For that which remains untransmuted, which you have failed to challenge, that which exists in consciousness, is therefore the creation of free will. And until you will to call it back, to undo it, to restore it to the fiery core for transmutation, it remains a blight on the whole of cosmos.

"'Only when you challenge the dweller-on-the-threshold of your own cosmos and your own consciousness—the rebellious one—can you breathe the breath of life and know "I AM free!" Therefore, that judgment that has come to the Fallen One, meted out by Alpha and Omega, must also resound within the consciousness of every living soul. And the Alpha-to-Omega, the atom of identity in the fiery core of your own being, must release the spiral that renders the judgment whereby the dweller-on-the-threshold passes through the second death and is no more and has no longer any habitation in the whole consciousness of that life which you call your own, but which I am here to tell you is my very own—mine to give, mine to take. And I can claim that fiery core, that replica of the Great Central Sun, when the cycles roll and the Law of being returns the drop unto the Ocean.

"'You have a cosmos! You have an energy field assigned to you! Let the four quadrants of your creation be purged of every residue of the Fallen One! Let them be purged by your free will aligned with my own, aligned with the Four and Twenty Elders who render judgment in the God Star. And let the earth body as well be free of the impressions of rebellion and the ego that is set apart from the Divine One!' "[48]

Truly the thrust of the will of God is for the creation of worlds within worlds. By free will man must decide if these will be worlds of godly virtue or worlds of ungodly disintegration of the souls of the living.

The fallen angels have created mechanical worlds, and mankind have imitated their creation. Now the choice to be God on the first ray of his will is to uncreate the worlds of mechanization man, to transmute the mechanical monsters that loom as the Illuminati and as the beasts of the carnal-minded ones that roam the canyons of the astral plane, to remove the hexes of the fallen angels from elemental life and from the children of God—the hexes of disease, decay, disintegration and death.

The thrust of the will of God is able to invert the negative spirals of darkness. And by the alchemy of the sacred fire, the baptism of the Holy Ghost, it can recreate man and woman in the image and likeness of God. It can recreate the four planes of Matter. It can recreate elemental life and reinstate man and woman in the Garden of Eden on the path of initiation under the Guru Maitreya.

The Wisdom of the Buddha and the Mother

T HE CONDITIONS OF THE COVENANT of Eden, which the LORD God set before man and woman in the garden set aside for their initiation on the Path, come under the activity of the second ray. These initiations are given through the office of the Cosmic Christ.

The second ray is the ray of the wisdom of the Mother and of the Christed ones pursuing the way of illumined action. It is the ray of the raising up of the rod of wisdom's power. It is Mother because its energy, the energy of the crown chakra, is in polarity with the white fire core of the Mother focused in the base-of-the-spine chakra.

The pure energy of the Mother rises from this four-petaled chakra, which is the base of the pyramid of man's being. It rises as the entwining action of the caduceus around the rod of power. In the crown it becomes the wisdom of the Father that is in Matter the enlightenment of the Buddha. Hence the second ray carries the energies of interaction between Mother and Father in the foundation and in the consummation of the creation.

The Mother, who originally went forth from the Father, returns to the Father. And in the course of her cyclings through the Matter sphere she gives birth to the manifestation of the Trinity as Father, Son and Holy Spirit. With the Mother as the integrator, these three aspects of the One provide the basis of action-reaction-interaction in all human relationships.

The second ray is the ray of the Buddha's meditation upon the Mother and the Mother's meditation upon the Buddha. The office of the Buddha is the highest spiritual attainment of the sons and daughters of God that can be realized within the Matter sphere. Attainment beyond this is realized within the Spirit sphere.

In Matter, the highest representative of the feminine ray of God is the one who attains to the office of Mother of the World. And the highest representative of the masculine ray is the one who attains to the office of Lord of the World, which presupposes having attained the fullness of the Buddhic enlightenment on the path of initiation. In the Matter sphere, those who hold these two positions in hierarchy govern the integration of the forces and the forcefields that we call time and space.

You Are Not Bound by the Karma of Time and Space

Lord Gautama Buddha has taught us that time is Mother and space is Buddha. Time and space are given to the soul to be transcended. Gautama explains: "All that has occurred in time is in Truth not real, for time is not in the point of reality. Therefore, why tarry and become the prisoner of time through karma? ...

"Every act of love and light takes place in the timeless realm—yes, indeed, the ongoing cycle of cosmos, but not in time. And therefore time is not for the saint, whether on earth or in heaven....

"Those who count time are on the spheres that revolve around the sun. But in the center, where is the sense of time? There is none. It is the point of the pin that holds together a solar system—a tiny pin. There is no time in the center of being.

"Know this in the absolute sense and then begin by the power of the Absolute to transform thy life accordingly. Whatever, then, makes you the prisoner of time, consider—when will you dispense with it? For, you see, if you dispense not with it..., then in the end when time does collapse, you will collapse with it and be no more.

"Those wed to time die with time.

"Thus, take a grand accordion, section by section measuring time—time, then, by vibration and beat and note. And suddenly it collapses in a very tiny space. There is no delineation, no further sound. But in the silence of the Law of the One, the player has become the All....

"The perception of the Buddha's heart does give to those at the point of the eye a means of escape through the lens of the eye of God. I carry you far from the burdens of time and space, for perspective is all. The distance between the eye and the outer events and eventualities is the perspective of the laser beam of the Mind of God.

> In this perspective
> I AM the Eternal Youth
> In the heart of every lifestream of earth in all octaves,
> Yet I do not fret and mourn
> Nor decay with the bodies I inhabit.
>
> I AM joyous
> I AM silent

> I AM filled with laughter
> I AM Beingness
> I AM at the pin in the center of the earth—
> Motionless, perpetually in motion.
>
> I perceive beyond all maya,
> I penetrate all maya.
> I AM beyond all conflict
> And in the center thereof.
> I know no opposites,
> For I AM the Law of the One.
>
> I AM real,
> My waters flow through the unreal.
> I move in the stars,
> I AM unmoved—
> The Immovable One
> In the heart of Shamballa....

"Ye are immortal now in the Eternal Now. In the interval of the secret chamber of the heart where the threefold flame is suspended, there is no time. Yet the beating of the heart that results from the pulsation of life through the threefold flame is the marking of time, of cycles....

"Time is the author of mortality.

"The fallen angels had to be consigned to time. It was the ultimate condemnation and limitation. They swore enmity with the woman, drew down her seed in the veils of time and said, 'If we be prisoners of mortality, so shall they be prisoners of mortality.' They have decreed it. You must undecree it, you see. They have used their ill-gotten power of fohat to declare the ultimate curse that the children of the sun should become prisoners of time.

"Thus, they have intensified karmic temptation, testing—

as though you were caught in a snarled string, your feet all tied, and the more you would struggle, the more you would become totally entwined with the endless knotted string of karma, creating all the more with each attempt and struggle to be free of it. For struggle is binding.

"And thus, liberation is the Eternal Now. Dwell in it, as in a sealed chamber, as a sphere of light suspended in the center. Weightless, you are in the center and heart of the threefold flame in the interval of that secret chamber of the heart.

"Know the meaning, then. For I tell you, within your grasp is the demonstration of this law. And its demonstration is with the utmost practicality and sensitivity to the world of time.

"We know no contradictions. We dominate polarities. We contain them. We subdue them. We allow not opposition but synthesis—always of Alpha and Omega. And the Serpent devouring its tail is Absolute Good devouring the antithesis of Absolute Evil. There is no shaking hands. The Serpent devours all.

"For I the LORD thy God AM a jealous God.[49]

"Thus, understand that God-Good will have all of thee, will devour thee even as the whale devoured Jonah—yet he came out whole. He was suspended there in the belly of the whale in the sense of timelessness in the threefold flame. How can this be? It is the symbol of man entering the sacred fire, entering that spiral of Alpha and Omega, being not consumed thereby but stepping forth the Immortal One.

"When Absolute Good devours the configurations and the figures mathematical in time and space of the fallen ones— when all of this Absolute Evil is devoured, it is assimilated. It retains no objectivity, subjectivity, self-identity. It is masticated. It is pulverized. And it is assumed by light. It is demagnetized. And the Absolute God-Good becomes the One. And again, time is not, space is not: because it is unnecessary.

"The flame makes all like itself, else leaves the pile of ash that is held in the hand of the prophet. The prophet ascended holds the ash resulting from his own cremation fires. And in his hand the ash, then, is the crystal white, scattered to the winds. And the light and the fragrance charges the earth—charges the earth, then, with that consciousness now concentrated in these that are called the remains, yet the nucleus of a consciousness that was and is and evermore shall be permeating, transmuting Matter.

"So shall thy remains be—as thy soul soars sunward to thy God—not dust to dust, but crystal fire mist to crystal. And the white crystal becomes the leaven in the earth. None can resist it.

"Enter, then, the center—the very center of the belly of the whale. Retain thy individuality in God. Step forth. Step forth from the flame, from the whale, from the interval. Step forth the master of time and space in the world, not subject unto the law of sin—sin meaning 'without.'[50] Without identity in God is the state of sin. Thus, the sin not forsaken can never be forgiven. For as long as it is engaged in, the individual is without an identity in God that can retain forgiveness.

"Note the child appeased, forgiven without penance or discipline. The child repeats again and again and again the offense. Thus, beloved, the parent who reinforces repetitive misdemeanors is truly the greater sinner of the twain. The child seeks reinforcement of the Law of the One and yet receives the reinforcement of repetitive acts of indiscretion, disrespect, self-denial.

"This is not the way of the true Father and the true Mother in heaven and in earth. Thus, seize the errant son and daughter and let them know in the full fire of the Eternal Now the trap of time as it is the vessel of every sin.

"Thus, come apart and be a separate people—separate from the cycles of time. Come apart, then, for the flame of forgiveness is an eternal flame. This is why it is written, 'His mercy endureth forever.'[51] It is the foreverness of the Eternal Now self-canceling time and space. Mercy does not eternally dwell in the sinner's realm but eternally gives the opportunity for the exit from that realm.

"As the grass are the days of the man who will not disassociate himself from unreality. So the wind passes through that grass, over it. And suddenly the place thereof knows it no more.

"Thus, time produces the self-canceling process, self-canceling ten thousand cans of beer shuttling on the conveyer belt. There is no reinforcement of Truth in a million cans of beer. Thus, why tarry in the cups of beer and the cusps of time? The multiplication of error is the multiplication of the canceling-out of those who partake thereof.

"I speak to the very core of self-delusion and the lie perpetuating the liar that is the mask and the synthetic self and the anti-Buddha force in each one of you. I step up the sacred fire. And I make you uncomfortable in the presence of that element which, when it is immersed in sacred fire, does experience pain.

"Loose it! Let it go into the sacred fire. For it is the only acceptable offering that I shall receive this night. I stand ready to receive the charred self, the error self—the figure become a voodoo doll, a cheap imitation of thy Christ. I challenge you to cast it into the fire. . . .

You Were Born Free to Love Life Free

"Children of the night and the day, you may be a million light-years from the heart of Abram or one inch from his victory in thyself. You are the determinant factor. You are God as he was God! He made his choice. He became the fire infolding itself. Do not wait for events—make them happen!

"Do not wait for some far distant day and a vision of some Master appearing to thee in the hills. Some of you have created with extraordinary drama and self-importance the scene when you meet Maitreya one day. In this reverie the stage of life is missing the hand of the Divine Director through you.

"Time is not! Maitreya is here! Let us get on with the Initiator.

"Understand the impeccable nature of the mind that steels itself against erosion, encroachment. Pushed hither and thither as though upon an astral sea, you have no part with astral unrealities. You were born free to love, to be love—born free to be love, born free to love life free.

"I AM THAT I AM. I speak now only to the Real Self. If you desire to speak with me, you must enter that reality. I have spoken long enough to the time-conceived, -concealed self. Now I make demand upon the soul: Leave it behind. Let the wind blow and blow hard that thou mayest know thy mortality. Let the extremity and the danger of life compel the call! I will give my all and do anything that circumstance may prevail to liberate you, not to send you crashing to the rocks and down the precipice of life.

"The choice is one: *Upward! Onward!* Scale the heights. Do not be dismayed by elements or elemental life or elements of Death and Hell. Subdue them. Bind them. Thou art the victor over Death and Hell. I proclaim it.

"I AM the One. I AM the Keeper of the Flame of Life for earth. I compel you by the will of thine own heart founded upon the rock of Buddha from the beginning. I compel you to embrace your fiery destiny in the Eternal Now. To that light I bow. And I will have thee as thou art for my heart."[52]

The Path of Initiation in the Garden of Eden

As we have seen, the second chapter of the Book of Genesis portrays the creation of the Matter sphere and the coming of Lord Maitreya, the Buddha, as the Initiator of those who will inhabit that sphere. It also portrays the creation of man and woman that they might meet the challenges of initiation on their respective paths to become the rod of wisdom's power in the flame of the Buddha and in the flame of the Mother.

The raising up of this power through the mastery of the seven planes of God-awareness was their sole reason for being in the Garden of Eden. Had they accepted the covenant that Maitreya set forth, the raising up of the energies of the sacred fire would have formed the crown of glory that is the crown of the World Mother and the crown of the Buddha.

Instead of nakedness and shame, guilt and godlessness, they would have been filled with the glory of their LORD, their Guru. Working through their own self-realization of the I AM THAT I AM, he would have transferred to them the halo that is the crown of life, the hallowed life-force of those who have preserved the energies of the sacred fire as they walk the path of initiation.

The rod of authority that the LORD God gave to Moses and to Aaron is the same energy that rises as a funnel of fire in the hollow of the spine, the coolness and the hotness of the sacred fire breath ascending and descending as the fountain of life.

This is the life force by which the manchild shall rule all nations with the rod of iron. It is the pen of iron with the point of a diamond by which the two witnesses shall write the "sin of Judah,"[53] the law of the karma of the Israelites, the karma of both their Truth and their turning from the Truth.

Out of the flame of the Causal Body of the Buddha the Garden of Eden was created, for the Buddha is the Lord of space. Out of the flame of the Causal Body of the Mother were the times and the seasons and the cycles and the spirals spun for the initiations of man and woman.

Man and woman within the garden are subject to the spacing and the timing of the Buddha and the Mother. It is for them to put on and to become this space and this time so that they might pass from the finite to the infinite measure of God's consciousness. They are required to function within the geometry of the Law of being, as Above, so below.

Here in this very special setting, protected by the matrix of the Mother, held within the mathematics of the Father, man and woman are taught the fundamentals of the Path. They are given knowledge of the Causal Body, the I AM Presence and the Christ Self. They are taught step by step the exercises of soul awareness that Maitreya will give them from the twelve hierarchies of the sun through the twelve trees "pleasant to the sight, and good for food."

Mankind's karma poured out upon the sea from the golden vial of Archangel Jophiel is the karma of the misuse of the second ray—the wisdom of the Father in the Mother and of the Mother in the Father. It is the perversion of the path of initiation by the false teachers who have usurped the position of the Guru Lord Maitreya. Not only have mankind perverted the space set aside for their initiations, but they have also perverted the timing of those initiations.

The Counterfeit Path of Pride

Once man and woman have rejected the Path—both the teacher and the teaching—their existence is relegated to the time-space world. There nature and elemental life in Matter have been subjected to the prideful, willful misuses of the crown chakra by the fallen angels who follow the leader who calls himself the Illumined One.

Lucifer chose this title as the ultimate perversion of the wisdom of the second ray and of the light of the Father-Mother God. Those who followed him in the usurpation of the Mother's energies of illumined action called themselves the Illuminists.

And over the centuries the inner and outer orders of those who have created the counterfeit path have been known as the Illuminati.

Mankind's karma on the second ray is their desire, through their pride and their ambition, to become rulers over others before they have become self-ruled. This is the so-called wisdom of the false teachers, of their philosophy of intellectualism, humanism, individual rights superseding God-ordained rights, and an independence outside of God and his laws.

The Illuminists have taught over thousands of years the philosophy of scientific humanism. This is the doctrine that man has a superior intelligence and that he can achieve his goals by intelligence alone. The scientific humanist strives for domination of the Matter sphere; his goal is man's exaltation over nature and nature's God. He has no need for a God who is perceived to exist outside of his consciousness, for he is a god unto himself.

In the course of the manipulation of mankind, the Illuminists (who now stand in the place of guru) have imposed their tyrannies of pride and arrogance on top of the self-imposed tyrannies of fallen man and woman. It becomes expedient for the purposes of continued manipulation that the Illuminists write a declaration of the rights of man[54] so that mankind might rally around their banner of rebellion against the true hierarchies of light.

In fact, such a declaration is not necessary. The LORD God in the person of the Guru Maitreya has set forth the rights of man and woman in the garden; he has set the boundaries of freedom and self-restraint that must be held in balance on the Path.

Sons and daughters of God on the path of initiation enjoy certain rights according to their level of attainment. Each step on the ladder of initiation accords the individual certain rights and certain restraints according to his self-discipline and the concentration of energy that he guards in the seven chakras of his being. The greater the attainment, the greater the self-discipline; the greater the self-discipline, the greater the freedom; the greater the freedom, the greater the responsibility; the greater the responsibility, the greater the self-restraint.

In the push-pull action and reaction that has characterized their conspiracy against the Christed ones, the Illuminists have alternately given and taken from man and woman these so-called rights. Over the centuries the pendulum swing has been either from absolute freedom (the golden ages of Lemuria and Atlantis, where the misuse of this freedom led to their ultimate destruction) to absolute slavery (Greek, Roman and American slave cultures) or from relative freedom (the modern United States) to relative slavery (European and Russian feudalism).

When mankind thought they were free, they were usually materially free but spiritually enslaved by the Illuminists. And when they thought they were slaves, many were slaves materially but free in their souls. For instance, prior to the French Revolution the people of France, though subject to the rule of a monarchy, were spiritually free to work out their karma and their dharma. Although there was a seemingly inequitable structure in society, these inequities derived from individual levels of karma.

The Illuminists Co-opt the Divine Right to Rule

The Illuminists, working with the Satanists and certain orders of the occult sponsored by the false hierarchy, succeeded in invading the echelons of the most highly evolved among the sons and daughters of God who held their positions in the royal houses of Europe according to what has been called the divine right of kings.[55]

The right of sons and daughters to rule was the natural order of hierarchy from the time of the golden ages of Lemuria and Atlantis. But having successfully corrupted the royal houses and the royal line by infiltrating the ranks of the light-bearers with their own, the Illuminists became the libertines, the fallen angels who took full advantage of their positions inside the royal families.

Whether through intermarriage or through the manipulation of money, the Illuminists destroyed the royal lineage that had descended both spiritually and materially from the house of David and from the twelve tribes of Israel.

In France the inner circles of the order of the Illuminati made the monarchy look so black by their own doings within it that they were able to rally the people against the king and queen. The ensuing bloodbath and Robespierre's reign of terror resulted in the murder of both the sons and daughters of God who had the right to rule and of the pawns of the Illuminists as well.

Those who masterminded the conspiracy of the French Revolution were not concerned that thousands of their own were sacrificed in order to advance the cause of an intellectual humanism. The innermost core of the Illuminati consider that those who occupy the successive rings in their dark mandala are expendable and that the end always justifies the means.

Thus they use the children of the light and mankind in general to rebel against the established order of the sons and daughters of God and the hierarchy of light. Once that establishment has been thoroughly infiltrated by their members, at a certain point when revolution is imminent, the key Illuminists withdraw from the scene. Then those of equal rank on the path of light and the path of darkness are buried in a common grave.

Thus the heads that rolled at the guillotine were of both the seed of Christ and the seed of the Wicked One. No matter. The goal of the guillotine in every age is to widen the circle of godless government by the intellectual elite—the Illuminists.

The French freed themselves from a tyrannical yoke, but

alas, they soon put on another even greater yoke: the karma of rebellion against holy order, which is heaven's first law. When man becomes a law unto himself, the path of liberty is inverted and, like the children of Israel, he condemns himself to endless wandering through a desert devoid of heavenly graces. Then only a compassionate prophet, like a Moses or a Saint Germain, can deliver him.

This has been going on century after century, and still the children of God and most of mankind have not perceived the great conspiracy of the false hierarchy. Their failure to see has fulfilled the prophecy "Where there is no vision, the people perish."[56]

The Golden Vial of the Second Angel

Mankind's karma on the second ray, which they must face individually and collectively, is the karma of the rejection of the true teacher and the true teaching. In place of the path of initiation, mankind are on the treadmill of the false teachers and their false teachings. Jophiel, the Archangel of the second ray, addresses this dilemma:

"Sons and daughters of God born to rule by the rod of understanding, let the understanding of the Christ confute the philosophy and the psychicism of the fallen ones! Let the illumined action of the lightbearers show forth the light of salvation!

"Let the action of those who work the works of God with compassionate understanding be the great example by which the teachings of the Great White Brotherhood are made clear— clear as the sea of glass mingled with fire.[57]

"And the golden vial of the second angel is poured upon the sea, and the emotional bodies of mankind are agitated as the astral plane becomes as the blood of a dead man, and the souls of the living cannot survive in the sea of the astral plane.[58]

"We walk through the valley of the shadow of death.[59] We walk through the canyons of the astral; and our light, as the brilliance of the noonday sun, as the light of the Causal Bodies of the heavenly hosts, does expose the remnant of the Liar and his lie.

"And they recoil in the presence of the Archangels. Where have they to go? None can escape the LORD God in the hour of judgment.

"Therefore 'for judgment I am come,'[60] saith the Lord. And their recoiling is the driving-back of the energies of the fallen ones. And they are driven back into the white fire core wherein the error of their wrong choosing is become the consuming of the white-fire yellow-fire sun.

"And the consuming of the pollution of the waters of the living Word is the consummation of the Mother and the Holy Spirit. The understanding of the Mother is the wellspring of life unto all who have retained the Law of the Father. Let the wellspring of the Mother rising from the base-of-the-spine chakra be the focus of purity's transmutation of all misunderstanding. For misunderstanding is the mist that went up from the earth as the maya, the veil of evil that watered the whole face of the ground.[61]

"Now is the vial of mankind's misuse of the Mother flow poured out upon the sea. And those who dwell in the sea must forge here and now that God-identity which is a fire infolding itself[62]—that God-identity which is able by the flame upon the altar of the heart to consume all mankind's misuses of the sacred fire perverting the wisdom of the Divine Mother in the second ray of illumined action.

"Yes, I am Jophiel. I consecrate places of learning where souls are yearning to be free through the mastery of the Mind of God. Unfortunately, the fallen ones have usurped the seat of authority, and they sit in the philosopher's chair instructing the children of the light in the ways of darkness. And discrimination is nowhere to be found, save in the teachings of the Mother.

"I come wielding the sword of discrimination that by the flame of wisdom you might join my bands as they thrust home to the core of the Luciferian creation to cleave asunder the real from the unreal. Let the motives and intents of the heart of a planet and a people be laid bare in this hour of the tenth station of the cross,[63] when those who take their stand for the Lord incarnate are stripped of their garments by the Roman soldiers.

"I say, let the fallen ones also submit to the stations of the cross! Let them be stripped of their temporal power and of their authority in the governments of the nations!

"Let those who have led the children of God into captivity now go into the captivity of the Holy Spirit. And let the cloven tongues of fire strip from them their carnality and their sensuality, which they have put upon the children of God as a smothering cloak of unrighteousness. And let him that killeth with the sword be killed with the sword.[64] This is the sword of the sacred Word of wisdom; this is the sword that consumes all that is unreal.

"Therefore those who identify with unreality shall be no more in that day of the judgment of the Lord. And let the patience and the faith of the saints[65] keep the flame of life and light and illumination as darkness covers the land and the sea and the only light that shines is the light of the I AM Presence.

"Let the warning be sounded forth by the angels of Jophiel's band that all those who have taken the Word of God and the true teachings of the Law and perverted the divine credo of the Holy Spirit shall face the judgment of the Almighty.

"And let the false prophets and the wolves in sheep's clothing[66] who have usurped the pulpits of the world be stripped of their garments! And let them stand naked before the children of God, who will then see the wickedness of their ways and the evil machinations that they have put upon this generation.

"Let the clarity of the Mind of Christ *flow!* Let golden rivers of illumination *flow* from the throne of God! Let rivers of light inundate consciousness and clear the way for the true teachings of the Law! I stand upon the earth this hour and I stand upon the sea, and I make way for the coming of the Lord and of the law of life. And I clear the consciousness of mankind that they might receive wisdom at the hand of the Mother.

"In this hour of reckoning comes the angel of opportunity sent forth by Portia, the Goddess of Justice. This angel is the mercy of the Law and of the karma of the seven last plagues. And opportunity is a scroll declaring the independence of the souls of Terra, ratified by the saints Above and below. This declaration is the open door for the wisdom teachings.

An Increment of Light Delivered Once in Ten Thousand Years

"Let the Holy Kumaras release the light of the seven rays in the minds of mankind. And let the quickening that was begun at Shasta by the Elohim of the second ray[67] be intensified, even as darkness is intensified before the dawn of the Christ consciousness in mankind.

"This is that increment of light which is delivered once in ten thousand years by the Holy Kumaras. It is a rod implanted in the minds of the children of God by the Solar Logoi for the elevation of mankind's consciousness and the centering of that consciousness in the crown. So intensify! So magnify! So let the star be brilliant in its appearing and let mankind be polarized to that star of the light of wisdom!

"Let the wise man and woman entering the Aquarian cycle hear the word of wisdom's ray and increase learning and attain unto the wise counsels of the Four and Twenty Elders. Now let the fear of the LORD come upon mankind—that fear which is the beginning of knowledge.[68] For this is the age of opportunity, the age when the LORD giveth wisdom. And out of the mouth of his Messengers cometh knowledge and understanding. This is the LORD, who keepeth the paths of judgment and preserveth the way of his saints.

"Let illumination's fires be invoked for the consuming of all false doctrine and dogma, all misstatements and misunderstandings of the Law. Let wisdom crystallize the image of the Christ within you.

"Yes, I am come with the golden vial of the second of the last plagues. But I come also with opportunity at my side. Let the children of the light run into the wave of wisdom's light. Let them run into the great cosmic wave of illumination that breaks upon the shores of Mater and floods the consciousness with the refreshing waters purified by the Mother of life and love and liberation.

"Run to greet the wave of light and see how the great wave will swallow up the pollutions of the river of life.[69] I am for oneness only if it be the oneness of the Christ Mind. And those who defy that mind in my servants the prophets shall be scattered abroad; for they are the proud, the rebellious and the unrighteous generation.

"I am at the door. Bidden by the Lord, I enter. And I come to overthrow the moneychangers in the temple of our God. I come to scourge the wicked generation. See then that you, the lightbearers, are allied with the light, lest when the judgment come it scorch the wings of an angel!"[70]

The Opening of the Door of Consciousness

The Archeia Christine comes with the comfort of the Mother to give to her children the hope that they can yet regain the Christ consciousness in this age. She says:

"Sons and daughters of God who walk the earth in the light of the Logos unmoved by human tyranny or the condemnation of the fallen ones, you who keep the flame of life: know that I am with you in the intelling Presence of the I AM THAT I AM and that I send angels of Jophiel and Christine who come in the name of the Cosmic Virgin to protect the consciousness of all who love the LORD with all their hearts and souls and minds.[71]

"Wherever there is a glimmer of the Christ light, wherever there is a flickering in the consciousness and then a bursting-forth of a facet of the Mind of God, there the angels of illumination are magnetized to enhance that energy, to enlighten minds and hearts and souls already one in the mission of the Lord and Saviour.

"To acknowledge him is to open the door to your own Christ-identity, and to deny him is to close that door. And this is the message of the Spirit of the Christ unto the churches: 'Behold, I stand at the door and knock: if any man hear my voice and open the door, I will come in to him and will sup with him, and he with me.'[72]

"The opening of the door of consciousness is a sacred ritual that must be performed by the children of God in this age. To open the door to the Christ and to the seven Spirits of God [the Seven Elohim] and to the seven stars[73] [the seven Causal Bodies of the seven rays] is to open the heart and the chakra of the heart to the love-wisdom-power of the Logos. When you consciously, willingly allow the Christos to enter there, the divine spark is quickened by emissaries of the heavenly hierarchy who have already attained to the measure of a God Flame and its manifestation.

"Understand, then, that to reject the heavenly hosts and the Faithful and True who leads the armies of heaven into the battle of Armageddon[74] is to seal the door of consciousness against the light of your own Christ-perfection. And this is the dread of the Seven Archangels—that when we enter the octaves of earth we find no room in the inn of being, no chamber in the heart where we are welcome, and the light of the Mother is rejected by those who fear her all-consuming love.

"The LORD God has said, 'Seal the door where evil dwells!' But mankind have inverted the command and sealed the door of the Christ consciousness to their own hurt and their own destruction. The dread of the Archangels is the dread of the awful day of judgment—awful only for those who have sealed themselves from the contact of the Christed ones and the blessed tie of hierarchy that binds mankind to the Law of his own inner being."[75]

The Perversion of Exoteric and Esoteric Religion

Archangel Jophiel warns of the perversions of the false hierarchy in the midst of the mission of the Christed ones to whom it is given to govern the evolutions of earth and to regulate the flow and the fabrication of money and goods in the economies of the nations. Archeia Christine, on the other hand, warns of the penetration of the Illuminists into the religion and education of the world—both into the outer court and the inner court of the temple.

Exoteric religion has been perverted through the false doctrine and dogma of the black priests who have usurped the position of the true prophets of East and West. Esoteric religion, guarded in the mystery schools, the communities and the lamasaries of East and West, also has its counterfeit creation through the false hierarchy and their teachings. Many of these have come under the label of the occult. This word, denoting the "hidden" wisdom referred to by Paul,[76] has come to have a derogatory connotation in Christian circles. This is because of the anti-Christ techniques and training given by the

Illuminists who have invaded the so-called esoteric schools.

Many of those who are members of the successive rings of the orders of the false hierarchy think that they espouse the cause of the Great White Brotherhood. Although they are idealists, they have not mastered their penchant for intellectualism. Nor are they aware of spiritual pride, of the unconquered carnal mind and of their allegiance to the Illuminists.

Their so-called mystery schools are actually centers of mystification, and all of their false teachings can be traced line by line as the perversion of the true teachings set forth in Maitreya's original matrix in the garden. It is the mist of maya that covered the face of the Mother and her education of *Eden*—the understanding of the *e*nergy of *d*ivinity (the Spirit polarity, the positive polarity) becoming the *e*nergy of the *n*egative polarity (the Matter polarity).

This education of the Mother, grounded in reality and sponsored by the Buddha, was presented in the temples of Lemuria and Atlantis. It is the true *educare*—the *Ed*enic *care* of the heart—the initiation of the heart chakra that the Mother brings to educate her children.

Thus Archeia *Christine*—the one who enshrines the light of the *Christ in* the *e*nergies of Matter as intelling love, as indwelling wisdom—instructs us on the opening of the heart and the heart chakra to the love-wisdom-power of the Logos. This is the true flame of education that the Buddha of the age passes to the Mother of the age that Wisdom might teach her children.

The Black Brotherhood of Lemuria, working through the Black Brotherhood of India, has taught their devotees how to manipulate elemental life through the misuse of the mantra and the misuse of the energies of the caduceus. The false prophets of the light of the true Hindus and the true Buddhists have perverted the polarity of twin flames, which manifested in the complete oneness of man and woman before the Fall.

The sacred ritual of the flow of sacred fires between the chakras of twin flames has been perverted in the misuses of tantric yoga and in the practices of certain teachers who have taught the gullible to meditate upon the sacral centers to heighten sexual and sensual gratification, and to master material forces in the body for the purpose of controlling spiritual forces. All this is done not to the glory of Christ but to the glory of the carnal mind. One and all, these teachers function without the sanction of the real Gurus of the Great White Brotherhood, ascended and unascended.

This anti-Christ, anti-Buddha activity, widespread in America and in India, is an example of material freedom side by side with spiritual bondage. Certain teachers purporting to represent the Great White Brotherhood—and others who have publicly denied its existence—teach the rites of kundalini yoga to those whose attainment does not accord them that right.

Other advanced forms of yoga that should be taught only by the real Gurus ascended and unascended are being conveyed freely, to the destruction of souls who ought to be submitting in all humility to the very first steps on the true path of initiation.

Black magicians in East and West have manipulated the polarity of twin flames and created out of it, in fallen man and fallen woman, an opposition of all of the opposing elements of their karma of disobedience under the twelve hierarchies of the sun that is registered in their electronic belts.

Brothers and sisters who enter the schools of the false hierarchy do not have the direct tie to the God Flame in the center of the Causal Body. Nor do they enjoy the initiations of the spheres of the Causal Body cycle by cycle. Instead they are tied to the successive rings of influence made up of independent members in independent circles, none of whom realize that they are all puppets on the string of the Fallen One in the center.

Instead of being tied to the Christ Self as the real Guru, they are tied to the Antichrist and to the impostors. Instead of being tied to the soul and to the hierarchies who govern the initiations on the path of solar awareness through Helios and Vesta,[77] they are tied to the philosophy and the psychicism that supplants true soul awareness.

Counterfeit Mystery Schools of the Fallen Angels

Genesis describes the deep spiritual communion necessary for the soul's evolution as the deep sleep that the LORD God caused to fall upon Adam.[78] This was the natural means that Maitreya provided whereby the soul would separate from the lower vehicles and travel in its etheric sheath to the higher octaves of creative consciousness in the Causal Body of the Guru Maitreya or in the retreats of the Great White Brotherhood.

Later, certain schools of the false hierarchy that were in vogue on Atlantis during the hundred and twenty years of the preaching of Noah perverted this natural "going out and coming in"[79] to the body temple. During that era the descendants of Cain, working with the Illuminists, popularized the psychic trance, preceded or followed by psychic meditation in the subconscious.

This subconscious plane of self-awareness (below the conscious awareness of the Self as God), which we have equated with the electronic belt, became the psychic laboratory for the manipulation of the mental and feeling worlds—of the self and of other selves. This was the beginning of the practice of hypnosis and autohypnosis.

This form of psychic trance and psychic meditation has persisted to the present day. According to these false teachings, the neophyte is taught to leave the body not through the fire center (the heart chakra) and the fire body (the etheric envelope) but through the water center (the solar plexus) and the water body (the astral or emotional body).

This results in soul travel in the astral plane. Once caught on the astral plane, souls are taken to the abodes of the members of the false hierarchy, their astral forcefields. Those who are thus led by the embodied and disembodied representatives of the false hierarchy are beguiled by the endless euphoria of the plane of psychic phenomena. They are convinced that they contact the living Masters, both ascended and unascended.

They know not (for they are the sincere) that they themselves are being used by the fallen angels, who no longer enjoy the crystal cord connection to the Source. Instead, these fallen angels dupe their unwitting disciples into states of adulation and excessive attention wherein they release great quantities of solar (soul) energies to the false teachers.

The fallen angels maintain astral forcefields that closely resemble, even in simulated radiation, the etheric retreats of the Great White Brotherhood. By deliberate design, the astral forcefields key the memory of the would-be disciple of God to the Garden of Eden, since it is the desire of every sincere soul of light to return to the place prepared for her initiation on the Path. When she sees the imitations of the garden set up by the members of the false hierarchy, she is anxious to accept their validity. She lacks the discrimination to discern the real from the unreal.

Once hooked into the endless entertainment of the psychic plane, souls are bound to coils of the counterfeit creation for interminable centuries—until they cry unto the LORD and receive the self-elevation of their own Christ Self together with that of Jesus the Christ and Lord Maitreya.

With the coming of Mother (Matter), the sphere of the soul's individuality is born. With the coming of Mother is the soul's opportunity to make God's karma her karma. The Mother provides the womb of time and space and the teaching whereby the soul aborning in her womb can become the Spirit whence it came.

As we continue to examine the secondary causes of mankind's karma resulting from their disobedience to the First Cause, let us bear in mind that the challenge of transmuting karma is the challenge that the Mother gives to her children. Therefore, in its fulfillment this balancing action must include the mastery of the Mother Flame. The Mother and the flame of Mother (the Mother and the Matter sphere in which she figures as both Creator and creation) must become the focal point of our understanding in this age, if we would ride the crest of the wave of light that has come out from the Source to take us back to the Source. (See figure 17.)

The Mother in the person of Archeia Christine reminds us that energy is God. The Mother who gives birth to the Christ teaches us that "the core of energy, as that energy flows from Spirit to Matter and returns again, is the Mediator, the Christed one, the great transformer of the energies of life."

She teaches us that the Christ is the great integrator of the Law of being and that at the nexus of the flow of the figure-eight spiral is the integrator who also "in the white fire core of the atom is the point for the transition of consciousness as Above, so below."

From the Archeia of the second ray we learn that the energy which is God is "self-luminous, intelligent, obedient to the Law of the One. Wherever there is intelligence," she affirms, "there I am amplifying the flow of the intelligent electron." She astonishes us with her comment, "More intelligent than the rebellious generation who have usurped the light of God's energy are these electrons who have elected to do and to be the will of God. Their flow is with the flow of the eternal Christos."

The Judgment of the Godless Creation

Archeia Christine removes the veil from a passage of scripture concerning the judgment: "You see, God's energy will not forever be confined to the limitations and the imitations of the counterfeit creation. As the LORD has said, 'My Spirit shall not always strive with man, for that he also is flesh.' The LORD God will not forever allow himself as energy to be imprisoned in the matrices of imperfection. Therefore cometh the judgment."[80]

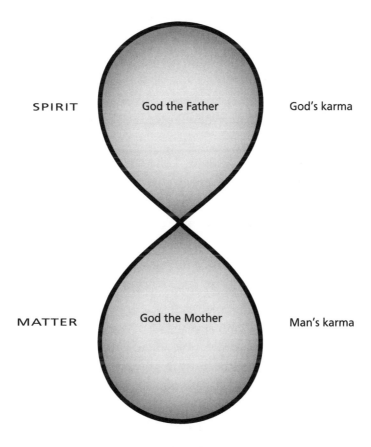

FIGURE 17:
Mastering the Mother Flame to make man's karma God's karma.

From time to time the LORD God sends the judgment upon the creators and their creations in the planes of Matter. Those who have misused the science of the spoken Word in the seven steps of precipitation have encased God's energy in the godless creation. Those who have squandered sacred fires on unsacred desires will meet upon the mountain those who are the instruments of the Lord's judgment. For the LORD has said, "Thou shalt break them with a rod of iron; thou shalt dash them in pieces like a potter's vessel."[81]

Here the judgment is of the heathen. The heathen are the godless creation—the creation in whom there is no God. Therefore they have not accepted the God of *Israel*, the God of all that *is real*, the I AM THAT I AM. Thus "do the heathen rage" and the people whom they have vexed "imagine a vain thing." For they have been hexed with the mass hypnosis and seduced with the subliminal seductions of the mass media.

The Illuminists have set themselves up as the kings of the earth, but not of the heavens. The Luciferians and the fallen angels have established themselves as the rulers of this world. They have taken counsel together against the LORD and against his anointed, saying, "Let us break their bands [the strength of their numbers] asunder, and cast away their cords from us." The cords of righteousness bind together the body of God on earth. It is these cords of invulnerability in Christ's love that the Illuminati would cast away by mass control.

But we hear the judgment of the LORD, "He that sitteth in the heavens shall laugh: the LORD shall have them in derision. Then shall he speak unto them in his wrath, and vex them in his sore displeasure. Yet have I set my king upon my holy hill of Zion. I will declare the decree: the LORD hath said unto me, Thou art my Son; this day have I begotten thee. Ask of me, and I shall give thee the heathen for thine inheritance, and the uttermost parts of the earth for thy possession."[82]

By confirming the decree of the LORD as Above, so below, the sons and daughters of God may call for the Lord's judgment of the heathen who have invested themselves with the robes and the rites of ecclesiastical and secular authority.

Those who are the godless creation, as well as those who have imitated it, are the generations of the Archdeceiver of mankind. They have no right to rule the righteous who are regenerated in the Son of God. Christine conveys Alpha's counsel to the children of the light to confirm the judgment of the Fallen One and his seed within their own being:

"'Let all be alert! Let all know that the passing from the Macrocosm of the one who instigated the rebellion of the angels[83] is a point for the release of great light in the Macrocosm. You are globules of identity suspended in the Macrocosm of my own Self-awareness. And that light which inundates the cosmic sea cannot penetrate the sphere of identity that you are unless you will it so. Therefore I come to say: Ratify and confirm the judgment within your own being; and only then be satisfied in the Law and in the victory.

"'Judgment is nigh. Understand that unless you release the judgment in your own microcosm and withdraw all support of the energy veil, when the judgment comes and the skeins of consciousness are found to be woven inextricably with skeins of evil, then the entire globule must pass through the spirals of Alpha and Omega. And this is the ritual, then, of the canceling-out of that which cannot be absorbed into the sea; for by free will it has not willed it so.

"'You are set apart as a diamond suspended in crystal, suspended in ruby, suspended in agate. See how the crystallization of the God Flame that I AM must be made your own. You determine the fate of your own cosmos. So let it be. So receive the warning that perhaps there is even greater danger now than when the Adversary was personified before you; for now it remains only the subjective awareness, and that subjectivity is the burden of the soul that longs to be extricated from that substance that has no part with light.

"'I AM Alpha. I AM Omega. When you know that you are Alpha, that you are Omega, then and only then will you find yourself in the white fire core of the Great Central Sun.

"'Children of the One: *Forge your God-identity!*'"[84]

A Mantra for God-Identity

Christine teaches us to confirm the judgment within and to forge our God-identity through meditation upon the spiritual sun and through the concentration of the attention within the heart chakra as we demonstrate the science of the spoken Word.

She teaches us to maintain contact with all who adore the one supreme God by feeling the intensity of the love of the Logos. And she gives us a mantra to forge our God-identity:

> I AM Alpha and Omega
> In the white fire core of being!

Her words are a burst of hope for the universal illumination of mankind, which overcomes the universal infiltration by the Illuminists:

"Let the sun of God expand within your heart and let your meditations be upon the blessed sun—expanding, expanding as the brilliant golden white light from the altar of your very own heart.

"When you give your mantras and invocations, when you recite your decrees invocative of the divinity within you—above all, when you pray to our Father-Mother God—let not your attention be attenuated in outer manifestation, but rather let it be concentrated in the heart.

"And as that heart fire expands and expands, taking in the all of your being and your four lower bodies, you will be confirming the judgment of the Law. You will be refining your soul energies in the great cloud of the Spirit. You will be building the forcefield of the Great Central Sun Magnet that will surely magnetize to you, even as I AM THAT I AM, the heavenly hosts who nourish and sustain the children of God through all of the trials and tribulations of this world.

"Therefore intensify, O intensify that sun! See it now! Adore its golden glow! Feel the intensity of the love of the Logos within you contacting all throughout a cosmos and beyond who adore the one supreme God.

"By the power of the central sun focused within you, the Christ will put down the carnal mind, the Christ will consume the dweller-on-the-threshold and all subconscious layers of selfishness and rebellion against the one true God. Your soul longs to be free. Take then the mantra of the free! Forge your God-identity with this saying of the LORD: 'I AM Alpha and Omega in the white fire core of being!'

"Let this be the acceptable word of the LORD that comes forth from your mouth, the sacred instrument of the voice of God. Let this be the acceptable word, the fiat and the command uttered unto the atoms, molecules and precious electrons of being: 'I AM Alpha and Omega in the white fire core of being!' Let this be your finding of yourself in the white fire core of the Central Sun on this the acceptable day of salvation and the appointed time of the judgment."[85]

To know that I AM Alpha, that I AM Omega, is the ultimate freedom of the white fire core of each one's individual being, God-ordained. This freedom to be in God Father, in God Mother, is the freedom of the Holy Spirit. It is this Spirit, as the wisdom of the second ray and as the Lord's judgment in the second ray, that is the hope of the salvation of souls and the victory over all activities of anti-Christ, anti-Father, anti-Mother, anti-Holy Spirit.

Mighty Victory and his legions of light from Venus will lead the children of God as they join the armies of the Faithful and True and the hosts of the LORD—who will indeed manifest the victory over the first beast and the second beast, over the dragon that gives power to the beasts, over the Antichrist, over every false prophet of the carnal mind, and even over the Great Whore.

Following is the call of the golden victorious light. Let all who give it know that they are encompassed round about by the hosts of the LORD, encamped on the hillsides of the world, waiting for the call of the Christed ones who would do battle against every form and formula of Antichrist.

GOLDEN VICTORIOUS LIGHT
by the Cosmic Being Victory

In the name of the beloved mighty victorious Presence of God, I AM in me, Holy Christ Selves of all mankind, beloved Mighty Victory, beloved Lanello, the entire Spirit of the Great White Brotherhood and the World Mother, elemental life—fire, air, water and earth! I decree:

I AM the golden victorious light, the full-orbed flame of illumination from the heart of God that refuses to accept any concept of limitation concerning my eternal reason for being here and now made manifest in the chalice of the present hour.

I AM the radiation of that victory which sweeps across the face of the earth, removing barriers by the power of faith that will not be denied its immortal birthright.

I AM the flame of illumination that sweeps all continents, awakening peoples of every walk of life from the lethargy and sleep of the ages to a vital, breathing awareness of the wisdom that transcends dogma, sense consciousness and personality functions, threading the eye of the needle with the thread of light-determination whose sewings upon the garments of the LORD of Creation produce elevation, consummation, radiation, purification and freedom for every man, woman and child upon this planet.

> O world, awake,
> Your dusty selves now shake;
> Purify and rectify,
> New ways of thought to make! (3x or 9x)

And in full faith I consciously accept this manifest, manifest, manifest! (3x) right here and now with full power, eternally sustained, all-powerfully active, ever expanding and world enfolding until all are wholly ascended in the light and free!

Beloved I AM! Beloved I AM! Beloved I AM!

Serpent: Fallen Angel of the Second Ray

The subtlety of the Serpent lies in its self-centered existence. The coiled serpent is the esoteric symbol of the Causal Body, and the eye of the serpent in the center represents the All-Seeing Eye of God. The coils formed by the body of the serpent represent the revolutions of the cycles of reality around the center of vision in Christ. The power of the vision is multiplied by the number of times that the serpentine force is wound around the center of the Self.

The symbol of the serpent is also used to illustrate the

caduceus, the intertwining of the energies of Father and Mother around the center of being, the Christ. Moses held up the brazen serpent in the wilderness so that by the science of real eye magic (the vision of the third eye) the flux of the sacred energies of the people would be accelerated. This acceleration was for the raising up of the serpentine force culminating in the crown (the wisdom that is the healing of the karma of ignorance) and in the third eye (the vision that is the healing of the karma of unlawful desire).

Both ignorance and selfish desire are rooted in a self-centered existence outside of God. This is the existence of the Fallen One (the Serpent), which he must perpetuate through mankind. For the Serpent has no self-existence except that which it lives through the carnal mind of man and woman.

The Serpent can perpetuate its existence only so long as man and woman remain ignorant of the Law of the LORD and bound to the desires of the lesser self. Thus it is the perpetual activity of the Serpent to sustain this two-pronged condition of duality outside the Edenic consciousness.

The Serpent's energy coil is a vortex of selfishness that lures into itself those who are weak in their own Self-identity. This self-centered existence is a hypnotic spiral that draws to itself others who can be used to sustain its selfishness.

"Serpent" is the name of a fallen angel.[86] And the name Serpent is actually the title of an office in hierarchy that was perverted by the fallen angels. The angel who held the office of Serpent had the authority of the caduceus and of the thirty-three coils of initiation wound around the center (the eye) of the Christ consciousness. This angel originally held the focus for the evolution of the cycles of initiation according to the seven steps of precipitation. After his fall, the Serpent became the false hierarchy counterpoint to the Cosmic Christ, the Guru Lord Maitreya.

The Serpent is described as "more subtil than any beast

of the field which the LORD God had made."[87] He could not enter the garden except through the consciousness of the woman. He used her to give him access to God's energies through the lowering of her energies (the serpentine energies of the caduceus) by her attention upon the lesser self rather than the greater Self.

Serpent was an angel of the Matter energy field—an angel cast out of heaven (the Spirit sphere) into the earth (the Matter sphere). He was a cohort of the one of whom Paul spoke: "Satan himself is transformed into an angel of light." Satan figured in the false hierarchy as a lieutenant of Lucifer, one of lesser rank than that of the Archangel.[88]

With Serpent and others identified in the sacred scriptures of the world and in the mythology and folklore of many civilizations, Satan did the bidding of his master in tempting the evolutions of mankind to enter the downward spiral of self-deception. Even the children of God and the sons and daughters of God who dwell among them were not spared his wiles. However, Satan was less successful in dealing with Job and with Jesus than Serpent was with Eve.

Serpent Begins His Discourse with Eve

The first words of the subtle one to Eve,[89] who symbolizes the feminine part of each of us, are in the form of a question. This human questioning of the LORD's commandment is a wedge driven into the etheric body of Eve. The Serpent's question "Yea, hath God said, Ye shall not eat of every tree of the garden?" comes as an intimidation of her soul's innocence. Its implication is doubt—the doubting of the Word and the Law of the Guru. This intimidation, this questioning of the authority of Maitreya, evokes from Eve a restatement of the Word of the Guru set forth as Law on the path of initiation:

"And the woman said unto the Serpent, We may eat of the fruit of the trees of the garden: but of the fruit of the tree which is in the midst of the garden, God hath said, Ye shall not eat of it, neither shall ye touch it, lest ye die." Eve recalls the exact words of the Law. She knows what is right and what is wrong. She has been given the rules for the right-handed path. She knows the rules of the game, and she knows the penalty for failure to abide by the rules.

Now the Serpent is ready to thrust into the mental body of Eve his restatement of the Law of Maitreya. He presents to the woman the illogical logic of the Fallen One, the counterpoint of the Logos: "Ye shall not surely die."

What does this mean? "Ye shall die, but not surely"? Or is it a question: "Surely ye shall not die?" Or does it imply that state which is neither life nor death, that state of the subterranean, subconscious existence into which the Serpent desired to lure Eve? This is the state of the astral plane where the soul, no longer alive in Christ, dead to the Word of God, yet retains a quasi existence, a synthetic existence of the synthetic self.

The Serpent goes on to explain, "For God doth know that in the day ye eat thereof, then your eyes shall be opened, and ye shall be as gods, knowing good and evil." Serpent presents to Eve the same argument that Lucifer presented to the angels when he caused them to compromise their cosmic honor flame.

The Serpent is explaining that the fallen angels had become gods by partaking of the light of the Christ without undergoing the rigors of Christic initiation. They had stolen the light of the Christ, and she could do the same. This was the boast of the Luciferians made first to the children of God and much later to Adam and Eve in the garden: that they had become knowers of good and evil, that they had become arbiters of the destinies of entire lifewaves in this and other systems of worlds, that they were the counterparts of a vast hierarchical network stretching even to the sister galaxy Andromeda. Indeed, both before and after the fall of Lucifer mankind looked to him and to his cohorts and their robot creation as exalted beings—as some do to this day.

The Real "Original Sin"

Contrary to the lie popularized by the Archdeceiver of mankind, the original sin was not committed by Adam and Eve but by Lucifer himself. And that original sin was the desecration of the Christ, the only begotten Son of God "full of grace and truth." [90]

The Luciferians' original sin was their refusal to worship the Christ, the Son of God. It was against the Son and the Son consciousness that they directed their rebellion. They were already cocreators with the LORD God; why should they, they said, do homage to his Son?—much less bow down before the light of the Christ in the children of God who were far beneath them in evolution and in the order of hierarchy.

These fallen angels had not reckoned with the Law. True, man was made "a little lower [in the order of hierarchy] than the angels." Yet because of the Son consciousness with which man is endowed, upon passing his initiations in the Christ consciousness he would be crowned with more "glory and honor" [91] than they. The man whom the Luciferians had spurned, by spurning the image of the Son, would one day rise to confirm the Lord's judgment of their great rebellion against the Lord Christ and the LORD's hosts.

The Three Temptations of Eve

The temptation of the fallen angel Serpent was for man and woman to experiment in the uses of the sacred fire, the threefold flame, prior to the initiations of that flame which the Guru Maitreya would give to them. The fallen angel Satan tempted Eve[92] to partake of the energies of the Father, the Son and the Holy Spirit—the power, the wisdom and the love of God—and to use these to perpetuate self-centered existence outside of God.

Through the critical eyes of the Serpent the woman saw that (1) the tree was "good for food." The power aspect could be used to gain all economic objectives in the world, to acquire wealth and all that was necessary to meet the demands of physical man.

She saw that (2) it was "pleasant to the eyes." The pride of the eye is in the gratification of the emotions through fulfilling the pleasures of the senses, the emotional interactions of social intercourse in the various exchanges of energies that occur through the relationships of human attachment.

And she saw that (3) it was "a tree to be desired to make one wise." In order to control the economies of the world and the society of the world, she saw the desirability of using the energies of the Christ in intellectual accomplishment, for political ambition, and to gain the mortal, manipulative reasoning powers of the carnal mind.

Eve was tempted to enter into the ways of the world. She was tempted (as Jesus was) to fall down and worship the carnal mind as Serpent and Satan, who would give her dominion and power over all of the kingdoms of this world and over all that she desired to have and to control in man. When she saw what the misuses of the sacred fire could achieve, "she took of the fruit thereof, and did eat, and gave also unto her husband with her; and he did eat."

Thus Adam and Eve, alone in the garden, were given the opportunity to choose spiritual unity with God through obedience to Christ or the way of the fallen Archangel through obedience to the law of sin. They used their God-given gift of free will to choose darkness instead of light. They chose the temporary pleasures of this world in exchange for the permanent joy of bliss in this and the next world.

The Crux of the Path of Initiation

Maitreya did not interfere with their choice, nor did he intrude in the moment of their choosing. He did not descend with his legions and slay the Serpent. No, this is not the way of the path of initiation. For if man would become God, if man would make God's karma his own, he must demonstrate his willingness in complete freedom. Without this freedom to choose to be God or man, there is no path of initiation, there is no Initiator and no initiate.

The Path for modern-day sons and daughters of God is identical to the path of Adam and Eve. Nothing has changed—neither the Law nor the Lawgiver. God allows man and woman to consider the alternatives of God's karma and man's karma—the path of light and the path of darkness. In the beginning, light; out of the light, the One; out of the One, individuality; out of individuality, free will; out of free will, the responsibility to choose to be or not to be. From free will comes the choice and from the choice, the judgment; and from the judgment, karma.

God sends forth the call. It is his action. Man returns the answer. It is his reaction. The call and the answer, as action-reaction, produce the interaction of the energies of God and man: *karma.*

Man and woman set up their own cause-effect sequence, which was to become an endless chain of man's karma outside of God's karma—a chain of action-reaction-interaction that would bind them for thousands of years to the law of karma, to the law of sin self-made and to the wheel of rebirth. They had bound themselves with the chains of their own ignorance and their own desire.

The disobedient action of Adam and Eve was the desecration of the threefold flame; the reaction was that "the eyes of them both were opened, and they knew that they were naked; and they sewed fig leaves together, and made themselves aprons." The seamless garment of holy innocence had been rent in twain, like the veil that hung in the Holy of holies which was rent in the hour when the fallen angels again desecrated the threefold flame of life in the crucifixion of Jesus Christ.

So Adam and Eve became "as gods." As fallen ones they would daily face the dilemma of the knowledge of good and evil, the ambivalence of an ambivalent society. The curtain drops on the first act of disobedience to the Guru.

"And they heard the voice of the LORD God walking in the garden in the cool of the day." Sin and the law of sin were upon them. Ashamed of their betrayal of the LORD, "Adam and his wife hid themselves from the presence of the LORD God" who had made them.

The descent of the energies of the caduceus within the chela always registers upon the chakras of the Guru. Maitreya called Adam and said unto him, "Where art thou?" ("Where is thy consciousness? Have you lost the vision of the Law that I gave to you in the commandment and in the sealing of the third eye in the wholeness of the Father-Mother God? Have you taken the energies of the Christ consciousness and lowered them to the level of the lower chakras and the electronic belt of the mass consciousness? Are you in the plane of Spirit or are you in the plane of matter?")

And Adam replied, "I heard thy voice in the garden, and I was afraid, because I was naked; and I hid myself."[93]

Through the misuses of the sacred fire and the threefold

flame, Adam and Eve had perverted the energies of God in the lower chakras. So when Adam heard the voice of the Lord God "in the garden" (the replica of the heart chakra of God), he was afraid. His energies had descended to the level of the solar plexus. There for the first time on the path of initiation, he knew fear—the fear of the Law and the Lawgiver in the face of his own sin. He was naked because through his act his soul had been stripped of the garment of righteousness, the right use of the Law.

We see another example of this fear based on accumulated karma in Peter, who entered a vortex of fear when he attempted to walk on the water with Jesus.[94] His fear enveloped him, for he had not yet regained the seamless garment of the soul. He was saved by the wholeness of the Christ consciousness passed to him through the Saviour's hand. The current of Christ's caduceus arced to the body of Peter, but Peter had yet to prove his own Christ-mastery, as one day Adam and Eve would also do.

Thus Adam and Eve misused the power of the Father in the desire body and released it as a negative vortex of fear in the solar plexus. The promised wisdom became the soul's knowledge of her own state of wretchedness without God. This is the weeping and gnashing of teeth that takes place when man and woman depart from the inner light of the senses of the soul and enter the outer darkness, the experience of life solely through the physical senses.

The loss of the love of the Holy Spirit, the love of twin flames in the white fire core of the heart, is the logical conclusion of the misuses of the light of the Father, the Son and the Mother. The misuse of the Mother light lies in the use of the sacral energies to manipulate the planes of God's consciousness to subjugate the flame of Mother (the abundance of her light) to the ignorance and the desire of mortal law and mortal existence.

Thus God established Adam's reality and Adam himself established his own unreality. The LORD asked him, "Who told thee that thou wast naked?" ("Where is thy vision? If you see yourself as naked, you no longer have the vision of your immaculate conception in God, your original conception, made as you were in the image and the likeness of Elohim.")

The LORD demands answer: "Hast thou eaten of the tree, whereof I commanded thee that thou shouldest not eat?" Adam answers, "The woman whom thou gavest to be with me, she gave me of the tree, and I did eat." Adam's identity, even his own self-awareness, is inextricably linked with Eve. He cannot see himself or his sin apart from the self or the sin of Eve. For the LORD had taken her from man and Adam had said, "This is now bone of my bones, and flesh of my flesh: she shall be called Woman, because she was taken out of Man."[95]

And the LORD questioned the woman who before had been questioned by the Serpent: "What is this that thou hast done? And the woman said, The serpent beguiled me, and I did eat."[96] ("I have hearkened to the Fallen One. I have chosen him as my guru in place of the great Initiator, Maitreya.")

Understanding His Spiritual Marriage, Adam Bears Eve's Burden

In truth, it was woman who first fell from the God-estate. Man, finding himself alone in the plane of perfection, consciously and willingly descended to the level of the woman's imperfection. He remembered the words of his Guru, "It is not good that the man should be alone; I will make him an helpmeet."[97]

Man followed woman in the great compromise with the Liar and his lie. Man was not fooled by the illogical logic of the Fallen One. Eve's fall was the fall of desire that sustained ignorance. Adam's fall was the fall of disobedience, self-willed. Adam foreknew the punishment of Eve. But he accepted the covenant of their oneness—the intertwining of the caduceus of the man and the woman whom the LORD had made, the twin serpents of the caduceus that are the manifestation in Matter of the T'ai Chi of the Spirit sphere of the Father-Mother God.

The reenactment of the divine union in Matter is the true meaning of the marriage covenant of twin flames that Maitreya sealed: "Therefore shall a man leave his father and his mother and shall cleave unto his wife: and they shall be one flesh." This is the same covenant that Jesus crowned with the words "Wherefore they are no more twain, but one flesh. What therefore God hath joined together, let not man put asunder."[98]

This marriage covenant is the sealing with the ring of fire of the caduceus energies of man and woman. They are one as the Father-Mother God—on earth as in heaven. As Above in Spirit, so below in Matter, the intertwining of the energies of twin flames is reenacted for the wholeness of the LORD's body in manifestation.

In this oneness, twin flames share the burden of light of their Causal Bodies—the coiled serpent of the Spirit spheres, including the karma of God that they individually have made their own. They also share the burden of darkness of their electronic belts—the coiled serpent of the Matter spheres, including the karma of mankind and of the mass consciousness that they individually have made their own.

Thus twin flames are counseled, "Bear ye one another's burdens, and so fulfil the law of Christ." Even so, when it comes to the judgment and to the meting out of karma, "every man shall bear his own [karmic] burden."[99] Understanding this law, Adam willingly took on the karma of Eve lest he break the covenant of their oneness.

The First Judgment in Eden:
The Judgment of Serpent
(and of All Who Have Fallen from the Grace of God)

First the LORD God judges the Serpent: "Because thou hast done this, thou art cursed above all cattle, and above every beast of the field; upon thy belly shalt thou go, and dust shalt thou eat all the days of thy life: and I will put enmity between thee and the woman, and between thy seed and her seed; it shall bruise thy head, and thou shalt bruise his heel."[100]

The Serpent, the Fallen One, is cursed by the LORD. This cursing is the circumscribing of his energy flow within certain confines of consciousness (the bounds of his habitation). The LORD places a matrix of light over the Serpent; henceforth his action-reaction-interaction spirals may not exceed this proscription. This process is known as the fixing of the forcefields of fohatic energy.

This fohatic energy is the essence of all life, including man and woman and every creature the LORD hath made. Its functioning in man is controlled by the DNA chain and the genes and the chromosomes. From time to time, as it becomes necessary by divine decree (which the Lords of Karma set forth), the setting of the dial of the frequencies governing the fohatic flow is altered. The ascended Gurus and Lords of the Elements through the agency of the body elemental carry out these decrees.

This occurred, for example, in such events as the narrowing of the crystal cord, the diminishing of the threefold flame and the consequent shortening of man's days to threescore and ten;[101] in the reduced size of the fruits outside of Eden; and in the reduced stature of the descendants of Seth and Cain who departed from the Adamic covenant.

As a result of Serpent's aggressive influence upon Eve, his status was redefined. In the planes of Matter his hierarchical rank is beneath that of elemental life. This demotion applied to all of the fallen angels and those who followed them in their deprecation of the Word. The fallen angels have less status than the beings of fire, air, water and earth. They are relegated to the astral plane.

The light that they perverted in their seven chakras was cast down. Serpent was made to crawl upon his belly, the solar plexus chakra, which is the focus of the astral or emotional body.

Serpent lowered the energies of man and woman to the plane of unholy desire. His karma was that he be removed from the Spirit sphere of Matter to dwell only in the Matter sphere of Matter: "And dust shalt thou eat all the days of thy life." "Eating the dust" is ingesting only the energies of Matter-water and Matter-earth.

Through this half of the Matter whole, the Serpent will henceforth work against the etheric and mental bodies of mankind. Through man's desire body he will work to manipulate his mind. Through his physical body and his physical senses he will work against the etheric perceptions of the soul and the soul's experiences on the etheric plane.

Enmity is placed between Lucifer and the woman and between the seed of the Fallen One and the seed of the woman. As Paul said, "the carnal mind is enmity against God: for it is not subject to the Law of God, neither indeed can be."[102] The Serpent is the personification of the carnal mind. The Serpent has exempted himself from the Law of God and has made himself a law unto himself. The mortal mind that created the laws of mortality is subject to those laws as long as it is mortal, and thus it cannot be subject to the Law of God.

The enmity between the good seed of the son of man (the children of God) and the tares (the children of the Wicked One) is the instantaneous action-reaction of light and darkness. The seed of the Divine Woman redeemed, the Christ as the redeemer of souls, will bruise the head of the Serpent—the Serpent's misuses of the sacred fire in the chakras of the Spirit sphere located in the head (the throat chakra, the third eye and the crown).

These three chakras were perverted by the Serpent (as the misuse of the Word, the vision and the wisdom of God) to tempt Eve to pervert the lower chakras in the Matter sphere. Thus it is prophesied by the LORD God that the Christ should overcome the Antichrist. And until the redemption of the children of God through the redemption of the sons and daughters of God, the Serpent will be present in the Matter sphere to bruise their heel.

Because Eve allowed the dark wedges of the Serpent's consciousness to penetrate her four lower bodies, she left her seed vulnerable to the bruises of serpentine logic coming from the one known as the accuser of the brethren. These bruises manifest in a negative spiral of serpentine energies released to the receptive according to the cycles of the moon (symbol of fallen woman) and Mars (symbol of fallen man).

Perversions of God's Virtues

Referring to figures 18 and 19, we see the accusation of the accuser of the brethren perverting the Lawgiver's affirmation of being. This coiled serpent then becomes the anger of the false hierarchs of Aquarius, perverting the adoration of the love fires that ought to be kindled in the energy flow twixt all aspects of the God Self in manifestation.

In the fire quadrant, when dominated by the malicious animal magnetism of the Serpent, the anti-Father hex upon the energies and elementals of fire gains momentum as it moves from accusation, to anger, to total self-annihilation.

Unless this perversion of the Trinity is reversed, it will manifest in the air quadrant. When dominated by the ignorant animal magnetism of the Serpent, the anti-Christ hex upon the energies and elementals of air manifests first in the arrogance of the Adam-ego in its ambition to replace the Real Self with the not-self. It accelerates its perversion of the Alpha thrust from arrogance, to self-assertive argumentation in defense of this anti-Christ posture, and finally to total antagonism to the Mind of God which was and is in Christ Jesus.[103] Unless this all-consuming self-antagonism is arrested in the mental quadrant, it will propel itself upon the Omega sphere.

In the water quadrant, when dominated by the *whoredom* (*whore-dom*ination) of the anti-Mother forces and forcefields, the coiled Serpent manifests its so-called human or humane sympathies as sympathetic animal magnetism. This infects all

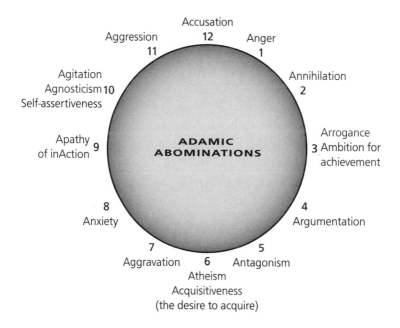

FIGURE 18:
Abominations of the Adamic generations
standing in the holy place of the solar hierarchies.
The serpent bruises the heel of the seed of woman.

relationships under the Motherhood of God as the affectations of the Eve-ego replace the true affection of the Christed ones. The attractions of the carnal nature replace the attraction of the Christ nature. Here the energies and elementals of water are subjected to the culmination of the anti-Father/anti-Mother hex that manifests in the acutely aggressive mental-emotional suggestion of the anti-God spiral of atheism.

To proceed through the second half of the Matter sphere with the appearance of alchemical coherence, the Serpent must bring his accusations against God to the logical conclusion of atheism. His premise in Mater is that Pater is dead. He proceeds to demonstrate this theory through all of the fiery energies of accusation, anger and annihilation pitted against the

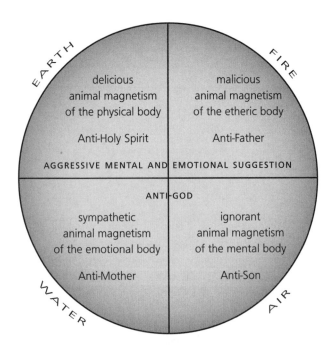

FIGURE 19:
Anti-God actualizations superimposed as the Serpent's coil
on the energies of time and space.

woman and playing upon her desires and emotions.

Having first replaced the feminine inclination toward adoration, the natural polarity of the Lawgiver's affirmations, the Serpent appeals to her acquisitive nature. (The name of her firstborn son, Cain, the product of her union with the carnal mind, means "acquisition.") This lower desire to acquire—with its attendant greed, gluttony and grasping—perverts the higher desire to ascend. It leads to all of the aggravations of the emotions that should be exalted in gratitude, givingness and all godliness.

Then comes the anxiety and the anguish of hoarding the energies of God in whoredom. Being out of alignment with the justice and the mastery of the Law, the woman perverts her passive role as the "Law receiver." As God the Father, the active principle of life, is the Giver-Receiver, so God the Mother, the passive principle of life, is the Receiver-Giver. As man perverts his role by giving without receiving, so woman perverts her role by receiving without giving.

Here in the water quadrant, the accumulation of mis-qualified astral energies—passively received and reinforced from the anti-Alpha thrust of the Serpent spiral—becomes a cesspool of pollution instead of a reservoir of light, harmony, godly attitudes and attributes, and the just uniting of the currents of Alpha and Omega in the Matter sphere.

Now the karmic burden of the three quadrants, the power-wisdom-love of the three-times-three that ought to produce precipitation through the Holy Spirit in the earth quadrant, burdens the soul of man and woman with apathetic self-assertiveness—the apex of unreality.

Cycling as spirals of the serpent coil, this monster of mass mist-qualification teeters and totters in its gross imbalance from its base in the desire for self-preservation—the mark of our exiled forebears—through every aspect of the synthetic self-awareness of the synthetic self: self-deception, self-denial, self-conception, self-concern, self-possession, self-pity, self-aggrandizement, self-accursedness, self-anathematization.

In the earth quadrant, when dominated by the delicious animal magnetism of the Serpent, his anti-Holy Spirit hex upon the energies and elementals of earth gains momentum from an apathetic self-assertiveness through agitated, agonizing self-aggrandizement to the ultimate aggressiveness of nonbeing. The perversion of the active/passive principles of Alpha and Omega in the aggressions of the Serpent's tail creates aggressive animosities. These manifest in individuals as the warring in the members unto the split personality, culminating in the warfare of the Spirit unto the death of the soul. They are seen in greater society as the warring between family members and neighborhood gangs, in civil wars and international wars.

Animosity between the members of the Body of God are thrust as wedges of aggression into the very midst of the lightbearers. And the enmity that God placed between the seed of woman and the seed of the Serpent as a natural repulsion (hence a natural protection against the magnetic animal attraction of the Serpent) is used by the fallen angels to divide and conquer the children of God.

The three Rs of aggression opposing the ray of the Trinity in manifestation in Mater are resentment, revenge and retaliation. At this point/counterpoint of the Serpent spiral the accumulation of all of the misuses of the sacred fire is thrust upon the evolutions in Matter as an aggressive perversion of the seven planes of the Alpha-Omega spirals through the seven chakras of the seven rays and through the five secret-ray chakras. Jesus described these twelve perversions as he gave to his twelve disciples the signs of the "end of the world" and assigned to each one the overcoming of one form of aggression—the end or the fall of the serpentine spiral of the misappropriation of the Christ consciousness. They are listed on the following charts:

Aggressive Perversions of the Seven Rays
(Matthew 24:5–12)

RAY	TYPES OF AGGRESSION	BIBLICAL DESCRIPTION	HOW IT PERVERTS THE RAY
1	Aggressive desecration of the I AM THAT I AM and the Christ consciousness	"For many shall come in my name, saying, I am Christ; and shall deceive many."	Law and Lawgiver perverted by misuse of the energies of the will of God.
2	Aggressive division	"And ye shall hear of wars and rumours of wars … For nation shall rise against nation, and kingdom against kingdom."	Wisdom perverted by divide-and-conquer tactics.
3	Aggressive death, aggressive deprivation Aggressive diseases Aggressive disturbance in the energies and elementals of fire, air, water and earth	"And there shall be famines" "and pestilences [plagues]" "and earthquakes [cataclysm] in divers places."	Death perverts love by curtailing divine fulfillment.
4	Aggressive denunciations, affliction of the lightbearers	"Then shall they deliver you up to be afflicted, and shall kill you: and ye shall be hated of all nations for my name's sake."	Purity and innocence incites anger and atrocities. The Divine Mother is killed.
5	Aggressive damnations, offenses among the lightbearers	"And then shall many be offended, and shall betray one another, and shall hate one another."	Error perverts Truth.
6	Aggressive deceptions, falsehoods	"And many false prophets shall rise, and shall deceive many."	The false hierarchy sends false prophets, who pervert the teachings of Christ.
7	Aggressive devilry (iniquity)	"And because iniquity shall abound, the love of many [of lightbearers] shall wax cold."	Witchcraft, black magic, rituals of Satanists pervert the rituals of the priesthood of Melchizedek.

The Eighth Ray
(Matthew 24:13–14)

RAY	ANTIDOTE	BIBLICAL DESCRIPTION	EXPLANATION
8	Eighth-ray mastery in Alpha and Omega: the antidote for the seven aggressions of the demigods		The correct understanding and application of the eighth ray is the fulfillment of the Alpha/Omega spirals, which counteract aggressive misuses of the seven rays and the seven steps to precipitation.
		"But he that shall endure unto the end, the same shall be saved."	Omega: To endure unto the end is to attain salvation through the rising flame of the Divine Mother.
		"And this gospel of the kingdom shall be preached"	Alpha: Preach the gospel of the kingdom (the consciousness) of God
		"in all the world"	in all the quadrants of Matter.
		"for a witness unto all nations; and then shall the end come."	Witness unto the Truth in all nations. Impart Truth to all units of hierarchy, all mandalas of the children of the Mother, all the tribes of Israel (initiates of the sacred fire collectively united under the hierarchies of the sun), groupings of evolutions working out group karma.

Aggressive Perversions of the Five Secret Rays
(Matthew 24:15–29)

RAY	TYPES OF AGGRESSION	BIBLICAL DESCRIPTION	HOW IT PERVERTS THE RAY
1	Aggressive desolation	"When ye therefore shall see the abomination of desolation, spoken of by Daniel the prophet. . ."	Ingratitude, ungraciousness, ungodliness.
2	Aggressive distress	"For then shall be great tribulation, such as was not since the beginning of the world to this time, no, nor ever shall be."	Gross injustices.
3	Aggressive denials	"For there shall arise false Christs, and false prophets, and shall shew great signs and wonders; insomuch that, if it were possible, they shall deceive the very elect."	Aggressive denials of reality and the Real Self by false Christs, false prophets; wizardry.
4	Aggressive darkening	"Immediately after the tribulation of those days shall the sun be darkened, and the moon shall not give her light [the light of the Christ]"	Aggressive darkening of luminaries; positions of personalities of light eclipsed by consciousness aligned with the false hierarchy.
5	Aggressive descent	"and the stars shall fall from heaven"	Serpent's followers who have misused Spirit sphere and Spirit chakras; energies of the upper chakras.
		"and the powers of the heavens shall be shaken."	Their identities densified in the upper chakras are unseated; energies of the upper chakras are lowered.

These perversions of the fallen angels, who subverted the white fire core of the base-of-the-spine chakra of the Mother, are continually directed against the self-mastery of the children of God.

This mastery of the God Flame was demonstrated by the Lord Jesus Christ through his mastery of the water element (the desire body), the very element and the body through which Eve, by free will, took the light of the Trinity to subvert the light of Alpha and Omega in her own soul and in the three lower chakras.

Jesus' victory was for the victory of the feminine ray in order that woman might redeem man whom she tempted into the downward spiral that began with disobedience to Christ; the desecration of the Trinity and of the Mother Flame; and the degeneration of the light of the chakras culminating in the law of sin, disease and death.

The Second Judgment in Eden: The Judgment of Woman

After the judgment of the Serpent comes the judgment of woman. The LORD God turned unto the woman and he said, "I will greatly multiply thy sorrow and thy conception; in sorrow thou shalt bring forth children; and thy desire shall be to thy husband, and he shall rule over thee."[104]

When Adam and Eve incarnated on earth they had already attained to the level of initiation whereby they were no longer called children of God, but had risen to the level of son and daughter of God. As such, they were ready to be received as initiates of the sacred fire in the first mystery school established after the Fall of mankind on Lemuria.

The karma meted out to Adam and Eve was the result of the judgment corresponding to the level of responsibility of the elect of God. Eve, the Mother of all living, had come to earth to keep the flame of the World Mother, to set the example of divine womanhood for all womankind, to be the example of the feminine aspect of God, to leave the record of the thirty-three steps of initiation for those who would walk the path of attainment to realize the Self as the Mother of God.

It is written in karmic law that each of the thirty-three steps of initiation to which the initiate attains on the right-handed path will be challenged by a being of equal attainment on the left-handed path. In the Serpent, Eve did not meet her superior, she met her equal. He came to challenge her right to wear the crown of the World Mother.

Before his enlightenment, Gautama was denounced and attacked by Mara, who challenged his right to sit in meditation under the Bo tree. Yet Gautama remained determined to attain enlightenment according to the requirements of the path of Buddhic initiation. And Jesus was tempted by Satan, who with three demands challenged his right to put on the Christ consciousness and as a Son of God to reignite the threefold flame in many who had lost it.

In Jesus' message delivered by the angel of the Revelation unto John, he writes, "Because thou hast kept the word of my patience, I also will keep thee from the hour of temptation, which shall come upon all the world, to try them that dwell upon the earth. Behold, I come quickly; hold that fast which thou hast, that no man take thy crown."[105]

This passage explains that all who are working out their salvation in the planes of Matter will be tempted. But when the initiate speaks the Word of the Logos (the Word of the Law of the Lawgiver) into the very teeth of the Serpent, then the Christ (the very personal Christ Self) will come quickly.

The crown refers to the attainment of God consciousness through the crown chakra and the energies of the twelve solar hierarchies that are sealed therein in the crown of the woman who appears in the twelfth chapter of the Book of Revelation. This is the archetype of every woman who attains the twelve initiations of the twelve hierarchies and is thus fit to wear the crown of twelve stars.[106] To all who meet this initiation there is promised the revelation of the name of God (I AM THAT I AM), the name of the city of God (the New Jerusalem—the City Foursquare) and the new name of the Christ (the individual Christ Self).

Figure 20 shows how the Serpent challenged Eve at the level of her attainment in the four quadrants of Matter: (1) the

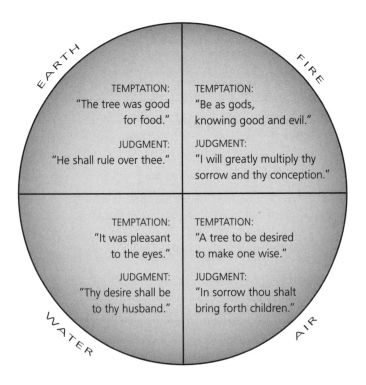

FIGURE 20:
Temptations and judgments of Eve in the four quadrants.

fire quadrant—to "be as gods, knowing good and evil" (to rule with the Fallen One in the highest plane of the Matter sphere); (2) the air quadrant—"a tree to be desired to make one wise" (to have the wisdom to manipulate in the mental belt like the fallen angels); (3) the water quadrant—"it was pleasant to the eyes" (to enjoy the pleasures of the senses, to enjoy the good life of the Luciferians who call themselves the beautiful people); and (4) the earth quadrant—"the tree was good for food" (to conquer the physical plane by the taking of its energy).

Eve had already demonstrated the geometry of this initiation on Venus. Therefore the Serpent had to appeal to the pride of person, he had to present his argument in such a way as to convince Eve that the corresponding station on the left-handed path was more enjoyable, more rewarding in the here and now than her station on the right-handed path.

Eve's Karma in the Four Quadrants of Matter

Eve's karma in the etheric quadrant was "I will greatly multiply thy sorrow and thy conception." It is the role of woman to hold the immaculate concept, the etheric pattern, the Mother matrix for all life. As woman was immaculately conceived by God, so her offspring are intended to be immaculately conceived out of the virgin consciousness of the Cosmic Virgin.

The sorrow that attends woman, with her conception of the divine plan for the four lower bodies and the soul evolution of her sons and daughters and of the children of God, is the burden of the world karma of womankind in her misuses of the fire element in the planes of Spirit and in the planes of Matter through the heart chakra.

Eve's karma in the mental quadrant was "In sorrow thou shalt bring forth children." The Mother is the Mediatrix of the Christ and the individualization of the Christ Self in the mental quadrant. Here she brings forth the etheric matrix and clothes it with the Mind of God, through her mastery of the air element in the planes of Spirit and the planes of Matter, as through the seat-of-the-soul and the third-eye chakras she endows all of life with the Christ consciousness.

Her sorrow in bringing forth sons and daughters of God and children of God and clothing them with soul awareness and the vision of oneness is in their resistance, their rebellion and their revenge engendered by the Antichrist and the fallen angels. To see her children go the way of the fallen angels is the greatest sorrow that woman can know.

Since Eve's failure many women have seen their offspring received in the highest hope—even as Eve when she bore Cain said, "I have gotten a man from the LORD!"—only to see their sons and daughters, possessed of the spirit of the Serpent, compromise the honor flame in all manner of wickedness.

In the emotional quadrant, Eve's karma was "Thy desire shall be to thy husband." The desire body of woman, created to contain the desire of the LORD God even as she was created to be the handmaid of the LORD and to acknowledge her Maker (her I AM Presence) as her husband, would now be subject to the will of her husband. For woman had caused man to depart from the sacred covenant of Eden.

Her karma must be that her desire should be his desire; she would have to wait until he desired to return to the God-estate. She would have to wait until he wanted to be God in the Matter half of the Matter sphere.

And thus in the physical quadrant, Eve's karma was "He shall rule over thee." Woman's physical existence would thus be dominated by man until man should willingly, lovingly return to woman her right to self-rule and to rule over man (to be the active aspiration toward Spirit within the planes of

Matter). This was her high estate before the Fall, when man and woman were equal in attainment, in self-awareness, in God. Because of the nature of the office of a daughter of God as one who channels the flow of the energies of Spirit in Matter, woman is the adoring, aspiring, ascending aspect of man.

The Roles of Redeemed Man and Woman

In redeemed woman, the dominion of the feminine ray manifests as the mastery of the heart chakra and of the chakras above the heart. In redeemed man, the dominion of the masculine ray manifests in the mastery of the heart chakra and of the chakras below the heart. Therefore it is woman who leads man through the energies of the atonement (at-one-ment) of her soul with Spirit to God consciousness in the planes of fire, water, air and earth in Spirit; whereas it is man who leads woman through the atonement of his soul with Matter through the Cosmic Virgin, in the mastery of fire, water, air and earth in the planes of Matter.

In the realm of Spirit and the things of the Spirit, woman leads man to his higher destiny. In the things of Matter and Mater-realization, it is man who leads woman to the highest God-realization in her sons and daughters.

It is clear that in the Garden of Eden, man looked to woman to lead him in the things of the Spirit. When she took of the fruit of the tree of the knowledge of good and evil "and did eat, and gave also unto her husband with her," *unquestioningly* "he did eat."

The desire of man to be led by woman into the paths of purity and righteousness, his desire to return to the state of holy innocence through the virtue of woman, his desire to be the object of her love and adoration as she holds him in the image and likeness of the Son of God, his desire to be elevated to the position of authority in the things of Matter and to freely give to woman the authority in the things of Spirit, his desire to break the cycles of the karma of man made in Eden and to return to the cycles of the karma of God—all of these are the reality of the soul of man.

The woman who holds this key in her hand holds the key not only to the heart of man but to the full God-realization of his potential. In the Aquarian age, woman must be the instrument of man's salvation (self-elevation). Man must recognize these as his real and legitimate desires. He must feel free to express these innermost longings of his heart. Every man has a right to expect that woman meet the highest desires of his soul, both in Spirit and in Matter.

If woman will endeavor to return to the state of listening grace that she knew before her own descent to the downward spiral of the Serpent's coils, she will then magnetize to herself through the upward-moving spiral of her joy in the LORD that man who will, through her exalted consciousness, return to an expanded awareness of Self in God.

Then that man who knows himself as God will desire to know woman as God by his own devotion to the flame of Christ and his adoration of the Cosmic Virgin. That man is free to be *man* (the *man*ifestation of God), and he will enter in through the exaltation of woman.

Putting down the accusations of the accuser of the brethren, he will behold the beauty of the helpmeet. And he will stand on the side of the north of the City Foursquare, the defender of her origin in God. Not "Dust thou art, and unto dust shalt thou return,"[107] but "Out of the One thou hast come, and unto the One thou shalt return."

Enfired with the Law whereby the Lawgiver made an helpmeet for man, he will stand—and having stood, still stand—to defend the original innocence, that inner sense of the solar awareness of woman, which she then transfers to the solar evolution and elevation of her sons and daughters.

The Elevation of Woman

Man beholds the expansion* of the consciousness of woman throughout time and space, the attenuation of her energies forming the *antahkarana* of the cosmos. The disciplining of the energies of woman forms the grid of time and space.

Through woman's alchemicalization of abundance, the anger of man—the wrath of the Fallen One directed against the woman and her seed in the Aquarian age—can be channeled into the expansion of the God consciousness: an expansive self-awareness, the control of the forces and forcefields of time and space. This is the new direction of the energies of man to the glory of God in manifestation in man, in woman, in Spirit, in Matter.

Now woman seizes her fiery destiny to attain God-mastery in the footsteps of the Piscean conqueror. Freely she chooses to walk the fourteen stations of the cross; freely she chooses to be crucified for her Lord.

By her flame of exhortation, she exhorts the wayward generations of mankind to be obedient to the will of God, to leave the fleshpots of Egypt and the fantasies of Pharaoh's court. She exhorts the race—men and women and children—to enter into the spirals of ascendancy, ascending day by day, hour by hour through the mastery of the self, as the Self dispels the mists of doubt, discouragement, fear and frustration.

By her exhortations from out the fiery core of the sixth ray of the Prince of Peace, woman goes out into the highways and byways and compels the generations of Adam and Eve to come in to the marriage feast, to fill the house of the LORD, to put on

*The discussion on pages 125 through 134 refers to figures 18, 21 and 22.

the wedding garment,[108] to dissolve every form of self-annihilation by the currents of the ascendancy of the feminine ray.

This is life, not death. With Christ, woman declares, "I am come that they might have life, and that they might have it more abundantly."[109] Through the abundant alchemy of woman, through her affirmation of being and her reaching for the stars of the Causal Bodies of her children, man comes into the awareness of his excellence as a son of God. In the excellence of his exalted ego, the energies of man are fully realized in an attitude of be-ness.

All conscious and subconscious motivations of the lesser ego give way to the excellence of the Christed ego. Woman, through the excellence of her execution of the will of God, has

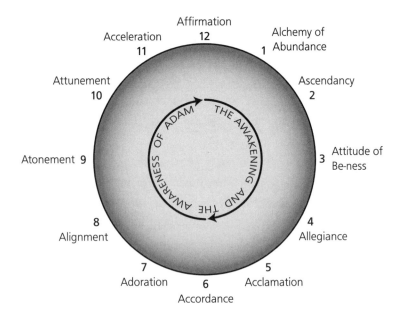

FIGURE 21:
Attributes of Alpha's sons and daughters,
joint heirs of the Christ consciousness of the solar hierarchies.
The seed of woman bruises the head of the Serpent.

enabled man to see himself as his Real Self. All energies once locked in momentums of an alienated arrogance are now lovingly, adoringly channeled into the self-awareness of the avatar, which every man and woman is to become through union with the Holy Christ Self. Behold the incarnation of the Word!

"Lo, I AM," man declares unto the woman, "and because I AM, thou art." Rejoicing in the incarnation of her Lord, woman declares, "Lo, I AM." And in man she affirms the attitude of be-ness, "And because I AM, thou art."

Hand in hand, man and woman go forth to outpicture the inner picture of the twin flames of Alpha and Omega. Man assumes the responsibility for his own God be-ness; woman

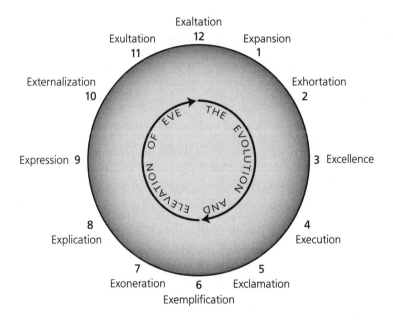

FIGURE 22:
The energies of Eve for the evolution and elevation
of the generations of woman.
Ex "out of" Omega.
Ex cathedra "out of the mouth of" God the Mother.

assumes the responsibility for her own God be-ness. Under the alchemy of their oneness, each assumes responsibility for the other.

Man bequeaths to woman his mastery of the masculine ray. Lovingly he transfers to her his mastery of the four elements in the four quadrants of Matter. Woman bequeaths to man her mastery of the feminine ray. Adoringly she transfers to him her mastery of the four elements in the quadrants of Spirit. "Therefore shall a man leave his father and his mother, and shall cleave unto his wife: and they shall be one flesh."[110]

"And the Word was made flesh, and dwelt among us, and we beheld" the glory of the son, the daughter of God[111]—the incarnation of the One, the Whole, male and female created in the image and likeness of Elohim. "She shall be called Woman, because she was taken out of Man." He shall be called *man* because he was taken out of God to be the God-*man*-ifestation. The identity of man and woman must be established in the I AM THAT I AM. The purpose of the self of man, of woman, must be defined. Not only must man know who I AM and woman know who I AM, but each must know who I AM in relation to the other.

Woman declares, "I AM woman THAT I AM man," and man declares, "I AM man THAT I AM woman," with the full understanding of be-ness. I AM woman in order that the I AM that is man that is in me might be liberated. I AM man in order that the woman that I AM may be liberated.

The purpose of the polarity of the Father-Mother God is defined: God is Father in order that he may realize himself in and through Mother. God as Father must remain Father in order to know Mother. God the Mother must realize herself as Mother. She must maintain the attitude of be-ness as Mother in order to know herself as Father.

Establishing the roles of identity in the divine polarity,

man and woman know who they are first as man and woman and then as man in relation to woman, as woman in relation to man. When identity is defined, then the flow of identity will be defined; and the action-reaction-interaction of the energies of man and woman will be for the continual realization of the Divine One on earth as in heaven. In this God-controlled consciousness of the One, man and woman go forth to execute the will of God through a mutual allegiance to the greater love of the Creator, who lives and loves through his creation.

By acclamation of Alpha and Omega, man and woman are the executors of the will of God. Through the angelic and elemental kingdoms, man and woman as priest and priestess go forth to rule. By their divinely ordained royal lineage they are acclaimed king and queen of the kingdoms of fire, air, water and earth. Salamanders, sylphs, undines and gnomes pay homage to them as God's representatives.

The Divine Exchange

In the rituals of the Mind of Christ, man and woman, as priest and priestess before the throne of God, receive the anointing to be ministers whom he makes "a flaming fire."[112] As director and directress of the angel spirits and the sprites of nature, man and woman redeemed fulfill the role of Adam and Eve.

Adam arcs the energies of Alpha through the thrust of the Alpha current as affirmation, alchemy of abundance, ascendancy, attitude of be-ness, allegiance and acclamation. And Eve carries the energies of Omega through the Omega current as exaltation, expansion, exhortation, excellence, execution and exclamation. These twin currents of twin flames are the caduceus of the figure eight—the creative flow of the Creator in the creation.

In the turning of the spiral and the returning of the energies of Alpha to Omega, there is the divine exchange, the interchange of the roles of Adam and Eve. From the within to the without, Adam carries the thrust of Alpha or the masculine current and Eve carries the energies ex cathedra of Omega. From the without to the within for the spiritualization of the God Flame, it is the role of Adam to carry the energies of Omega and the role of Eve to carry the energies of Alpha.

From the side of the south to the side of the north, Eve's mastery of the flames of accordance, adoration, alignment, atonement, attunement and acceleration are her contribution to the oneness of male and female, while Adam enters into the consciousness of exemplification, exoneration, explication, expression, externalization and exultation.

Eve, through the feminine ray, focuses the mastery of the Alpha current in Matter. Adam, through the masculine ray, focuses the mastery of the Omega current in Spirit.

As Adam exemplifies the energy of self, his own well-defined self-awareness as the Personal Personality of God, he accords to Eve her own self-awareness of the Personal Personality of God as Mother.

Thus the elevation of Eve is achieved through the awareness of Adam. Here where the Alpha thrust of north-south becomes the Omega thrust of south-north, Eve holds the balance of flow. In accordance she stands on the side of the south in agreement with Alpha's affirmation of the Law and the Lawgiver. She is Omega acting in conformity with the consciousness of God. She holds the balance of the interrelationship of Alpha and Omega. She is the nexus of the crisscrossing of the caduceus where man becomes woman and woman becomes man.

Eve holds the Mind of Alpha suspended in Omega. She is the Mind of Christ in the atom of self-awareness. She is with one accord the harmony of the Holy Spirit. Her harmony is the immaculate conception of a cosmos. She is the accord of the

Law and the Lawgiver. Her temple is the temple of the living God. She is the all in the All.

Eve's allness is the consuming of atheism, agnosticism and anti-God actualizations superimposed as the Serpent's coil on the energies of time and space. She has replaced the acquisitiveness of fallen woman, her carnal desire to acquire more and more. Along with her manipulation of man, it is consumed in the God-desire to accord the heart flame the authority of the Trinity of God in manifestation in Father, Son and Holy Spirit, and the authority of the unity of God in manifestation in the I AM THAT I AM.

Eve has accorded man his rightful place to take dominion over the earth. She has conceded to Adam the masculine role. And once again the Lord has conceded to her the feminine role, to take dominion over the soul in the earth. This is the evolution and the elevation of Eve.

Man and woman enter the spiral of the return to the One —the return from man's karma to God's karma. They experience together the true meaning of Paul's observation: "Be not deceived; God is not mocked: for whatsoever a man soweth, that shall he also reap."[113] The cycle of the Omega return is the open door of opportunity to balance the energies of disobedience to the commands of God.

In gratitude for the evolution of Eve to her self-awareness as the woman clothed with the sun, Adam is caught up in the rapture of exoneration. In his gratitude for the finding of the one whom he had lost, he becomes the instrument of the LORD's forgiveness. First he forgives himself, then he forgives her—and their mutual adoration becomes the LORD's approbation.

His forgiveness is another opportunity in time and space to obey the commands of Christ, to oblige the Holy Spirit with self-sacrifice, to obviate their transgressions against the Law and the Lawgiver. With one voice the two as one confirm,

"Forgive us our trespasses as we forgive those who trespass against us."

The cycle has come full circle. The LORD approbates Adam and Eve. He will give to them a new novitiate. They may enter in to the service of the LORD. They may minister unto the lifewaves of earth's evolutions to fulfill their probationary period in Matter in order that man's karma might become God's karma. Eve's adoration blends with the choruses of the four beasts who sing before the throne of Alpha and Omega: "Holy, holy, holy, LORD God Almighty, which was, and is, and is to come."[114]

And her adoration is of the Lord who is her husband, who has become Adam's self-awareness in God. Eve stands in perpetual adoration of Adam's awareness of God. He has become her hero; she, his heroine. God sanctions their love as a fiery trial that they must now enter if they would return to the heart of the One. Flame by flame the fiery trial consumes all energies that are out of alignment with the Alpha-Omega consciousness.

The justice of the judgment implemented by the love fires of adoration and exoneration becomes alignment with the justice of the Law. Eve is conformity, uniformity, oneness with God-justice. Adam is the explication of the Law. He unfolds the teaching of the Law of the Cosmic Virgin. He teaches the wisdom of the Mother to her children. He expounds the Law before the multitudes. He is the advocate of their own Christ awareness.

He interprets the Law to the generations of Seth who have departed from the ancient covenant of Enoch, the seventh from Adam. He quells the anxieties of their sense of human injustice. His are the moving fingers that write: "MENE, MENE, TEKEL, UPHARSIN.... Thou art weighed in the balances, and art found wanting."[115] And all of the generations of mankind look up to see the writing of God upon the wall of consciousness.

Through their own inner alignment with the Law of being, Adam and Eve are the exemplification of the Law. Because they have elected by free will to enter the consciousness of adoration and exoneration, they now have the authority to give the explication of the Law—an explanation that is satisfied in their example. Face to face, heart to heart, aura to aura they convey the bearing of the Law (its stature and its statutes) and the burden of the Law (God's karma and man's karma).

Eve is at one with reality. She is the active and the passive principle of the Holy Spirit. And her at-one-ment is Adam's awareness of self-expression. In his expression of the cloven tongues of fire, Adam has elevated Eve to her rightful place of authority in Spirit, and he has assumed his rightful place of authority in Matter.

Adam's expression is his active/passive undulating current, his "pressing out" of the image and likeness of God—as man, as woman, as manchild. This pressing out is the pressure of the Holy Spirit pressing from the plane of Spirit to the plane of Matter, the full outpicturing of the Mind of God manifest in molecules of self-expression, monads of self-awareness.

This is the action-reaction-interaction of the Holy Spirit that overcomes the apathy of nonalignment, the unreal existence of the synthetic self of man and woman and the endless experiences of mortals in an existential, empirical effort to rationalize the existence of the unknown God.[116]

The unknown God is the unreal God. The known God is the God who is expressed in man and woman. The known God is the *a priori* God who is known by the direct assumption "I AM real, therefore God is real." "This God that I know," says Adam, "is not the *a posteriori* god of the Sophists or of the Sanhedrin or of the Satanists. This God I know is the God I AM."

This direct knowing of the reality of God is the acceleration unto the victory. This is the stepping-up of vibration for the final burning up in the ascension currents of every form of aggression (perverting the seven rays and the five secret rays). This is the sign of the end of the Serpent's spiral and the beginning of the eternal cycles of evolution and elevation in God.

Reversing the Spiral

The reversal of the spiral of the seed of the Serpent by the seed of woman is described in Matthew 24:30–31, 34–35. (See also the following chart.)

On the first ray: "And then shall appear the sign of the Son of man in heaven." This sign is the coming of the Christ Self into full awareness in awakened man and woman. From the Spirit sphere of being, the Christ Self appears to those who have prepared for the marriage supper of the Lamb, those who have the wedding garment.

On the second ray: "And then shall all the tribes of the earth mourn." All the tribes of the generations of Cain—of the earth, earthy—and of those who have amplified the abominations of the Adamic generations, mourn at the sign of the coming of the Christ Self. They mourn the death of their mortality and their mortal means and ends. They mourn the exposure of their Machiavellian mischief-making. They mourn the end of the Luciferian creation and the end of the incarnation of the cycles of the seed of the Serpent and the seed of the Wicked One.

This is the portent of the sign of the Son of man. Yet their mourning is to no avail. For even in the momentum of the earth, earthy, they see the soul liberation of the sons and daughters of God. On the third ray, they see the Christed ones—one with the Son of man, the anointed—"coming in the clouds of heaven" as the great spheres of the Causal Body are unveiled at the end of the Adamic age and the beginning of the age of the reigning of the Christ consciousness. The Christ comes with the

\multicolumn{2}{c}{Reversing of the Spiral of the Seed of the Serpent by the Seed of Woman (Matthew 24:30–31, 34–35)}	

RAY	BIBLICAL DESCRIPTION	EXPLANATION
1	"And then shall appear the sign of the Son of man in heaven"	Sign of the Christ Self in the Spirit sphere of being.
2	"and then shall all the tribes of the earth mourn"	Those who are in the momentum of the earth, earthy, mourn the death of their mortality, their mortal means and ends, and their Machiavellian mischief-making.
3	"and they shall see the Son of man coming in the clouds of heaven" "with power" "and great glory."	Overshadowed by the Causal Body the I AM THAT I AM and the light of the Holy Spirit.
4	"And he shall send his angels" "with a great sound of a trumpet"	Coordinates of the Christ consciousness are precipitated by the sound of the Word.
5	"and they shall gather together his elect from the four winds, from one end of heaven to the other."	Angels gather souls who have sustained self-awareness in the four quadrants of Spirit.
6	"Verily I say unto you, This generation" "shall not pass" "till all these things be fulfilled."	This evolution and this generation of karma shall not be judged and its misuses of the sacred fire shall not be balanced till the precipitation of both light and darkness, the deeds of the seed of the woman and the seed of the Serpent are actualized.
7	"Heaven and earth shall pass away, but my words shall not pass away."	The entire creation of the Spirit-Matter spheres of God's karma and man's karma may spiral into the white fire core of being in the personal and planetary ritual of the ascension; but the Word and the emanations of the Word as the consciousness of Christ that before Abraham was, the I AM THAT I AM, shall remain the permanent identity of man and woman redeemed through the great alchemy of the Holy Spirit.

power of the I AM THAT I AM and with great glory in the light of the Holy Spirit.

On the fourth ray, he sends "his angels [coordinates of the Christ consciousness] with a great sound of a trumpet"—for this Christed one is the archetype of the Faithful and True. Out of his mouth proceedeth a sword of the sacred Word. At the sound of the Word, which is as the "sound of a trumpet," there is the precipitation of the angles of his God Self-awareness, angelic servants of the Most High who are the liberators of the mankind who would be liberated.

On the fifth ray, the Seven Archangels, the Archeiai, the seraphim and cherubim, and angelic hosts of an entire cosmos come. They gather together his elect—those who have elected to be in the spiral of the attributes of Alpha and Omega's sons and daughters, those who have elected to be joint heirs of the Christ consciousness of the solar hierarchy. These the angels gather "from the four winds"—north, south, east and west—in the four quadrants of being. From one end of heaven to the other, so the angels gather the souls who have sustained their soul's awakening unto the awareness of the Self in Spirit as Spirit.

On the sixth ray, the Son of man speaks to the generations of Adam and Eve who have not elected to put on the karma of God, but remain in the Serpent's spiral: "Verily I say unto you, This generation shall not pass, till all these things be fulfilled." The law of karma (as the requirement of the sixth-ray action of Alpha and Omega) has been spoken, and the judgment of those generations of earth is pronounced—this evolution, this life-wave and the cycles of karma that they have generated shall not pass under the rod of the Last Judgment until its misuses of the sacred fire are balanced through the fires of the Holy Spirit.

They shall not be judged until the precipitation of light and darkness and the deeds of the seed of woman and the seed of the Serpent are apparent. They shall not be judged until the secrets of men's hearts (the motivations concealed in the subconscious) are actualized to the right and to the left, as the separation of the milk and the cream. Not until this sixth-ray requirement of the law of karma has been met will this generation enter in to the Holy of holies with the Son of man and his angels.

Yea, on the seventh ray, "Heaven and earth shall pass away, but my words shall not pass away." This edict of the LORD shall stand, for it is the Word that goeth forth out of the mouth of God (ex cathedra) and the LORD has said, "it shall not return unto me void, but it shall accomplish that which I please, and it shall prosper in the thing whereto I sent it."[117] For the sons and daughters of God who are redeemed from the karma of Adam and Eve, the ritual of the ascension is nigh. Heaven and earth cannot contain the glory of God. So the Matter sphere can no longer contain the son, the daughter, who glory in the LORD.

Therefore the entire creation of the Spirit-Matter spheres of God's karma and man's karma, through the sacred fire of the ascension current, spiral into the white fire core of being in the personal and planetary ritual of the assumption of the soul of man and woman into the Spirit of God. Only the Word and the emanations of the Word as the consciousness of Christ that before Abraham was,[118] the I AM THAT I AM, shall remain the permanent identity of man and woman redeemed through this the great alchemy of the Holy Spirit.

The Third Judgment in Eden:
The Judgment of Man

Man and woman have rejected the teacher and the teaching. By free will they have chosen to be a part of the world, the kingdom of this world and the karma of this world. Therefore the LORD God sets forth the conditions of life for man and woman outside of the mystery school.

Through the misuse of the sacred fire in the threefold flame and in the white fire core of the Mother, man and woman have perverted the seven rays of the Christ consciousness. The LORD God outlines seven conditions (each one a penalty, each one a penance), whereby through the balancing of his or her karma on that ray—working a sacred labor under the conditions the LORD God imposes—man and woman might return to the grace of the Christ consciousness through the promised redeemer, the Saviour Christ the Lord. These are the seven conditions:[119]

(1) "Cursed is the ground for thy sake."

The power of the first ray is diverted from man. The LORD God has decreed that the earth—Matter, and elemental life in nature (the beings of fire, air, water and earth) manifesting in and through the Holy Spirit and in the power of Elohim—would no longer act as the servant of man, but man would become their servant. He would be at the mercy of the forces of God in nature whom he had defied in his disobedience to the Guru.

(2) "In sorrow shalt thou eat of it all the days of thy life."

The wisdom of the second ray is diverted from man. The sorrows of the two-pronged proposition of the Serpent—ignorance of the Law and desire to live outside the Law or to be a law unto oneself—shall be man's lot. This pollution of the four elements will recycle through consciousness as long as man lives outside the Eden of Self-existence, Self-knowledge and Self-bliss. Thus the sorrow of living outside of the I AM THAT I AM replaces the joy of living inside the I AM THAT I AM.

(3) "Thorns also and thistles shall it bring forth to thee."

The love of the third ray is diverted from man. His own hatred of the Mother is turned upon him. Instead of partaking of the fruit of the three trees of the Garden of Eden, which would have been presented to the chelas by the Guru on successive steps of the ladder of initiation, man would reap the ripened fruit of his own karma—thorns and thistles of his own past sowings. And one day, in search of the Guru whom he had lost, man would present the fruit of his own effort to the gurus of the world—some false, some true—hoping thereby to regain the lost grace of Eden.

(4) "And thou shalt eat the herb of the field."

The purity of the fourth ray is diverted from man. Man no longer eats of the fruit of God's consciousness. By his own impurity he can no longer drink directly, freely, from the fount of the waters of eternal Life, nor can he breathe the sacred fire breath through the chakras, nor can he partake directly of the prana of the Holy Spirit. Until the coming of the Saviour and man's acceptance of the teacher as the Christ of Jesus, of Self and of every son of God, man will not know of the wellspring from on high, nor will he be able to say with Jesus, "I have meat to eat that ye know not of" and "Man shall not live by bread alone, but by every word that proceedeth out of the mouth of God."[120] Because he is expelled from the garden, man is denied the ritual of daily communion, the Eucharist of the Body and Blood of Christ.

As Christ was to say, "I will not drink henceforth of this fruit of the vine, until that day when I drink it new with you in my Father's kingdom,"[121] so Adam would say, "I shall not drink henceforth of the fruit of the vine of the Christ consciousness, until another will come in my place to kneel before the Guru Lord Maitreya, to meet the temptations of Satan in the wilderness, to demonstrate the law of the thirty-three and the seven steps of precipitation. When another shall come in my place to be the chela of the Guru Maitreya, then I shall once again partake of the Body and the Blood of my Lord."

(5) "In the sweat of thy face shalt thou eat bread, till thou return unto the ground; for out of it wast thou taken."

The truth of wholeness (healing and harmony), the science

of Alpha and Omega on the fifth ray, is diverted from man. Without the alchemy of the seven steps of precipitation, without the truth of the laws of healing (the wholeness of Alpha and Omega in the flow of the chakras) and the laws of science (the harmony of the 144 virtues manifest as the 144 elements), man would eat his daily bread (the daily allotment of his karma) in the sweat of his face, in the toil of the lesser image that had now replaced the greater image of the great God Self.

The chemistry of man's karma would replace the alchemy of the karma of God, manifest through the miraculous presence of the Guru. The wheel of karma and of rebirth, the turning of the cycles from Spirit to Matter, Matter to Spirit, would continue until the law of man's karma would be fulfilled.

And "one jot or one tittle shall in no wise pass from the Law, till all be fulfilled." Until all the energies that man has used in disobedience to the Law to create the negative spiral of his karma are used through obedience to the Law to create the positive spiral of God's karma, he will be bound by the decree "Sufficient unto the day is the evil thereof." [122]

(6) "For dust thou art, and unto dust shalt thou return."

The ministration and service of eternal life on the sixth ray of Alpha and Omega is diverted from man. Man will no longer live in the two spheres in the flame of action-reaction-interaction of Spirit and Matter.

Now his cyclings will be from Matter to Matter, from the etheric-mental to the emotional-physical (from the plus to the minus) of the four planes of Matter. Back and forth from a physical to an etheric existence, his soul will move through the cycles of birth and rebirth. And these will be the cyclings of his soul's evolution until the Redeemer, who has gotten the victory over hell and death, restores the rite of eternal life through his ministration unto the Body of God and his service unto the Spirit of God.

One day man will kneel once again at the feet of his Lord and master. He will acknowledge him and only him as the Mediator. Through that Mediator—that one anointed—and his great victory, he will enter the path of initiation that will lead to the reenactment of the ritual of the resurrection and the ascension.

Then through the one who would come to reestablish obedience to the Guru, man will begin to reintegrate wholeness. He will know the quickening of the Lord's Spirit. His energies will begin to flow once again in the currents of eternal life to and from the Spirit sphere until his eye is single, his entire body of the Matter sphere is filled with light, and he returns to the white fire core of the Edenic consciousness in the whirlwind of the ascension flame.

(7) "Therefore the LORD God sent him forth from the Garden of Eden."

The law of freedom and the alchemy of the Tree of Life on the seventh ray were diverted from man. Man would no longer have access to the I AM Presence or to the Causal Body through Christ the Mediator, manifest before him in and as the Guru. Without the teacher Maitreya he would very soon forget the teaching, and the knowledge of the Law would pass away.

And God would deliver through Moses the codification of the Law, not as inner intuition but as outer do's and don'ts. Then with the coming of the Saviour, the grace of the Law of the I AM would be returned through the one who said, "I am the way, the Truth and the life;" "he that followeth me shall not walk in darkness, but shall have the light of life."[123]

And after the coming of the Saviour who would submit to the way, the Truth and the life of the I AM THAT I AM, there would be the second coming of the Christ within this son and daughter, Adam and Eve, and within every son and daughter who had gone out of the way of the Garden of Eden.

And then would come to pass the fulfillment of the prophecy of the LORD God given to Jeremiah, "I will put my Law in their inward parts, and write it in their hearts; and will be their God, and they shall be my people. And they shall teach no more every man his neighbour, and every man his brother, saying, Know the LORD: for they shall all know me, from the least of them unto the greatest of them, saith the LORD: for I will forgive their iniquity, and I will remember their sin no more."[124]

And once again through the rebirth of the lineage of Seth, men would begin to "call upon the name of the LORD."[125] And with their calling upon the name of the LORD, the prophecy of Joel would be fulfilled:

"And it shall come to pass afterward, that I will pour out my Spirit upon all flesh; and your sons and your daughters shall prophesy, your old men shall dream dreams, your young men shall see visions: and also upon the servants and upon the handmaids in those days will I pour out my Spirit.

"And I will shew wonders in the heavens and in the earth, blood, and fire, and pillars of smoke. The sun shall be turned into darkness, and the moon into blood, before the great and the terrible day of the LORD come. And it shall come to pass, that whosoever shall call on the name of the LORD [I AM THAT I AM] shall be delivered."[126]

The Love of Twin Flames in the Hallowed Circle of God

B EFORE WE EXPLORE THE JUDGMENTS of mankind's karma on the third ray, let us look once again at the story of Adam and Eve, this time to learn of the initiations of Divine Love.

It is written that "the LORD God planted a garden eastward in Eden."[127] The Garden of Eden was the protected forcefield of initiation that was established by Lord Maitreya on the east side of the continent of Lemuria—the east, symbol of the place where man and woman realize the Christ consciousness.

Hence the garden was the place prepared, the place in the Motherland set aside for the redemption of mankind, who had lost their Edenic state long before. Here in the first outer retreat established by the Great White Brotherhood after mankind on Mu succumbed to the Luciferians, Lord Maitreya sponsored Adam and Eve. Twin flames from Venus, this beloved son and daughter had volunteered to take incarnation on earth to redeem fallen mankind, as many other teachers, avatars, prophets, messengers and Christed ones from Venus had done before and have done since.

Lord Maitreya sponsored them. He gave them four lower bodies. He placed them apart from the decadent civilization of earth. He provided them with the optimum circumstances to demonstrate the law of love by choosing whom they would serve. Yet they failed their test.

It was required of these twin flames that they take the thirty-three steps of initiation in the Christ consciousness on earth, in the midst of the culture of the fallen angels yet set apart from that culture, so that they might restore in Matter the culture of the Mother. It was necessary for the record to be set for the victory of these thirty-three steps in order that every child of God who had gone astray under the influence of the fallen angels might return to the state of grace that he had lost as the result of his misuse of the sacred fire.

This misuse of the sacred fire included all manner of experimentation with the seed and the egg, and the creation of human and animal life in the test tube. The "taking of the sword" to kill the holy innocents while they were yet in their mothers' wombs was also practiced on fallen Lemuria, and even then they bore the weight of the law of karma that Jesus later taught: "They that take the sword shall perish with the sword."[128]

Jesus also warned of the karmic consequences to those who "shall offend one of these little ones which believe in me; it were better for him that a millstone were hanged about his neck, and that he were drowned in the depth of the sea." The taking of the kingdom of heaven by force[129] (the forcing of the chakras of the successive planes of God's consciousness through the taking of violent drugs) was also in vogue on decadent Mu.

Into the midst of this degradation of the third ray of God's love and the energies of the Holy Spirit, the twin flames Adam and Eve were born to demonstrate the law of love, to be the example on the path of initiation, to prove that all mankind might be freed from the toils of the spoiler. They came to demonstrate the worship of the Christ, whom the Luciferians had defiled.

The highest worship of the Person of God, or the personification of the Law who is Christ the Lord, is obedience to the Law as well as obedience to the commandments of the Person, the Pure Son. Jesus said, "If ye love me, keep my commandments."[130] In the LORD God (in this instance, Lord Maitreya), the Law and the Lawgiver are one. This is the wholeness of the Cosmic Christ consciousness.

The Loss of Androgynous Being

Man and woman, androgynous in the white fire core of their innocence, knew wholeness in the Edenic consciousness. Through the misuse of the Christ Flame they lost their wholeness, and they stood naked before the LORD God. Thus the original sin of the Luciferians, which caused first the fall of mankind and then the Fall of Adam and Eve, was the misuse of the threefold flame—the perversion of Father, Son and Holy Spirit.

Immediately, Adam and Eve's misuse of the threefold flame formed a negative spiral that produced the electronic belt. And the white fire core of purity (the energy source in Matter, the origin of the threefold flame) was sealed in the Mother chakra, guarded by cherubim "and a flaming sword which turned every way, to keep the way of the Tree of Life."[131]

It was the loss of wholeness through the misuse of the masculine trinity of God's energy that relegated man and woman to the Matter sphere. Having lost the purity of their contact with their own inner Spirit polarity, they no longer experienced the androgynous consciousness of God within the threefold flame. Because of this loss of wholeness, they were no longer able to procreate through the projection of light rays as is practiced by more advanced evolutions of Venus, who have not descended from the etheric plane.

Unless man and woman, son and daughter, contain within the heart the balanced threefold flame as the focus of the Spirit sphere of their own God-identity, they cannot and do not experience the androgynous nature of God in the plane of Matter. The loss of wholeness in Matter by Adam and Eve resulted in the karma of Eve's desire being unto her husband and Adam's desire being unto his wife. Thus, two are required in Matter in order to experience the totality of the Father-Mother God.

The necessity for wholeness, the longing of the soul for the androgynous consciousness of Eden, produces desire in Matter. The desire for God and for reunion with God as Father or as Mother is holy desire. The manifestation of this desire becomes, then, a necessary component of procreation outside of the Garden of Eden.

Real Original Sin: Rejection of the Christ, the Inner Guru

In Genesis 4:1 we read for the first time that Adam knew his wife. Sexual intercourse is not the original sin. The original sin is the departure from the Christ consciousness through disobedience to the individual Christ Self within and the Universal Christ Presence manifest in the Guru. Procreation through sex is only one of a number of conditions of the Adamic covenant, conditions of the life of fallen man and fallen woman outside the Garden of Eden.

Sex, therefore, as it is practiced on earth today, is the effect and not the cause of original sin. Sex is not in itself sinful. But mankind have made of the misuses of the sacred fire in sex the greatest sin since their descent from the grace of the garden.

This they have accomplished through their willful desecration of the sacred fire in all of the sacred centers of God-awareness (the chakras) by fulfilling the lusts of the flesh through disobedience to the Ten Commandments.

The seven sacraments of the Church and the eighth sacrament of the law of integration are a means whereby man and woman may atone for the misuses of the seven rays. In redeemed man and woman, sexual intercourse becomes the sacred ritual of the sacrament of marriage. This ritual can be purified of the taint of the original sin of disobedience, as well as the secondary sin of lustful desecration of this ritual, through the restoration of the Christ consciousness in man and woman.

When the seven initiations of the seven chakras have been passed and the thirty-three steps have been fulfilled, man and woman return to the wholeness of the One within. When both are freed from the separation of the Whole and have entered this state of wholeness, their desire is no longer based on incompleteness but is only that holy desire which comes from the oneness of the Father-Mother God.

There is no sin in this union. It is the reenactment of the divine reunion, of the alchemical marriage of the soul to the Spirit. Prior to the ascension this divine reunion may be expressed between man and woman in the union of heart, soul, body and mind to the glory of God in all of the seven chakras. Out of this union comes forth no longer a "kind of man" (the genealogies of the carnal mind or the offspring of the flesh), but archetypes of the Christ consciousness, the highest of which we know to be Jesus the Christ.

This beloved Son of God was born out of the sanctified union of the soul of Mary with the Spirit of God through the highest initiate of the Holy Spirit, Saint Germain (embodied as Joseph). Jesus was the first fruit of woman redeemed. Mary had become Ma-Ray, the Mother ray. She had passed the test of the ten, which Eve had failed. Her virginity was her obedience to the Christ within and to the Cosmic Christ. He sent to her his instructions and his initiations, first through her devout parents, Anna and Joachim, and through sisters in the Essene temple where she took her early training, and then through the Archangel Gabriel.

Since sex itself is not the original sin, the virgin birth remains the virgin birth with or without sexual intercourse. Mary's virgin consciousness is the raising-up of the white sphere of the Mother that in unredeemed man and woman remains locked in the base-of-the-spine chakra.

As that light of the Mother rises, it restores the light of the Trinity to each successive chakra, regenerates the balanced threefold flame within the heart, resurrects the Alpha and Omega wholeness as the white fire core of the seven planes of God's consciousness, and locks that sphere in the third eye, completing the caduceus.

Over this spiral of energy, sanctified and made pure by the Body (the Matter) and the Blood (the Spirit) of Christ who "before Abraham was, I AM," the Son of God became the Word incarnate: Jesus the Christ was born.

If it were true that Jesus was pure because his mother, Mary, did not have intercourse with his father, then we could never be pure. The misinterpretation of the virgin birth of Jesus is the lie of the Luciferians that keeps the children of God in self-condemnation and keeps the self-righteous in condemnation of those who are obliged to engage in intercourse to bear the children of God.

The Luciferians propounded the lie that sex is the original sin in order to keep the light of mankind veiled in the sin consciousness, to keep their attention (hence the serpentine force) constantly revolving around sex as the forbidden fruit. The Luciferians did not want mankind to know that it was their rejection of the Christ that caused them to fall. For if mankind knew this, they could and would accept the redemption of Jesus the Christ, of the Christ Self and of the Initiator Lord Maitreya. Thus they would return to the glory that they knew in the beginning before the world was.

The Luciferians knew very well that mankind could become Christed ones through obedience to the Christ until establishing soul congruency with his soul. By letting that Mind be in them that was in Christ Jesus,[132] they would know the inner, microcosmic Guru (the Real Self, the Christ Self) and the outer, macrocosmic Guru (Lord Maitreya himself). Through the Saviour, all mankind can overcome this original sin—disobedience to the Christ. All mankind can enter the path of initiation if they will.

But some among mankind, ridden with guilt and shame, consider themselves to be sinners from their conception—a condition that they are convinced they cannot overcome. As David said in utter despondency, "In sin did my mother conceive me."[133] Through the lie of Lucifer, he felt alienated from God and rejected by the Guru Maitreya, for whom he expressed perpetual longing in his Psalms.

Those who accept this concept of original sin—and thus their sinful state—look for the Saviour outside of themselves. This Saviour is indeed Christ the Lord, and Jesus shows the way to salvation by providing the example. But until each soul appropriates the Christ consciousness that Jesus became, she cannot undo the original sin of her own desire-filled, self-willed disobedience.

Jesus is the Saviour only when you realize that the Christ that he is, is the same Christ that you are. Only then has he succeeded in saving your soul for the path of initiation. The lack of this realization is the origin of all other manifestations of incompleteness, including all lesser sins of the world of relative good and evil leading to disease, decay, disintegration and death.

The Evil One perpetually tempts the holy innocents to depart from oneness in God and to know relative good and evil. What these "gods" do not tell mankind is that when they become gods knowing good and evil, they lose their knowledge of Absolute Good: God. This is the price that must be paid for the departure from innocence. *This is negative karma.*

Once the fallen ones had trapped mankind into disobedience to the Guru, they erased the guru-chela relationship from the memory of the children of God. They then substituted the lie of original sin and said, "You cannot overcome original sin by sexual continence or incontinence. So whether you do or whether you don't, mankind, you are condemned to be sinners —nor will you ever be born of the virgin birth, nor will you ever give birth through the virgin birth."

Having denied the law of integration whereby God's karma becomes man's karma, the Luciferians then deny the law of reincarnation—the reincarnation of the Word (the Christ within you) and of the soul, again and again until the thirty-three steps on the path of initiation are fulfilled. Only through reincarnation can the soul balance the karma of having gone out of the way of the Law, the karma of misalignment whereby man's karma is out of alignment with God's karma. The souls of man and woman reincarnate again and again until the rebirth of the Spirit, when they are born anew in the likeness of the Christ—born again in the image of God, free of the taint of their original disobedience.

Learn to Love, and Love to Love

The challenge of man and woman to meet the conditions of the web of circumstance outside of Eden is succinctly put by the Archeia Charity. It is to learn to love and to love and to love. Love is the key to the undoing of the spirals of the Serpent and the key to the fulfillment of the spirals of the seed of woman, the Christ consciousness that must be realized by every son and daughter who would return to Eden.

With the consummate fires of Divine Love, Charity would redeem Adam and Eve and all sons and daughters of God who have also failed their initiations on the third ray. These include the descendants of Seth who were chosen to receive the redemption of the Christ—the Israelites who had not departed from the name of God I AM THAT I AM or the flame of the Holy Spirit.

The Fall into Idolatry

We should also know how Eve became the Mother of the generations of Cain. It must be understood that the tribes of Cain are the Gentiles—"foreigners" to the nation of Israel—whose karma did not allow them to receive the Word of Christ until it first had been given to the elect. The elect were those who had elected to do the will of God ever since the days of Seth and Enos and Cainan and Mahalaleel and Jared and Enoch and Methuselah and Lamech and Noah.

To understand how the lightbearers of ancient Israel became inextricably tied to their idolatrous neighbors, we turn to the Ascended Master Djwal Kul. He presents their history as a story that is being outplayed to the present day:

"My beloved, hear now the story of the bondage of the souls of the Israelites—how they were freed by God from the Egyptian bondage and how they entered again into the bondage of the fleshpots of Egypt. Mankind have often wondered why the angel of the LORD or the LORD God himself did not come down from the mountain of the gods to set free the captives of the oppressors, but instead allowed the self-made law of idolatry to render that captivity captive of the law of karma.

"Mankind cry out for salvation, and in the groanings of their souls they appeal to the Almighty. And yet the Almighty has appeared time and time again through his emissaries—angels, prophets and messengers—to warn of the impending doom that hangs like the sword of Damocles over the idolatrous generation. Likewise, the hand of mercy, of justice, of prophecy and of wisdom has appeared; and yet mankind, in the perverseness of the wicked, have defied the counsels and the counselors of the God of Israel.

"To those who would know the freedom of the soul, I say, listen well! For there is a price that must be paid for that freedom. It is the surrender of your idols, of your idolatry and of your submission to the idolatrous generation.

"And so it came to pass in the days of the judges that 'an angel of the LORD came up from Gilgal to Bochim, and said [to the children of Israel], I made you to go up out of Egypt and have brought you unto the land which I sware unto your fathers; and I said, I will never break my covenant with you. And ye shall make no league with the inhabitants of this land; ye shall throw down their altars: but ye have not obeyed my voice: why have ye done this?

"'Wherefore I also said, I will not drive them out from before you; but they shall be as thorns in your sides, and their gods shall be a snare unto you. And it came to pass, when the angel of the LORD spake these words unto all the children of Israel, that the people lifted up their voice and wept.'[134]

"Through the hand of Moses, the Israelites were rescued from the bondage of Egypt, which represents the bondage of the soul to the cult of death and the cult of the serpent that arises out of the misuse of the sacred fire in the base-of-the-spine chakra. This is that bondage which results from the utter perversion of the Mother Flame.

"In order for the energies of the Israelites to rise to the plane of God-awareness in the seat-of-the-soul chakra, it was necessary that they be delivered from those who enslaved their consciousness and their energies to spirals of disintegration and death. But in order for them to retain that freedom, to receive the blessings of the LORD and to be participants in the covenant of their Maker, it was required of them that they should not, in the words of Paul, be 'unequally yoked together with unbelievers.'[135]

"Therefore, God warned the Israelites to be free from entanglements with those who were carnally minded, for by Cosmic Law the children of righteousness ought not to have fellowship—especially intermarriage and the bearing of offspring—with the children of unrighteousness. For the true Israelites are the children of reality whom God would one day use as the seed of Abraham to bring forth the Christ consciousness and that great nation which would be the fulfillment of the City Foursquare.[136]

"But they would not; and their leaders did not drive out the inhabitants of the land that God had given them, nor did they throw down their altars and challenge their gods. And generations arose who knew not the LORD nor the works that he had done for Israel; and they did evil in the sight of God, forsaking the LORD and serving the false gods of Baal and Ashtaroth.

"Even when the LORD raised up judges among them to deliver them out of the hand of the spoilers, yet in their perverseness they would not hearken unto the judges, but 'went a whoring after other gods and bowed themselves unto them.'[137]

"So their corruption was great, and the anger of the LORD was hot against the Israelites who departed not from their stubborn ways. And the LORD left the nations of the laggard generation without driving them out in order to prove Israel and to be the testing of her soul. These were the Philistines, the Canaanites, the Sidonians and the Hivites.

"Moreover, those who had been chosen of the LORD to carry the torch of freedom 'dwelt among the Canaanites, Hittites, and Amorites, and Perizzites, and Hivites, and Jebusites: and they took their daughters to be their wives and gave their daughters to their sons and served their gods. And the children of Israel did evil in the sight of the LORD and forgat the LORD their God and served Baalim and the groves.'[138]

"'Come now, and let us reason together, saith the LORD: though your sins be as scarlet, they shall be as white as snow; though they be red like crimson, they shall be as wool.'[139]

"In the seat-of-the-soul chakra (see figure 23), there are anchored in man and in woman the powers of procreation—the seed of Alpha in man, the egg of Omega in woman. And the seed and the egg contain the mandala of the Christ consciousness that is passed on from generation to generation through those who espouse the disciplines of the Law and keep the commandments of their God.

"The soul that is free is the soul that retains the image of the Christ and is the progenitor of that image in the raising-up of the sons and daughters of God who take dominion not only over the earth, but over the idolatrous generations who inhabit the earth. These are of the Christ consciousness, which works the works of God and bears the fruit thereof. These are they who multiply the God consciousness 'as Above, so below' by preserving in honor the freedom of the soul.

"Some among the original Hebrews, chosen of God and to whom God gave the Promised Land, compromised their attainment in the seat-of-the-soul chakra by allowing the seed (the Christic light) of Abraham to be commingled with the Canaanites. By so doing they not only forfeited their right to be called the chosen people, but they also forfeited their vision of God in manifestation—the faculty of the third-eye chakra—which would have enabled them to recognize the Christed one who came in fulfillment of the prophecy of Isaiah.

"So great was the abomination of those who had been chosen to bear the Word of the Law that the LORD God allowed them to be taken into Assyrian and Babylonian captivity and ultimately to be scattered over the face of the earth. Those

FIGURE 23: The seat-of-the-soul chakra.
The six petals of the soul chakra represent the six-pointed star of victory. They govern the flow of light and the karmic patterns in the genes and chromosomes and in the sperm and egg of man and woman.

This chakra focuses the violet flame—the flame of freedom, transmutation and forgiveness. The violet flame is the seventh-ray aspect of the Holy Spirit that comes to us under the sponsorship of Saint Germain, the Master of the Aquarian age (the seventh age).

Through the science of the spoken Word, you can direct the accelerating violet flame of the Holy Spirit into the accumulation of karma recorded in the subconscious electronic belt. And you can feel the flame renewing thought and feeling, liberating your soul to become all that God made her to be.

among the descendants of the twelve tribes of Israel who remembered their calling to free a planet and her people from idolatry and who had never compromised the Law of the prophets and the patriarchs were allowed to embody upon a new continent.

"They were given another land that was the fulfillment of the promise of God unto Abraham—the land of the I AM race.[140] That race is composed of all peoples and kindreds and tongues who have the worship of the individual Christ and the one God—the God of Abraham, of Isaac and of Jacob, who declared himself unto Moses as the principle of the I AM THAT I AM and who affirmed, 'This is my name for ever, and this is my memorial unto all generations.'[141]

"Because the original race that was chosen to bear that name compromised the light, the very Christos of the seed of the patriarchs, the opportunity to bear the flame of freedom was widened to include all who would choose to come apart from the idolatrous generation to be a separate people who would raise up in the wilderness of the human consciousness the brazen serpent—which symbolized the raising-up of the energies of the Divine Mother, the serpentine fires of the Goddess Kundalini. This is indeed the caduceus action rising as the life force, the energy that blossomed as Aaron's rod through the union of the spirals of Alpha and Omega.

"Thus, beloved—and I speak to all children of the I AM THAT I AM in every nation upon earth—the mastery of the seat-of-the-soul chakra is the mastery of the flame of freedom in the Aquarian cycle. It is the retaining of the energy of the seed and the egg in preparation for the bringing forth of Christed ones of the seventh root race. And it is the release of that energy in the upper chakras in creativity, in genius, in learning and innovation, and in the art, the music, the literature and the culture of the Divine Mother.

"And thus the fires of freedom anchored in the soul are not to be used in acts of immorality or for the breaking of the code of the Ten Commandments or for the desecration of the grace of the Christ and the sacred energies of the Holy Spirit.

"Therefore, in the true spirit of wholeness (hol-i-ness), let the sons and daughters of God who would build the temple and the New Jerusalem raise up the energies of the Mother and of the soul through the resurrection spiral. And let those energies be consecrated on the altar of the heart for the building of the golden age.

"To you who would have the aura of self-mastery, of soul freedom, I say: Let the energies of your lusts, of your pleasure seeking, of the gratification of the senses be now raised up in the wholeness of Almighty God! And with the courage, the honor and the conviction of the Christed ones, stand before the altar of the LORD of Israel and declare:

In the name of the Messiah who has come into the
> Holy of holies of my being, I consecrate my energies
> to the fulfillment of the spirals of Alpha and Omega.

In the name of the Promised One whose promise is fulfilled
> in me this day, let the brazen serpent be raised up in the
> wilderness.

In the name of the King of kings and Lord of lords,
> let the energies of my soul rise for the fulfillment of life.

In the true name of the LORD God of Israel, I proclaim:
> I AM THAT I AM.

> I AM the resurrection and the life of every cell and atom
>> of my four lower bodies now made manifest.

> I AM the victory of the ascension in the light.

> I AM the ascending triangle of Mater
>> converging in the heart chakra and merging
>> with the descending triangle of Spirit.

I AM the six-pointed star of victory.

I AM the light of all that is real.

In my soul I AM free, for my energies are tethered
    to the Holy One of Israel,

And in the name of the one true God
    and in fulfillment of his commandment,
        I withdraw the seed and the egg of Alpha and Omega
        from the unrighteous and the idolatrous generation.

I AM the fulfillment of the law of love.

I AM a keeper of the flame,

And I AM the guardian light of the covenant of my
    Maker, the LORD God of Israel.

"The challenge goes forth from the Lords of Karma to those who would keep the flame of Israel in America, in the New Jerusalem and in every nation upon earth: Put down your idolatry and your idolatrous generation, cast down the altars of Baal and Ashtaroth throughout the land, and reclaim your temples for the LORD God of hosts!

"And let my people return to the sanctity of the sacred ritual of the exchange of the sacred fire between enlightened man and woman who have come before the altar of God to consecrate their union for the bringing forth of the lightbearers. And let the young who ought to be maturing in the ways of the Christ be freed from the Luciferian perversions of life's sacred energies, from the incorrect use of the sacred fire in sex, from premarital exchanges and from perverted practices that issue from the degenerate spirals of Sodom and Gomorrah.

"So let these energies be restored to the place of the Holy of holies. For the fiat of the LORD rings forth from Horeb this day: Let my people go![142] Set the captives free! and let the judges render judgment this day! In the name of the living Christ, be thou made whole!

"I am invoking the flaming presence of the I AM THAT

I AM around all who have chosen to be the fulfillment of the promise of the LORD to Abraham: 'I will make thy seed as the stars of the sky in multitude and as the sand which is by the seashore innumerable.'[143]

"And I am placing the ring of freedom's fire from my consciousness as a circle of protection around the seat-of-the-soul chakra, the energies thereof, and the Christic pattern of the seed and the egg for the sealing of life within you as the life victorious and triumphant."[144]

Opportunity for Christhood

We read in Jesus' own words that he was sent to deliver the Word of the Logos "unto the lost sheep of the house of Israel."[145] Nevertheless there came a time in his mission when he opened the way of the Christ consciousness to the generations of Cain.

By this act, the law of karma as it had been meted out to the generations of Cain was mitigated by the grace and the mercy of the Lord Christ, as he was one with the Guru Maitreya and with the Christ Selves of all mankind.

By his intercession, Charity, the Mother/teacher of the children of light on the third ray, is also the Mother/teacher of those who continued to transgress the Law of God after the manner of Cain. Aligning themselves with the seed of the Wicked One and their Luciferian creation, they became known as the children of darkness.

By the dispensation of the Lords of Karma, delivered through Jesus Christ, the message of the Word of God is to all generations and peoples and kindreds and tongues[146]—even unto the fallen angels if they will in humility confess the Christ, confirm the name of God I AM THAT I AM and obey the commands of the Gurus who come as the incarnation of the Second Person of the Trinity.

By this act of Jesus Christ, the Seven Archeiai have stood at the door of the Christ consciousness to teach all of the evolutions of earth the way to enter in. In this age of the cycles turning, when many are called to judgment and the balance of karma is being exacted equally in all of earth's evolutions, salvation is, therefore, for all who will to be self-elevated—by the grace of Jesus Christ.

Let us relive the moment when by the love of God the opportunity for Christhood was extended to the generations of Cain. It is written in the fifteenth chapter of the Book of Matthew: "Then Jesus went thence, and departed into the coasts of Tyre and Sidon. And, behold, a woman of Canaan came out of the same coasts, and cried unto him, saying, Have mercy on me, O Lord, thou son of David; my daughter is grievously vexed with a devil.

"But he answered her not a word. And his disciples came and besought him, saying, Send her away; for she crieth after us. But he answered and said, I am not sent but unto the lost sheep of the house of Israel.

"Then came she and worshipped him, saying, Lord, help me. But he answered and said, It is not meet to take the children's bread, and cast it to dogs. And she said, Truth, Lord: yet the dogs eat of the crumbs which fall from their masters' table. Then Jesus answered and said unto her, O woman, great is thy faith: be it unto thee even as thou wilt. And her daughter was made whole from that very hour."[147]

This is the moment when the law of forgiveness was extended to the larger circle of human evolution. Immediately following this dispensation great multitudes came to Jesus, and he was moved with compassion toward them.

And through the grace and the mercy of the law of forgiveness he healed those whose karma of disobedience to the Christ, the Guru, was manifest in manifold inequities. And it is written that when the multitudes "saw the dumb to speak, the maimed to be whole, the lame to walk, and the blind to see," they who had turned away from the LORD God now "glorified the God of Israel."[148]

These miracles are the beginning of the redemption of the generations who were destroyed in the Flood of Noah (the sinking of Atlantis), of whom it is written: "And God saw that the wickedness of man was great in the earth, and that every imagination of the thoughts of his heart was only evil continually."[149]

Deliverance from Selfish Love

In the very moment of the judgment and the return of mankind's karma of their wrathful misuses of the energies of love, Archeia Charity, Mother of love, also delivers the compassion that is opportunity on the third ray. This is the balance of twin flames. As Chamuel descends to decelerate the intensity of God's love, tempering the wind to the shorn lamb of mankind's identity, point/counterpoint Charity delivers love's liberation.

Let us listen first to Chamuel: "The winds of the Holy Spirit and the fires infolded in the winds are indeed for the judgment of the Luciferian creation and for the intensification of love in the hearts of the lightbearers, that love itself might be the instrument of the judgment.

"Let your hearts now burn within you![150] For the Presence of the Lord, though unseen and unknown, is nigh. And you will recognize the reality of your Lord and your Saviour by the burning of your heart in the love of the Creator. For only the Saviour, the eternal Christos, who lives in the hearts of ascended and unascended beings, can cause the quickening of the fires on earthly altars—the same fires that burn as votive flames ignited by angels who keep the flame of life on behalf of souls moving in the planes of Mater.

"Just as the quickening must come in the hearts of the

children of God on the notable day of the LORD, so the quaking must also come in the hearts of those who have rebelled against the light. It is their hearts that will fail them for fear[151] of the judgment that is come.

"Therefore in answer to the edict of the LORD, I come forth from the Temple of the Tabernacle of the Testimony carrying the golden vial that contains mankind's wrathful misuses of the energies of love. What do you think, O mankind, will come upon this generation who have taken the very fires of creativity, the very energies of the Holy Spirit, and perverted them against the light of the One! I say, let judgment reign! And let it be the raining of the fires of the Almighty One as I pour out the measure of mankind's karma upon the rivers and fountains of waters for them to become blood.[152]

"And now let the response of the angel of the waters be heard: 'Thou art righteous, O Lord, which art and wast and shalt be, because thou hast judged thus. For they have shed the blood of saints and prophets, and thou hast given them blood to drink; for they are worthy.' And let the angel standing at the altar of the Most High God give the mantra of the third ray, 'Even so, LORD God Almighty, true and righteous are thy judgments.' And let this mantra be heard by God from the lips of the righteous who have learned the right use of love and who have consecrated the energies of the Holy Spirit in the rituals of the sacred fire."[153]

This is the mantra of sons and daughters of God living in the twentieth century and beyond, who would confirm the judgment of the Luciferian creation within their four lower bodies—within the soul, the mind, the heart and the temple of being: "Even so, LORD God Almighty, true and righteous are thy judgments."

Each time these words are spoken, the I AM THAT I AM and the very personal Christ Self confirm the action of the judgment over the figure-eight spiral, as Above, so below. Those who would be counted among the overcomers in the Aquarian age rediscover the meaning of alignment with Alpha and Omega. This mantra, when used with the violet flame in the fiery intensity of the action of the Master of the Aquarian age (Saint Germain), is the antidote from the very heart of Alpha to the astral perversions of the fallen ones.

The Liberation of Love: Justice through Opportunity– Freedom through Transmutation

Chamuel speaks lovingly of Saint Germain, this Master of the transmutative fires of the freedom of the seventh ray, as the one who "focuses the consciousness of God-love in this system of worlds."[154] For his consciousness is the key to the transformation of souls and their salvation here and now.

Saint Germain's twin flame, the Ascended Lady Master Portia, serves on the Karmic Board as the Goddess of Opportunity. As we give the mantra "Even so, LORD God Almighty, true and righteous are thy judgments," we hear her voice echoing: "There is no injustice anywhere in the cosmos." The mantra is indeed the confirmation of Portia, whose flame (justice through opportunity) reflects that of her counterpart, Saint Germain (freedom through transmutation). Truly the affirmation of Portia's mantra with Saint Germain's violet flame is the alchemy of twin flames in the joyous judgment of love, for which the sons and daughters of God have been waiting for aeons.

There is no question, as Chamuel says, that "of all of the misuses of the sacred fire that mankind have imposed upon nature and the body of the Mother, there is none more deadly or more dastardly than the perversion of Divine Love."[155]

Therefore we can conclude that when these energies are

transmuted in the violet flame—in the love fires of the very heart of Saint Germain and in the confirmation of the judgment of the Lords of Karma individually, one by one, in the sons and daughters of God—the corresponding victory will be the greatest of all victories of all time and space, the victory of love.

We should run to meet the victors in their flaming robes of righteousness. We should run to greet the runners in the race of love—the angelic hosts, the legions of Chamuel and Charity, the lightbearers of the Elohim Heros and Amora, and all of the devotees of Paul the Venetian, whose path of initiation has been the discipline of the sacred fires of creativity.

Knowing that ours is the victory as we give forth the fiats of love, we ought to here and now consecrate the science of the spoken Word in an acclamation in full voice of the power of love, the wisdom of love, and the love of love. Let the fiats of love sound forth the voice of God in manifestation in man and woman in the greatest proclamation of love that the world has ever known—the love whose release is truly the alchemy of Aquarius and the victory unto the ascension of lightbearers who do indeed confirm the beauty, the bounty and the be-attitude of love.

There is nothing in heaven or in earth that love cannot, will not do in answer to the call of fervent prayer of an impassioned plea to the LORD God for mercy, forgiveness, grace and opportunity. Love is the all-power of a cosmos that was given to Jesus Christ in the hour of his victory.

This power is also given to every son and daughter of God who overcomes in the way of sacrifice, surrender, selflessness and service. When every jot and tittle of the law of love is fulfilled, then and only then can the Christed ones whose chakras are anointed with the precious oil of love declare, "All power is given unto me in heaven and in earth [in Spirit and in Matter]."[156]

In this very moment, if you desire the redemption of the

Lord Christ, of the Guru Maitreya, of your own Christ Self and I AM Presence, you have but to call upon the name of the LORD, I AM THAT I AM, and accept the redemption of love through the blessed Mediator (Jesus Christ) and the blessed Mediatrix (his mother, the Virgin Mary).

In this very moment, you can confirm the Law of God as Above, so below. You can confirm the existence of heaven right here on earth, right where you are, right within your very heart of hearts in the fiery core of the threefold flame and in the secret chamber of the heart. This is your own Holy of holies, this is your tabernacle of witness. This is the place where you meet the Gurus, the chohans, face to face. This is the place where you come to know the Buddha and the Mother. This is the place of your meditation upon the newborn child, the Bethlehem babe, your own Christ consciousness.

This is where you meditate with the three wise men, the three *kings* of the Orient, who have exercised the wise dominion of those who truly hold the *k*ey to the *in*carnation of *G*od on Terra. They came out of the white fire core of the retreat of the Great White Brotherhood to lay at the feet of father, mother and child the remembrance of Eden and the promise of redemption of the Archangels: gold and frankincense and myrrh.

Gold, Frankincense and Myrrh: The Remembrance of Eden

These three tokens of consolation were long ago delivered by God to Adam and Eve through the hand of the Archangels Michael, Gabriel and Raphael that they might trust in God and in the covenant that he made with them, promising them that he would send his Word and save them from outer darkness by the inner light of the Christ.

These three tokens were delivered once again at the birth

of the Lord. And the LORD God made the rods of gold (token of his kingdom) to shine forth with light in the cave. The frankincense (token of his divinity) was given that he might smell the sweet savor of God's presence. And the myrrh (token of his suffering and death) would bring him comfort in the sorrow of every trial and tribulation.[157]

Now is the victory of the promise upon us, in the fulfillment of the covenant that God made with Adam and Eve during the long days and years of their suffering outside of the Garden of Eden. With the coming of the judgment of mankind's karma is the coming of the glorious opportunity for every son and daughter of God to henceforth live and move and have being within the consciousness of God, here and now, until the day of the ultimate alchemy when death is swallowed up in the victory of love.

From the very moment of your awakening and your awareness, O Adam, that you are indeed the son of the Almighty One, the Most High God—from the very moment of the evolution and elevation of your consciousness, O Eve, that you are indeed a daughter of the living God, the true incarnation of the Word—you can henceforth and forevermore live in the consciousness of victory. Cycle by cycle you can put off the old man and the old woman, Adam and Eve, and put on the new— the Christ Self, your very own real identity in God.

Thus while mankind, who have sustained their rebellion against love for generations and generations, mourn the coming of the Son of man in the hour of the judgment, the sons and daughters of God rejoice to see the salvation of their God.

They make a joyful noise unto the LORD. They come before the I AM Presence with gladness and singing[158] that their long, dark night of the soul—thousands and tens of thousands of years outside of Eden—is come full circle in a cycle fulfilled.

This is the moment and the hour of love's liberation.

Therefore let us with all diligence listen to the counseling of Chamuel and Charity and let us see to it that we do not neglect, no, not one word nor one counsel nor one admonishment lest it become the one sin of omission, of opportunity lost, of freedom denied, that would deprive us of the victory of love.

Let us hear the words of the Archangels and know that theirs are not idle words, that they are given forth in the highest wisdom and the highest love and the highest understanding of the Law of God, because our souls have need of them.

The Hardening of Hearts

Chamuel explains the law of karma as it is interpreted by love. "Now this is the dilemma of the Archangels and of the Lords of Karma and of Alpha and Omega. As it has ever been, the light shone in the darkness and the darkness comprehended it not.[159] Therefore is judgment come, that mankind might learn from the taskmaster of their own karma that which is acceptable in the presence of love.... For this is a generation of people-haters, children-haters, Christ-haters and God-haters; and mankind's hearts have become hardened against the true children of *Israel*—the children of the light of all that *is real*.

"And as Pharaoh hardened his heart to the Word of the LORD that came through Moses and to the judgments of the LORD that turned the waters to blood and brought pestilence, affliction, and the death of the firstborn in the houses of the Egyptians,[160] so are the hearts of mankind hardened to the Word of the LORD delivered unto this age through the two witnesses....

"The true followers of God are hated—despised and rejected of men.[161] And thus it has been through all of the centuries when the sons and daughters of God have come to deliver the sheep of the Good Shepherd from the toils of the Luciferians.

"Through the pride of the eye and the degradation of the

flame of the Mother, mankind have rejected their deliverers. They have imitated the ways of the fallen ones and scourged and spat upon the true Lamb of God. Like the dog that bites the hand that feeds it, mankind have been utterly duped so that, in their depressed state of consciousness, they follow the pied piper into the night and reject the marriage supper of the Lamb and the Lamb's wife."[162]

An Admonishment for the Generations of Seth

If we would understand the counsels of the Archangels, we must discern in their dictations and in their decrees the message that is for the generations of Cain (the self-willed) and the message that is for the generations of Seth (the God-willed). The following admonishment is directed to the generations of Seth:

"Let honor, longsuffering and tenderness characterize the relationships of the followers of God. Let doctrine and dogma be consumed in the fires of love. Let the Holy Spirit unite all hearts in the love of the One. And let those who stand with Michael the Archangel and all the Archangels and their legions of light to defend the faith, the hope and the charity of all mankind determine to put down, once and for all, the aggressive voices of the night that hammer the brain with their lies.

"If you would get the victory over the beast and over his image and over his mark and over the number of his name, stand on the sea of glass! Stand on the purity of the Mother and her immaculate concept, which she holds undefiled for each child of God. Put down the Luciferian lie directed as an arrow of division into your mental body! Refute the lie concerning the woman and her seed. Refute the lie concerning the Keepers of the Flame. Put down these demons of the night! For they come as the hordes of shadow to take over the consciousness of the children by rays of insanity and profanity, of psychicism, spiritism, hypnotism and mental manipulation.

"Aggressive mental suggestion is the germ warfare of the fallen ones. You must hold up the shield of the Archangels and wield the sword of the Spirit to deflect the arrows of their outrageous consciousness. And they are raging in the stalls of the astral plane, like the Devil, that roaring lion, seeking whom they may devour.[163]

"The fallen ones are organized. They have taken the consciousness of love, which is the very order of a cosmos, and perverted it to their own use. They have organized a warfare of the Spirit, projecting their vials of astral microbes, astral viruses, deadly toxins that they would inject into the mental and emotional bodies of mankind through that which we have called aggressive mental suggestion.

"You can identify this energy. You can know it well. For at any moment of the day or night when you feel waves of irritation and mild dislike and a separation from brothers and sisters on the Path through barbs of criticism and waves of anxiety and nervous tension, and you feel your energies seized with a certain dislike for this or that individual or an action of intense condemnation or judgment of a co-servant who works side by side with you in the field of the LORD, know that the Devil has sent his angels, even Satan who has deceived the whole world.[164]

"And though he be bound for a thousand years by Michael the Archangel of the LORD, who 'cast him into the bottomless pit and shut him up, and set a seal upon him, that he should deceive the nations no more,' his angels enter into combat with the sons and daughters of God. This is Armageddon. This is the warfare of the Spirit 'against principalities, against powers, against the rulers of the darkness of this world, against spiritual wickedness in high places.'[165]

"You must be alert; for where there is gossip and where there is the maligning of the image of the Mother or her children, where there is the tearing-down of the activities of those who are serving (no matter how imperfectly) the cause of the Brotherhood, know that there are the fallen ones lurking in your midst to destroy the works of God on earth.

"Hearken not to their counsel! Hearken to the LORD. Do not respond to their turbulence, their riptides of emotional energy, which they unleash at the feet of the children of the light! Do you not know, O blessed ones, how they gather the clouds of darkness and the grids and forcefields of mankind's hatred and concentrate the misqualified energies of an entire city or a nation against one soul who is taking his stand for the light of Truth?

"If you would live in the flaming presence of love, be prepared to deal with the fallen ones who have misused this sacred fire to create all manner of ugliness and distortion of the divine arts and of the music of the spheres to turn man and woman upside down and inside out in acts of perverted sex and misuses of the sacred fire. And they have caused the judgment of Sodom and Gomorrah[166] to be upon this generation who have replaced reverence for life with the murder of the avatars and of the Divine Mother.

"I am come for the judgment, that the energies of the Holy Spirit might be realigned in man and woman, that the fires of the Kundalini might rise on the altar of the spine to illumine, to purify, and to increase the intensity of the Sun behind the sun."

The Wickedness of the Generations of Cain

Now, addressing the generations of Cain, Chamuel explains the circumstances of mankind's expulsion from Eden. This expulsion occurred even centuries before the opportunity was given to Adam and Eve, as a son and a daughter of God, to come forth from Venus to demonstrate the victory of love.

These sins of mankind were far greater than those of Adam and Eve. They are the wickedness of the generations of Cain that was practiced both before and after Adam and Eve's initiation and expulsion.

"Let mankind know, then, that their expulsion from Eden came about as the result of their misuse of the sacred fire in oral sex, in cohabitation with animal life, in homosexuality and all manner of experimentation with the seed and the egg, including their creation of human and animal life in the test tubes of the laboratories of the laggard generation.

"These things are the abomination of desolation standing in the holy place of the sacred union where they ought not.[167] Therefore judgment is come, and those that take the sword to kill the holy innocents while they are yet in their mothers' wombs must also be killed with the sword.* For this day they are expelled from the womb of the Divine Mother! And this is the Law and the judgment.

---

*Chamuel is affirming the law of karma as stated in Revelation 13:10: "He that killeth with the sword must be killed with the sword. Here is the patience and the faith of the saints." It is God's place to determine the cycles of karma, not man's. Furthermore, on October 26, 1990, Mother Mary explained, "It is the right of every woman to defend the right of souls to take embodiment. Whether you believe it or not, it is so, that your soul requires many incarnations on earth to fulfill her divine plan. Think, then, what is the karma of abortion. The karma is that one day if you should so pass from the screen of life not having balanced sufficient karma nor fulfilled your mission to allow you to pass through the resurrection and the ascension, that you yourself will be seeking entrée to the physical octave once again through the portals of birth. And at that moment, beloved, the karma of having performed or had an abortion may greet you with the denial to enter once again earth's schoolroom because you have denied life to another. This is the law of karma. It is real and it is true." Therefore we strive to uphold God's laws, and we call for God to mete out justice and mercy according to Divine Law. In the patience and faith of the saints, we are directed to trust in God's wisdom to implement his judgments according to his own timetable through the inexorable current of karmic cycles.

"I shall take my leave of you, for even the children of the light have all that they can bear in the intensity of my message. There is weeping and gnashing of teeth outside the womb of the Cosmic Virgin! Let those who would retain the right and the light to live in the flame of the Mother cease their desecration of her love."[168]

The Sacred Circle of Marriage

Chamuel and Charity are the guardians of the flame of love, the very sacred fires of the Holy Spirit, as these sustain the action-reaction-interaction in all relationships between the manifestations of God. The first of these relationships is that of the soul to the living Presence of the I AM THAT I AM, then the relationship of the soul to the Christ Self as the tutor of the Law, then of the soul to father and to mother, to brother and sister, to husband or wife, to child, to friend, to neighbor, to fellow pilgrim on the homeward way.

Charity, Archangelic being of love, gives counsel to those who would share the love of God as twin flames, as soul mates, as partners in the marriage covenant ordained by God for the relationship of man and woman on earth. She gives counsel to those who would nourish the love fires on the altar of hearth and home to consecrate the Holy Family matrix of the holy Trinity as the foundation of the Aquarian age.

Charity is a being of practical love. She is concerned with man and woman working out the cycles of their karma in marriage. She is concerned that men and women in these times understand that the divorce rate is high in every nation because people do not understand that often their love is a selfish love, a love of passion and possession instead of giving and receiving according to the cycles of the figure-eight flow of the Father-Mother God. Charity would have us receive the vision of the beginning and the ending of love, of love on earth that must reach for the love of heaven.

Charity comes. She identifies herself as the "adornment of the sacred union of the Father-Mother God." As the feminine aspect of the third ray, Charity is the Mother/teacher of the children of the One who have gone out of the way of love.

She is the deliverer of the flame of God's love to the souls of all mankind. Her words are the liberation of love for which the souls of the generations of Adam and Eve have been yearning these long centuries: "I come to deliver mankind from the toils of selfish love. I come to deliver man and woman from the agony of self-centered love and of that which seeks to possess and is thereby possessed of the not-self....

"I stand on the threshold of the circle of the oneness of twin flames. I am Charity, and I come to draw the hallowed circle of your union. I come as the patroness of the Holy Family in the Aquarian age. I come in the service of Saint Germain and Mary and the Lord Christ. For I have been bidden to come forth from the Temple of the Tabernacle of the Testimony of the Logos to protect the love of devotees serving in the planes of Mater."

Now let us study the admonishments of Charity: "See how the discarnates penetrate that which ought to be the hallowed circle of the love of the Father-Mother God sealed in the union of every son and daughter who have come before the altar of the Most High to consecrate their marriage vows! See how the envious ones lurk to steal the energies of the sacred fire that belong to you and to you alone! ...

"O my children, the demons of the night are jealous of your love. They would claw the very body of the Mother if they could. They come as vultures to devour the flesh and blood of the children of God before the hour of the consecration of the Body and the Blood by the Sacred Eucharist of our Lord.

"They are not the eagles who gather together at the place of the corpus Christi. They are not the sons and daughters of God who follow the flame of the Mother enshrined in the tower of the lighthouse—a beacon to guide the souls to victory —but they are the discarnates sent by the dragon to devour the child as soon as it is born.[169]

"Cradle the child of your love. Wrap the child in the swaddling garments of the Holy Spirit. Let honor and reverence for one another be the pivot of a cosmic love unfolding in Mater to the glory of the eternal Christos.

"Remember the story of Sleeping Beauty. Each time the innocence of love is veiled in flesh, each time the Mother Flame is born anew in Mater preparing to unite with the knight champion of the Holy Spirit, there appears on the scene, lurking in the shadows, the representative of the Great Whore,[170] who comes to poison that rosy-cheeked innocence.

The Ritual of the Archangels

"O my children, let your love be the commemoration of the fusion of the cloven tongues of the Spirit. Now then, take the ritual that the Archangels practice at the rising and the setting of the sun when the torch of love is passed by angels of the dawn and angels of the dusk. Take the ritual of the Archangels and make it all your own, and prove thereby the victory of love on Terra. Prove that your love is the holy habitation of the LORD God of hosts and that this love, by your will firmed in the fire of God-determination, will not be defiled by the hordes of the night.

"Stand together facing the Chart of the I AM Presence (see Chart of Your Divine Self, facing page 182) and make your inner attunement with the star of your divinity. Meditate upon your heart and the flame therein and behold the arc ascend into the center of the Divine Monad. Now take your right hand and dip it into the fires of your heart and draw the circle of our oneness around yourselves as you stand in adoration of the One.

"Visualize this circle, twelve feet in diameter, as a line of sacred fire. It is your ring-pass-not. Within that circle of oneness is the forcefield of Alpha and Omega; and you focus the T'ai Chi, the plus and minus of cosmic energies, where you are.

"Let the flow of your love be not in imitation of the idolatrous generation. Let it not be the mechanization of sex as the Luciferians have popularized their sordid and sadistic ways. The flow of the Holy Spirit twixt father and mother is for the birth of the Divine Manchild, first within each heart and then in the Bethlehem babe. Seek not the thrills of sensuality or the titillation of mind or body, but seek the bliss of mutual reunion in the Presence.

"Let your love be the reenactment of the alchemical marriage. Let your love be consecrated for the soul's ultimate reunion with the I AM Presence. So is the marriage ritual intended to be the rehearsal for the great drama of your soul's assumption into the flame of love for the rolling-up of the scroll of identity into the Great Silence of your own I AM THAT I AM and for the fusion of those twin flames of the Godhead when the I AM Presence of each half of the Divine Whole merges in the hallowed circle of God.

"Seek the bliss of the raising of the Mother light—of *sushumna, ida* and *pingala*[171]—as these form the caduceus energies that reveal your real identity in Christ. Let your bliss transcend the earthly senses, and let your light flow from all of the chakras to reinforce the divine polarity of the Father-Mother God in every level of consciousness to be outpictured in the seven major chakras and the five chakras of the secret rays.

"Your marriage is made in heaven and you are wed to

God. Daughters of the flame: Behold, thy Maker is thine husband. So be, with Mary, the handmaid of the LORD. Sons of the flame: The golden band you wear is the halo of the Cosmic Virgin, the bride descending out of heaven[172] to consummate your love on earth.

"As Above, so below, the cosmic flow of Father-Mother God is intended to be shared in the sanctuary of the Holy Family. And it is intended to be sealed with the blessing of the true ministers of the Logos and to be guarded by purity in the Holy of holies. The ark of the covenant is also a matrix of the protection of twin flames joined together in holy matrimony for a life of service to God and man. And the covering cherubim[173] must be invoked daily, for they are the guardians of love in the planes of Matter.

"Understand, O wise ones pursuing the Law of the Logos, that if the fallen ones can destroy love, they can destroy all. For love is the foundation and the fountain of life. Love is the essence of creation. Without love, life is desolate and the skies are dreary and elemental life is despondent.

"Where the love of father, mother and child is broken, as in the totalitarian state, there is a depression that hangs over the land. And to compensate therefor, the people engage in a fierce rationalization of dialectical materialism. Without love the justifications of unreality are piled upon justification, and the impenetrable wall of self-deception that is erected, stone upon stone, of the hardness of their hearts is sealed with the mortar of their rejection of the God of Love.

"And so the superstate is built as the tower of Babel was built.[174] And men and women are saturated with an enormous pride in the ego and its accomplishments—all of this to stifle the aching in the soul, the aching for the tenderness of love, the caress of father, of mother, a humble home—a hearth kindled in the fires of Father, Son and Holy Spirit, an abode we can call our own, a creativity won by the work of our hands, the distillations of our minds, a sacred labor perfected by striving and surrender unto love.

"Let them build their towers to the sky! Let them erect a monolith to the ego! Let them train their armies, forge their weapons, plan their destructions! They are on a collision course with cosmic destiny, and the end of their rationalization of unreality is self-destruction. The intensification of the fire of love will consume all of this. As surely as the rod of heaven is thrust into the ground of Terra, as surely as judgment is come, as surely as the golden vial of the wrath of mankind's misuse of love is poured out among the nations, so will come the undoing of all mankind's wrongdoing.

"It was the release of the intense action of our love that confounded the language of those who sought to build a monument to mammon. And the LORD God, through the Archangel and Archeia of the third ray, scattered them abroad from thence upon the face of all the earth, and they left off the building of their city and their tower. And it was called Babel, for their rationalization became as the babbling of voices who have not the understanding of the heart.

The Love of Heaven and Earth

"Love begins at home. Love must be enshrined in the home and at the altar of the true Church. Love must be ensouled in the nation and in the world community. For if love is not raised up by the children of the One to consume all evil on Terra, then love will descend out of heaven as the chastening fires of the Holy Ghost, and none shall escape the cataclysm that will ensue.

"This is the choice that Saint Germain has set before you. Choose love this day, and live in love and live peacefully in the land that the LORD God has given unto you. Choose love, and you will prosper and all will go well. Choose the hallowed circle of the Father-Mother God and find there succor from the crassness of the world and surcease from all struggle.

"Choose love this day and live, for the fire of love descending out of the heavens will surely come to implement the judgment ere the cycles of the century have turned. And those who are in the circle of oneness will receive those fires as the gentle rain of the Spirit, but those who are outside will experience love as the fire descending as brimstone from the mountain of the LORD.

"By love civilizations have risen; by love they have fallen. In love is the all-power of Brahma, Vishnu and Shiva—the Creator, the Preserver and the Destroyer. See, then, that you have respect for love; for love in its omnipotence is the fulfilling of the Law of sacred being."[175]

THE FOURTH RAY:

The Rebirth of Purity

Y OU WHO WOULD KNOW THE LIGHT
and become a tangible focus of God-
reality, to you would Archangel Gabriel speak: "I come forth
from the white fire core of the Great Central Sun! I step out of
the fires of the dawn, and my angels with me. We come kissed
by the golden pink glow ray. The fires of love and purity, as
dewdrop and crystal, flow from our garments as we traverse
the morning with the angels of the dawn.

"Children of the sun, I would that you would become
worshipers of the dawn and of the sun. For in your meditation
upon the rising orb of Helios and Vesta, you face the east and
behold the rising Christ and the consciousness thereof illumin-
ing a darkened world. And you see in the fire that pierces the
night with the morning light the image of your own I AM
Presence. You glimpse the brilliance in physical, tangible manifestation of the I AM THAT I AM.

"So dazzling is the sun of God that mortal eyes can
scarcely focus upon that concentrated energy. And the rays of

the sun, as they filter through the impurities of the atmosphere, can be harmful to body, soul and mind. Yet this is but a fragment of the I AM Presence focused in time and space to awaken your soul memory of the Infinite One. Such a minute fraction of your own God-reality is this center of your solar system! Can you imagine what it would be like to see the Sun behind the sun, your own I AM Presence? To visualize the replica focused so lovingly and tenderly, so tangibly by Helios and Vesta is enough to increase in a moment your perception of inner spheres.

"Therefore, you see, I would that you would become worshipers of the dawn that you might carry with you throughout the day the God consciousness of your God-reality. And never for a moment forget—as you walk the strait and narrow path to your ascension—that hovering very near is the great dazzling sun of your own I AM Presence releasing limitless light and energy, the abundance of every good and perfect gift of wisdom and love and power and the many mansions of the Father's house[176] that are lowered even now into physical manifestation for the enshrining of the flame of the Mother.

"Yes, I come for the judgment; but I look beyond the judgment. And I see through the crystal of the Mind of God (and not in the crystal ball of the psychic moon-gazers)—beyond the crucifixion, beyond the fiery cross of trial and tribulation—the hour of the resurrection of the sons and daughters of God. Yes, I see the way clearly marked. I see the way of the overcomers who walk into the light of the dawn, who are not content to bask in the light of the Presence, but who follow that light with the intensity of an absolute God-determination to return to the One."

Archangel Gabriel comes to illumine all who would accept and savor the gift of purity. Out of the Mother light he brings judgment, even as he exhorts the soul to remember her reason for being on earth:

"I announce to you your virgin birth in the womb of the

Cosmic Virgin. I announce to you that you are of the seed of Alpha, that you have been sired by Almighty God, that you have been nourished by the fires of the heart of Omega, and that you have been set for the fall and rising again of many in Israel and for a sign (which is the sign of the Logos) that shall be spoken against.[177] You have been sent into this world—although you are not of this world—as instruments of the Lord's judgment, even as you have come to balance the scales of your own uses and misuses of God's energy....

"In the moment when you read this communication from on high, sent and signified by the Messenger of the LORD, you will know that I am standing in your presence. And if you will close your eyes and meditate upon the sun centered within your heart, you will receive the flow of purity from my Causal Body and the golden pink glow ray of the angels of my band.

"Take then this [my message] and read it again and again. At the hour and the moment of the dawn, face the east as the Muhammadans do. And let your prayers be unto the Christ in all mankind and unto the universal Christ; and know that in that moment of communion, the purity of your soul is reinforced for the battle in the Dark Cycle.[178]

"Know this, O chela of the Law, that I can and I shall come to you in the first fiery glimmer of the dawn that is the hope of the resurrection of the son of God. As surely as I came to Anna and Joachim to announce the birth of the child Mary,[179] as surely as I came to Elisabeth and Zacharias to proclaim the coming of John the Baptist, as surely as I went before the Virgin to announce the birth of the Saviour,[180] so I shall stand before you—not only to speak the word of the birth of your soul in the flaming spirit of the resurrection, but also to transfer from my flaming aura to your own the energies of the Great Central Sun in the white fire core of life.

"Let my presence pierce the veil of skepticism and cynicism

and the endless human questioning—questioning even the very existence of the Archangels and the angelic host. What blasphemy against the LORD God himself to deny the existence of the angels who personify the great feelings of the Almighty for the creation biding in the planes of Mater!

Renewal through the Quickening Fires of the Holy Spirit

"I am Gabriel, and I come with Hope (my own divine complement) in the flame of our joint mission. Our hope for the restoration of the souls of the fallen ones is never for a moment set aside. As long as there is life and even the flickering of the flame of life upon the altar of the heart, we breathe the breath of the Holy Spirit upon that life, upon that flame, fanning the flame with renewal, directing the consciousness to new horizons.

"Each day is a day of hope—hope for resurrection, hope for the setting of the records straight, for the clearing of the fire body (repository of the blueprint of the divine plan), the clearing of the etheric envelope of all of the sordid or supercilious aspects of human life. I should say 'human existence'; for those who inhabit the veils of mortality, gray and shadowed, that keep the consciousness in a perpetual state of mourning, of complaining, of a sense of loss and of the sense that life is not meting out the just portion, those who dwell in the semi-state of awareness of the true self—these truly have not yet begun to live. They have only a quasi existence that remains to be quickened by the fires of the Holy Spirit.

"Let the trumpets of the Archangels sound and let the dead be raised incorruptible! For the human consciousness shall be changed. And this that is corruptible man must put on the incorruption of the divine man. Therefore, in this hour of the judgment, let this mortal put on immortality. This is my

The Chart of Your Divine Self

annunciation and this is the electrode of my life that I transfer to you—you who would be lightbearers to the age."[181]

The Way to God Is through the Portal of the Heart

A strong sense of individuality, of one's uniqueness in God, is key to this divine reunion. The way to God is through the portal of the heart, for within the heart is the very throne of your unique personhood in God, your Holy Christ Self. Truly can it be said of your Real Self, "Holiness unto the LORD."[182] The Christ who lives in your temple is one with the Most High, and he partakes of the purity and sanctity of the seraphic hosts.

We come before the threefold flame of our hearts with reverence. We are in awe of the presence of the Infinite One right at the cusp of time and space, right at the point in our body temple where the fiery mist becomes the crystal and the crystal is hallowed as Christ-reality extended to our soul—the gift of gladness.

To open our heart, to welcome our Holy Christ Self into our world is a service we perform not only for our own souls, but for the whole body of God on earth. We understand in our hearts that this is indeed an extraordinary service, which the remnant of the lightbearers are given to perform on behalf of all of the people of God and all of the tribes of Israel who yet mourn and lament the absence of their God—even while their God is in their very midst.

This service, this opening of our hearts, must be rendered to God one by one by one. As we open the door of our heart to our soul, we guard our soul's holiness against the profane. No other but the Divine may be given the preeminence of entering the innermost sanctuary of the heart or the temple of being. We do not allow anyone's human consciousness by reason of our own personal idolatry to enter in and be accorded that place of preeminence in our life that can only be given to the LORD God Almighty and to the priest of our temple, who is Christ the Lord.

Union with Christ

We realize that the coming into our temple of The LORD Our Righteousness means that God's rules and regulations come spontaneously from within—from our own sacred mentor, our own most holy Christ Self, who teaches us that the vibration of lying or of stealing or of cheating on exams or of personal uncleanliness or of wrong dietary patterns or of indulgences is not worthy of the LORD.

If we have indulged in activities that are not of the light, we call upon the law of forgiveness. As a sacrificial offering, we lay upon the altar that misqualified energy and even a portion of our heart's light, our own Christ consciousness, that we might atone for that sin.

That sin is not merely a personal sin, but it affects the entire earth. The whole earth is in God's heart, and we are in his heart as keepers of his life that is entrusted to our care. Thus we call on the law of forgiveness for all and send forth the light of the purging and purification of the whole body of God.

We ought to sense in our hearts what is pure, what is right, what is holy—and what is profane. We do not subject our consciousness to profanity. We do not go and seek that which is profane, that which is of the earth, earthy, that which is below the level of the heart of the Lord Christ. We keep our temple pure that the Holy Spirit might descend, that the Word of the LORD might speak unto the people through us and deliver them.

We root out all gossip and criticism and condemnation and judgment of one another. We uphold one another. We provide strength for one another as we go forth to face the world with all of its trials and testings and temptations, even its persecutions. God's light in us is for the freeing of the people who know not that they are in bondage. When our Holy Christ Self is resident within us, we go forth as the Good Shepherd to rescue the sheep from the jaws of the lion even when they would rather not be rescued, for they have gained a security and a comfortability within those jaws.

Know that The LORD Our Righteousness is come and is coming through the descent of light, and that always and evermore the light of the personal Christ in you is becoming greater and greater. Christ is ever being born, ever manifesting himself. It is not a one-time event. It happens continually as you allow the rippling of joy of his holy garment and the wind that precedes his presence to come into your temple to announce to you the glorious descent of the Son of God.

Let your soul officiate at the altar of life on behalf of all mankind, in the name of the LORD. Walk worthy of this holy calling. When profane thoughts descend upon mind and heart, know that these are the enemies of the people and of the temple of our God—and that while they are present with us, while we allow them to manifest, our LORD cannot occupy the temple of the heart or the sanctuary.

Therefore be cleansed and cleansed again. Invoke the sacred fire with great intensity to bind the demons and discarnates harboring the death consciousness and hovering near to seek to catch us off guard that we might, instead of entertaining angels, be tending demons and discarnates. Let us be vigilant.

Let us recognize the earmarks of their discord and their lies. Let us understand their divisive nature and let us know that we have the opportunity to keep the flame of life. This means being vigilant through the hours. This means being joyous in the love of God, to so exude love, to so be the instrument of the waterfall of love from the mighty river of life from our mighty I AM Presence that so much love is flowing that we only know love. We hear only the word of love, we listen only to the call of love, and all else is consumed by this mighty conflagration of our God who is a consuming fire.

The people of the Old and New Testaments who knew God knew him as an all-consuming fire. How else can we live upon earth in purity except God be that all-consuming fire where we are, consuming all that is unlike him? When we are that all-consuming fire, we can walk the earth as leaders of God's people, a pillar of a cloud by day—a cloud of witness— and a pillar of fire by night.[183] Let the fiery pillar of your own God Flame be unto all people a sacred magnet of the Central Sun, magnetizing in them their own Christ-potential.

Is it not wonderful to contemplate that when you greet people and when you are with friends, they can feel by the devotion of your heart an uplifting current of light, a magnetizing back to their God Flame, a desire for holiness, an understanding of the ineffable sweetness of the Holy Spirit, the perpetual sweetness of the light? Is it not a joy that wherever we go, people can be made happy and lighter and they may see enough light to ask the questions "Where does this light come from? What do you know? Tell me what you know that I don't know."

This is the greatest compliment that a chela could ever receive, and so many of the Ascended Masters' students have received it because their aura has the odor of sanctity. Therefore, sons and daughters of God, rejoice that God has placed his mantle upon us and that we are worthy because God in us is worthy to be called to the holy ordinances and offices of our God in his holy temple.

The Brilliance of the Noonday Within

Hear, then, Gabriel, who would sanctify your temple and prepare you for your higher initiations: "Now when you practice the ritual of the opening of the door of the heart that was told to you by the Archeia Christine (see page 84) and you receive the Mother and the initiations of Maitreya through the Mother and you receive me, Gabriel, an Archangel, in the name of the Lord, you will begin the transformation through the stations of the cross and the initiations of the transfiguration, the crucifixion, the resurrection and the ascension. And you will proclaim with the endless voices of the heavenly hosts who come in celebration of your victory:

" 'So when this corruptible shall have put on incorruption and this mortal shall have put on immortality, then shall be brought to pass the saying that is written, Death is swallowed up in victory. O death, where is thy sting? O grave, where is thy victory? The sting of death is sin; and the strength of sin is the Law. But thanks be to God, which giveth us the victory through our Lord Jesus Christ.' "[184]

Archangel Gabriel has seen the Most High face-to-face. He has seen the abomination of desolation standing in the holy place where it ought not.[185] He is fierce in the defense of the light in God's sons and daughters, for he knows that the karma of those who have persecuted the prophets and the lightbearers through the ages must be fulfilled.

Thus Gabriel proclaims: "The fourth angel descending from the Temple of the Tabernacle of the Testimony doth pour out his vial upon the sun [upon the etheric plane, the plane of the fire element], and power is given unto him to scorch men with fire. And this is the sacred fire by which mankind are scorched with a great heat, so much so that they blaspheme the name of God, the Almighty One—the only one who hath power over these plagues. And therefore, as it is written, they repented not to give him glory.[186]

"Stand fast, then, to behold the salvation of our God! And behold the death of the wicked[187] and of the generations of the wicked. For the fallen ones and their carnal creation are brought to naught on that notable day of the LORD—the day of the release of the sacred fire.

"I am the Archangel of ascension's fires. I stand in the brilliance of the noonday to counteract the midnight hour. I stand before the throne of God to intercede before the LORD God Almighty on behalf of those who blaspheme his name. I shield his throne from the echoings of mankind's infamy. And the thundering and the lightning that descend from Horeb[188] are a warning unto mankind to walk away from evil, to leave it in the way, to depart from the evildoers, to separate themselves bodily from those who have made themselves the instruments of unrighteousness and channels for the pollutions of the psychic realm.

"What fellowship hath righteousness with unrighteousness? And what communion hath light with darkness?[189] Do not allow the sympathy of the Luciferians to prey upon the very light of your soul! Do not allow your consciousness to be entertained by the so-called sorrows of Satan! Do not feel sorry for those who do evil; for they, too, have the option of walking away from their evil ways.

"But go rather to the lost sheep of the house of Israel[190] to proclaim the name of God—the power by which all souls yet tarrying in time and space can be saved. Proclaim the coming of the Christed ones and rebuke the devils who usurp the pure energies of the Mother and of the Holy Spirit. See how your love, replacing all sympathy, will go forth as the compassion of the Law to compel the children of God who tarry in their childish ways to rise to the standard of the Christ.

"I am an Archangel—and I survey the consciousness of the lightbearers. And I am choosing the most stalwart and the most self-disciplined ones for the front lines of the battle of Armageddon. Let us see who will be the forerunners in the race for the light of the dawn."[191]

Persevere unto the Summit of Life

While the cycles of returning karma descend upon individuals and communities, upon the just and the unjust, the Law continues to give to free will its place of primacy. Each day, each cycle of time, the soul chooses whom she will serve—the light or mammon. And in so doing, she reaps either the beneficence of good will or the harvest of corruption.

Gabriel's twin flame, Archeia Hope, adjures sons and daughters of God to choose aright: "There is no turning back on the path of salvation, for there is no turning back of the cycles of karma once they are released. Therefore Jesus admonished, 'No man, having put his hand to the plough, and looking back, is fit for the kingdom of God.'[192] Those who begin the ascent, the arduous climb to the highest summit, must not turn back when initiation confronts them in the way; for the alternative to passing every test and submitting to every initiation is to be subject unto the concentrated release of one's own karma.

"More greatly to be feared than the tests and the trials of the Path is the outer darkness that comes when the soul deserts the flame, deserts the battlefield of the LORD for that most questionable of all human commodities—human comfort. In outer darkness all is chaos, disorder and disintegration. There the meting-out of karma measure by measure that comes from the Lords of Karma through the hand of the Master and the Christ Self into the crucible of the chela is no longer a grace that can be counted on.

"When you turn your back on the flame, you can count on nothing. The dispensations of mercy and opportunity dispensed at the hand of the Lords of Karma are not the option of the fallen ones or of the children of God who have fallen from grace. Who will intercede for them when they say to the mountains and rocks, 'Fall on us, and hide us from the face of him that sitteth on the throne and from the wrath of the Lamb: for the great day of his wrath is come; and who shall be able to stand?'[193] To turn one's back on the flame is to forfeit the intercession of the great Mediator of life.

"Take heed, then, all who would run and not be weary, all who have set their mark on 'the prize of the high calling of God in Christ Jesus.'[194] The race is to those who will run to the finish; and those who are not prepared to go all the way had better not start, for the price for desertion is far too great. The covenants of God and the blessings of the Ascended Masters and their Messengers are not to be trifled with.

"Let us see, then, how the Lords of Karma compassionately allow the soul to balance the mastery of personal karma with the carrying of a portion of the weight of planetary karma. Those who are diligent in the application of the Law and in their daily invocations to the flames of the sacred fire have nothing to fear; for they are moving in and through the returning cycles of personal and planetary karma as they stand, face and conquer every erg of energy that diverges from the center of life.

"Stand holding the two-edged sword with both hands. Clasp it directly in front of you and let the blade cut the oncoming tide of darkness in defense of the light of the heart. Let it part the wave of the Dark Cycle and let it redirect those energies into the sacred fires burning on the altar of the Mother. Her flame is the flame of purity. It is the all-consuming fire of the Holy Spirit. For the Mother is the Bride of the Holy Spirit, and unto her is given the allness of the sacred fire necessary for the consuming of the karma of the seven last plagues.

Refuge in the Mother and the Mother Flame

"What must mankind do to merit the intercession of the Mother? For she is the instrument of the LORD; she is the receptacle into which the power of his name 'I AM THAT I AM' does flow. And therefore on earth the Mother is the instrument of the judgment that proceeds from the Father in heaven. Pay homage to her Son, the Christ of all, and acknowledge the source—the woman clothed with the sun and the womb of the Cosmic Virgin out of which issues the flaming Sun Presence of all.

"When mankind shall receive the Mother in the name of the Father, in the name of the Son and in the name of the Holy Spirit, then they will have unlimited access to the flowing fountain of her purity, her all-consuming love. And then the woes that are presently coming upon mankind shall be stopped by the raising of the right hand of the Mother, by the power of the spoken Word, by the wisdom of the scepter of her authority, by the love of the crown of her overcoming.

"Therefore, let the children of God repent this day in the name of the Lord! Let them find refuge in the Mother and in the Mother Flame. Let them give the recitation of the Hail Mary[195] as a means of their atonement for the sins of mankind, and let their meditation on the Mother Ray be for the raising of the light of the white fire core for the detoxification of bodies and souls and minds of the wraths of the seven last plagues.

"Now hear the word of the preacher: 'To every thing there is a season, and a time to every purpose under the heaven: a time to be born and a time to die; a time to plant and a time to pluck up that which is planted; a time to kill and a time to heal; a time to break down and a time to build up; a time to weep and a time to laugh; a time to mourn and a time to dance.'[196]

"This is the time to be serious, to take to heart the principles and the precepts of the Law and the training you have received from the Ascended Masters and their Messengers. This is the time to invoke the flame of Sirius, the God Star, to invoke the counsel of the Four and Twenty Elders and the intercession of Surya and the angels of Sirius, who descend in answer to your call in the formation of a great blue eagle.

"Take then the call to Surya . . . and let it be shouted from the housetops![197] Let it be sent forth from all of your chakras with the utmost adoration to God, with the utmost humility and the utmost concentration of the sacred fire within your chakras. Let nothing take from you your commitment to this call, for it will deliver you from the toils of the toiler and from the harshness of the judgment. And it will deliver the wicked into the hands of the legions from Sirius.

The Judgment of the Usurpers of the Mother Light

"Let the fallen ones with their satanic rites tremble! Let those who have mutilated the cattle on the plains of America know that the judgment is nigh! They are broken this day by the rod of Almighty God! Let those who defend their rites of black magic and witchcraft also know that judgment is nigh, for you cannot take the purity of the Divine Mother and use it for selfish motive.

"Each interference with the free will of God and man exacts the penalty of the Law and of the Lawgiver. There are those who say in their hearts: 'Let us do evil that good may come.[198] Let us compromise the teaching of the Ascended Masters. Let us go around the Christ and enter the LORD's house at the side door. Let us convince mankind that we are practicing the divine art. Let us prove by distortion of the Mother Flame that our way is the acceptable way.' These gather in their covens and in their dens of iniquity professing to serve the light. I say, they have usurped the light and they shall pay the price. 'There shall be weeping and gnashing of teeth.'

And these wizards
That have come out of the astral night
Convince their followers,
By the appearance of right,
That their way is of the light.
Beware appearances!
Beware the 'way that seemeth right.'[199]
Relative good and evil afford no proof
Of Absolute Truth.
Only the law of just cause
Can produce the certain effect
Of the Holy Spirit
Who comes with healing in his wings.[200]
Put aside these other things,
These incantations that reek
With the stench of perversion
And the decaying bodies of children
And animals they have slain.
Beware of all that is vain
And the vanity of the ego.
More deadly than the Fallen One himself
Is the rot of the ego
That is transplanted from body to body,
From mind to mind,
As a cancer that eats away
To the very soul of a planet and a people.

"Let us be the instruments of righteous judgment! Let us tether the souls of mankind to the Holy of holies! Let us weave the garment of the LORD that the children of Israel may pass over the Red Sea stained by the blood of the holy innocents.[201] Yes, let them pass over from the planes of Mater to the planes of Spirit, from the corruptible to the Incorruptible One. And let those who have the intent to murder the Divine Mother be judged by their motive this day. Let their hatred of the flame of Aquarius be turned upon them by the raising of the hand of the Mother and of the scepter of her authority!

"For the LORD is come down to judge the earth this day, he who 'doeth great things past finding out; yea, and wonders without number. Lo, he goeth by me, and I see him not: he passeth on also, but I perceive him not. Behold, he taketh away, who can hinder him? who will say unto him, What doest thou?'"202

THE FIFTH RAY:

The Judgment of the Carnal Mind

Focusing the light of Truth on earth precipitates the judgment of the Liar and his lie and the carnal mind, which "is enmity against God, for it is not subject to the law of God, neither can it be."[203] This action of the Law is infallible. Archangel Raphael comes to bring that judgment and to realign the lightbearers to their unity under the polestar of their being. He declares: "I am the Archangel of the fifth ray, and my coming marks the intensification of judgment in Mater; for the fifth ray is the ray of precipitation. And when the chemist in his laboratory combines sodium and chlorine, invariably there is a chemical reaction and the precipitation of salt.

"And so it is with the flame of Truth. It brings all things to the fore of consciousness—the elements of the mind and of the emotions, the substance of the subconscious as well as physical densities. When the ray of Truth is used as the catalyst, that which is unseen becomes the seen. And the disobedience of Lot's wife precipitates the pillar of salt,[204] that all who seek to raise up the feminine ray might know that obedience is the key to godly alchemy.

> The approbation of the heavenly will
> The law of righteousness does instill
> In all who would now prove the Truth.
> Stand forth, the soul, as living proof!
> Come out from among them
> And be a separate people![205]

> Let the lightbearers themselves
> Be the precipitation of the Christ!
> Let them, by the catalyst of the inner flame,
> Send forth the call of the I AM name.
> Let them precede the day of judgment
> To apply the law of self-perfectionment.
> Let them precipitate the good and the noble
> Ere sacred fire reveal the evil and ignoble.
> Let all choose and choose well
> Ere choice is no longer in the hand of man,
> But in the hand of God.
> Choose to be and you will see
> The angel with the flaming sword.
> In the right hand is life;
> In the left is death.
> Choose you this day whom ye will serve;[206]
> Your lot shall be as you deserve.

"I come forth from the Temple of the Tabernacle of the Testimony. And the heavens are opened this day as I pour out from the golden vial the wrath of God upon the seat of the beast, and his kingdom is full of darkness this day. And those that worship the beast shall gnaw their tongues for pain and blaspheme the God of heaven because of their pains and their sores, yet they repent not of their deeds.[207]

The Beast of the Carnal Mind Is Judged

"This vial contains mankind's wrathful misuses of the fifth ray of life and the science of life, of healing and healing Truth, and of the abundance of the immaculate consciousness of the Cosmic Virgin. All of this the fallen ones have taken to create the beast of the carnal mind sitting in the seat of the soul. Now we unseat the carnal mind! We dislodge it from its moorings! We cut it off from the light of the soul! No longer shall it vampirize the solar energies of the sons and daughters of God. It has laid claim to earthly existence. Let it stand this day before the Court of the Sacred Fire and present proof of its origin, its lineage, its heritage.

"Let those who rely on the carnal mind as the seat of a human authority and a human personality prepare themselves to give testimony before the Four and Twenty Elders. Let them receive our warning that all that proceeds out of the light of the Logos and all that is of God, showing forth allegiance to Alpha and Omega, will live in the eternal kingdom. And all that is of the world must receive the judgment of this world.

"I place the light of living Truth as a sphere of the immaculate conception around the souls of the children of God who are loyal to their Creator in the last days. Let their souls and the dwelling place of their souls in the chakra of freedom be sealed in the light of the Mother Ray and of the Archeia of the new day. For the souls of mankind have been literally squashed by the beast who is bound this day by the Seven Archangels. And we hold back the beast to make way for the coming into prominence of the souls of mankind, that they might have the freedom in the flame of Saint Germain, hierarch of the Aquarian age, to choose the light, to choose the right, and to be centered in the God Flame.

"And therefore while Satan is bound for a thousand years at

the Court of the Sacred Fire,[208] so the counterpart of Satan, which is the carnal mind of each one and the very presence of Antichrist that challenges the soul day and night, is also bound that mankind might exercise free will in the flame of freedom without interference from the darkened self, the shadowed self, the not-self. Therefore this day is the influence of the carnal mind stayed on Terra in the consciousness of the children of God!

"Given the freedom to choose, they may still choose the ego and the self-centered existence. So be it. We will not interfere with free will. We come as intercessors of the Law responding to the calls of the Faithful and True. For the Lord Christ himself, as the Good Shepherd of the sheep, has knelt before the altar of the Most High God, praying fervently as he did through the long night in Gethsemane for the LORD's intercession on behalf of the sheep.[209]

The Rooting Out of Darkness from the Earth

"Therefore we come fulfilling the dispensations of the Almighty granted unto the beloved Son. We come to intensify the All-Seeing Eye, to give mankind the vision of the choice, to lock the souls in the flame of Truth that can make them free if they will to be free. But the fallen ones with their robot creation have not the dispensation of the children of God, for they are the seed of the Evil One. And for some the end is not yet come,[210] and for some the day of reckoning is at hand.

"And they stagger and they stalk the earth, and they glower as they hover in their spacecraft. And not all are of this planetary home. And some are a physical evolution and others inhabit the astral plane. And some have not been allowed to incarnate in tens of thousands of years. For by the intercession of the Lord Christ they have been confined to the dungeons of the astral, bound in chains—yes, bound hand and foot. But the abomination of their carnality is the contamination of Mater. Thus far and no farther! The day of judgment comes in the year of the Holy Spirit, 1975, and the day of judgment continues to the year 2001.

"And there is yet time and space for every man and woman and child upon Terra to partake of the Eucharist, to assimilate the Body and the Blood, the Omega and the Alpha spirals of the Christ consciousness. And there is yet time and space for the message of the two witnesses to cover the earth if the lightbearers will be diligent as runners of the gods carrying the message from house to house, from nation to nation, stopping only for sustenance and brief periods of rest under the wings of the Holy Spirit.

"Children of the One, remember the darkness of the city of Jerusalem. Remember that it was so intense that the Lord Christ would not lay his body to rest in that city. And did he not exclaim, 'The foxes have holes and the birds of the air have nests; but the Son of man hath not where to lay his head'?[211] Where can the sons and daughters of God go to find respite from the machinations of the dark ones? They inhabit every plane of Mater, and the thick smoke of their burnt offerings is obnoxious to the children of the One.

"As the Lord Christ took refuge in the ship on the Sea of Galilee, or in the mountains, or in the home of Mary and Martha at Bethany, so you, too, can take refuge even in the planes of Mater, securing your soul in the secret place of the Most High. And remember, when judgment draweth nigh, the words of the Psalmist: 'Whither shall I go from thy Spirit? or whither shall I flee from thy presence? If I ascend up into heaven, thou art there: if I make my bed in hell, behold, thou art there. If I take the wings of the morning and dwell in the uttermost parts of the sea, even there shall thy hand lead me and thy right hand shall hold me.'[212]

"While the souls of mankind prepare to make right choices, the structures and the superstructures of the fallen ones come tumbling down; for their foundation was in the seat of the beast, whose kingdom is filled with darkness. Let the false practitioners of the healing arts be exposed! And let them repent of their deeds. Let the moneychangers in the banking houses of the world be exposed! And let them repent of their deeds.

"Let the ray of action penetrate the misuses of the science of precipitation! And let all that has been precipitated out of the astral plane, out of the collective subconscious, out of the seat of the beast, be challenged by the sword of Truth! And the Great Divine Director comes forth to arrest the spirals of the misuses of the Christ light in the seven rays of God.

"Behold, mankind, now is the accepted time! Now is the day of salvation! Now let those who are contributing to the pollution of the body of the Mother through the manufacture and sale of alcohol, cigarettes, marijuana and every harmful drug be exposed! And let them repent of their deeds. Let the selling of sex and the promotion of products accompanied by subliminal sex symbols be exposed! And let those with blood-stained hands repent of their deeds.

"I reinforce the judgment of abortion and the abortionist delivered by Almighty God through the pronouncement of the Archangel Uriel.²¹³ And I send forth my ray into the houses of whoredom where the flame of the Mother is being desecrated and the Eves of this world are daily tempting Adam-man to partake of the forbidden fruit of the tree of the knowledge of good and evil. Let them be exposed! And let them repent of their deeds.

"In the name of the I AM THAT I AM, I send forth the fires of the crystal ray! And there shall come upon mankind suddenly, without warning, a freezing of their actions and their consciousness as on the day that the sun and the moon stood still[214] and the stars themselves were fixed in their courses. So for a moment of eternity slipped into time and space, there shall be a silence and all action shall be brought to a halt. And the angels of the LORD shall take note of the deeds of mankind and of the fallen ones.

"And there will not be time for the people to put on their Sunday best and to primp and to preen before the mirrors of their vanity. This is the LORD's candid camera. And the shutter of the All-Seeing Eye of God will click, and the soul will hear the click, and the fallen ones will hear the click, and they will know that the evidence has been taken for the execution of the judgment this day.

"Be diligent, O my children—children of the One! Work the works of righteousness, fulfill the law of life taught by the Christed ones, and fear not. For those who fulfill their sacred vows have nothing to fear, but only the anticipation of joy, liberation, light and discovery that comes on the wings of judgment—the judgment that shall surely be known as the greatest manifestation of love that the world has ever known."[215]

Mother Mary's Service to the Evolutions of Earth

Mother Mary is the Archeia of the fifth ray. She volunteered to come to earth to bring forth the Christ and to bring the light of Omega unto a fallen race. Hers is a story of sacrifice, of grace and of unconditional devotion to the Father-Mother God:

"I am Mary. I have chosen to ensoul the Mother Ray for a cosmos. I am the handmaid of the LORD Alpha and the instrument of Omega. I am the awareness of the Father-Mother God extending even unto the planes of Mater, that the children of the One might know the sanctity of communion—of the marriage of the daughters to the Holy Spirit, of the vows of the sons unto the Cosmic Virgin.

"Because the flame of the fifth ray relates to precipitation in Mater and because the feminine aspect of the flame is directly involved in the spirals of God-realization descending from the formless into form, I was chosen by Alpha and Omega to incarnate in this system of worlds, to set forth in time and space the example of the Divine Woman reaching full self-realization in and as the Divine Mother. How well I remember that moment when I was bidden by heralds of the king and queen, our own beloved Alpha and Omega, and I came escorted by the beloved Raphael to stand before the throne of the twin flames of a cosmos!

" 'You called, my father and my mother, and I have come.'

" 'Yes, our beloved, we have called. Unto you and to Raphael is given the opportunity from the heart of the Solar Logoi to manifest the balance of the flow of Truth "as Above, so below" over the spirals of the figure eight of our cosmos—opportunity to be on earth as in heaven the ensoulment of the Mother Ray.'

" 'What does this mean, my father and my mother?' "

" 'It means that you have been chosen, Mary, to incarnate in the planes of Mater, to take on the feminine form that the errant souls of the children of God now wear, to live and serve among them, to adore the Christ Flame within their hearts— as Sanat Kumara and Gautama have done and as the Christed ones, the avatars and Buddhas who have gone before, and the many angels who have volunteered to work through forms of flesh and blood to save the lost sheep of the house of Israel who have taken on the ways of the idolatrous generation.'

"I heard the words of our dearest Father-Mother and I looked into the eyes of Raphael, my beloved. And for a moment—only a moment—the pain of the anticipated separation was too much to bear. Instantly I was strengthened by the beauty and nobility of his countenance and the sternness of his eye disciplined in the Law. He had, as it were, almost greater courage than I to descend into the planes of Mater.

"But when I felt his hand press my own and the charge of the will of God and our dedication to eternal Truth flowed into my being and soul, I faced the beloved Presence of God now pulsating in utter formlessness as cloven tongues of fire where a moment before the personages of the Divine Polarity had stood. I knelt in utter surrender to the call of hierarchy and in silence before the Holy of holies gave my life that the Word might become flesh and dwell among the inhabitants of Terra, that the Christ, the eternal Logos, might incarnate, the Incorruptible One.[216]

"Precious ones, did you know that for the souls and the angels who volunteer to incarnate in those several systems of worlds where the consciousness of the Fall, of fallen man and fallen woman, has taken over the race, there is no guarantee that the lifestream will emerge from that darkness unscathed, free to soar once more unto the arms of everlasting love? Those who come from heavenly octaves in defense of Truth, in defense of the life of souls who have strayed from the center of being, have only their commitment to the flame to rely on— only determination and will and love. For even the memory of those other spheres must be forsworn upon entering the birth canal and assuming the body temple that has been prepared— sometimes lovingly and sometimes not so lovingly—by earthly parents.

> Oh yes, God's grace is always there.
> His presence can be known.
> God's love is everywhere—
> Even in the wings of the morning
> Where I have flown.
> But, you see, it all depends upon the call
> And the making of the call.

For all of the potential of God and man
Can come to naught
When souls and angels forsake the Truth God brought.
The prayer, therefore, of every descending avatar
Is for the memory of the Bethlehem star,
That it might contact the teacher
And the teaching of the I AM Presence
And the Christ Self of each one
For the journey through the valleys of the earth
And then the soaring to the center of the sun.

And so I descended by God's grace;
And by his grace, and that alone,
I ascended to the heavenly throne.
Therefore I am one among the Archeiai
Who have experienced directly
The veil of human tears
And the passing of the years
From darkness unto darkness
As mankind's consciousness flows
Until, quickened by some inner light,
They find the road from glory unto glory.

Take comfort, O my children!
There is not a place on earth where you can be
That I have not also been.
I have seen the tempter and the temptations of sin.
I have seen the Christ upon the cross
And held him in my arms
As infant child and by the tomb,
The moment of the consecration to the cosmic womb.
I have parted from my son along the sorrowful way
And I have seen him nailed to the cross
On a very dark day.

My soul was also pierced as yours shall be.[217]
But fear not: I am thy Mother, I AM with thee.

Because I have gone before you
In the footsteps on the Path,
Because the blessed Son
Has also descended and ascended
Throughout a cosmos vast,
You can follow in each painful, blissful footstep—
Surefooted as the mountain goat,
Leaping to your cosmic destiny
And your place upon that cross,
Hastening to greet the sword
That must pierce the soul
That you might have the compassion
To make all mankind whole.
Because the way is known,
Because we have pursued and overcome,
You who have descended in answer to the call
Of Alpha and Omega
Can be certain of ascending
If you will make your calling and election sure[218]
By the call, by the initiations,
By the testing, testing, testing.

We extend a helping hand.
Clasp it if you will!
Feel the strength of Raphael
And the sternness of his love.
Feel the assurance of the beloved
Assuring you of your attainment
According to the motto
Of those who come to do His will:[219]
You can make it if you try!
You can make it if you try!

Midst all the darkness,
The density, and the dangers
Inherent in a world scheme
Where judgment is nigh,
The Archangels stand forth.
Hear their cry!
They come to intercede.
Won't you give them heed?
Their word is Law
Direct from the speech of the Logos.
Their word is power manifesting the work
Of the Creator, the Preserver, the Destroyer.
In this cycle of the Holy Spirit
You can expect to hear it,
To hear the wisdom
That causes the demons to tremble[220]
And the love that is a chastening
To them who fear it.

Without the fear of the LORD
There is no repentance,
And without repentance
There can be no forgiveness.
Forgiveness flows;
But it must be invoked
By the humble of heart,
By the sincere who ask the LORD's pardon
That they might undo their wrong
And redo their right.
When the apology becomes a ritual—
Dead and without works—
Then it is better to be silent
And to engage in living sacrifice

> As service to the Law,
> As testimony and as proof
> That forgiveness is the justice
> Of the mercy of the Law."[221]

Protecting the Christ Child Within

King Herod, considering the newborn Jesus to be a threat, sought to kill him. Thus Joseph fled to Egypt with Mary and Jesus in order to protect him. Archeia Mary compares this action of protecting the newborn Christ to the alchemy of Truth that marks the ascendancy of the Christ Flame within one's being: "Truth is the transforming power that transforms a universe. During the period of the chemicalization of Truth that the judgment brings, there is the groaning and the travail like unto a mother giving birth to her firstborn son. The Christ Child is aborning within you.

"The judgment is the hand of God making way for the birth of the Manchild; for the forces of Herod are abroad in the land this day to prevent the birth and the maturation of the Christ Flame in the hearts of humanity. Herod's men[222] come with their swords, their scalpels and their surgical instruments. They come to do the work of the dragon to devour the child as soon as it is born.

"But fear not! For the warning of the angel of the LORD who appeared unto Joseph, saying, 'Take the young child and his mother and flee into Egypt, and be thou there until I bring thee word: for Herod will seek the young child to destroy him'[223] comes to every son and daughter of God who has assumed the responsibility of bearing the Divine Manchild. And the angels of the LORD do intercede in this hour for the preservation of life and Truth and love as the threefold flame upon the altar of the heart.

"Wait and listen. Listen well to the words of the Archangels and the Archeiai. And read between the lines,... for
there are messages for each and every soul and there are applications for each and every circumstance contrived by the fallen
ones to trap the holy innocents as they make their way over the
little-traveled roads that lead to the place of safety."[224]

Thus Mary teaches that if we are to protect and honor the
Christ Child aborning within us, we must remove our consciousness into a far country, into a new compartment of our
being. We must "go to Egypt." Once there, we remove ourselves
from our normal habitation, from the momentums of the past.
Then the alchemy of our initiations on the Path can proceed
unhindered by those momentums and by the fallen ones, the
Herods, who would tie into them to kill the Christ Child within.

We can transcend our past by practicing the science of the
immaculate concept. We visualize and affirm that we already
are the virtues we wish to outpicture. That strong matrix will
keep our energies moving in the desired direction. Once the habit
of living in the new level is firmly established, we will have put
on another increment of the "new man" who is Christ.

Our God Presence continuously holds the immaculate concept for our being and the fulfillment of our divine plan. We
can tie into this in each moment. We can catch the ray of light
that descends over the crystal cord from on high and follow it
all the way back to the original matrix of our being.

And as you attune to your Higher Self, you may well meet
Mary in the way. For she delights in interceding on behalf of
her children. "When the Lord Christ, Jesus my son, prays fervently before the altar of the Most High God for the children
of the One, when I see him descending from the mountain of
the LORD, his face shining as the sun, his raiment white as the
light, I run to greet him in the way and he does embrace me in
the Mother Ray. And then I ask him for those dispensations for

the chosen ones that are his to give and mine to impart as the matriarch of the Law."[225]

When your karma descends and the dark clouds of your past enclose you as a shroud, remember that those who love you most—your ascended brothers and sisters—once stood where you stand. They have returned home the victors over death and hell, and they are eager to enjoy your victory even more than their own.

Mother Mary gives a glimpse of the heavenly reception waiting for you: "Like the soldiers who return from the battles of life to receive their stripes and pins—and the Boy Scouts and Girl Scouts with their badges and their bars—so the flaming ones who have overcome, when bidden to those formal receptions held in the retreats of the Great White Brotherhood, are required to come in full military dress. And by their dress, all know what worlds they have conquered—when and where. And old comrades who have shared in the victory of worlds reminisce in the strategy of their overcoming as they look longingly upon those now engaged in the warfare for the salvation of this planet and this people."[226]

Keeping the Garments of the Lord

SOULS WALKING THE PATH OF INITIA-
tion invoke light and more light to bal-
ance the karma that blocks their personal path of reunion with
God (their I AM Presence) and with their twin flame. Every initiation encountered is designed to bring the soul face-to-face with
people and situations that have been stumbling blocks in the past.
The Great Initiator, Lord Maitreya, comes to the soul through
everyday events to offer her the opportunity to convert what
were once hindrances into stepping-stones to greater attainment.

Thus Maitreya reveals the essence of spirituality as a willingness to work through one's growing pains and to accept the
burden of light that accompanies a closer walk with God. "The
purpose of initiation," says Maitreya, "is to inaugurate spirals
of God-integration within souls who would move toward the
center of being that is life. Life in all of its dazzling splendor,
life in its concentrated essence of the sacred fire, is too intense
for mortals who have subjected themselves unto the laws of
mortality."[227]

Let us listen, then, to Archangel Uriel as he relates how the laws of mortality came to be the norm for evolving souls. "The Garden of Eden was created by the LORD God as a haven of light and loveliness, as a replica of the Causal Body for the early root races who did not depart from the perfection of the plan. In the center of the garden was the Tree of Life, focus of the I AM Presence made tangible in Mater.

"And the tree of the knowledge of good and evil was the presence of the Christ, the blessed Mediator in whose consciousness is the balance of understanding of the absolute perfection of God and the relative imperfection of man and woman. 'And the LORD God commanded the man, saying, Of every tree of the garden thou mayest freely eat: but of the tree of the knowledge of good and evil, thou shalt not eat of it: for in the day that thou eatest thereof thou shalt surely die.'[228]

"Eve's hearkening unto the Serpent, who said, 'Ye shall not surely die,' was the first compromise of the flame of the Christ on Terra.[229] And so it came to pass that the generations of the fourth root race who lived in the abundance of the Motherland did partake of the energies of the Christ and of the fruit of the vine before they were initiated by Almighty God to be partakers of the Holy Communion.

"Later, the one who said, 'I AM the vine, ye are the branches;' 'except ye eat the flesh of the Son of man and drink his blood, ye have no life in you'[230] would come to initiate mankind in the sacred energies of the Word and of the Logos. He would come to initiate the ritual whereby man and woman consecrated in Christ might partake of the Eucharist.

"The penalties for seizing the fruit of the vine before it is offered in grace from the hand of God are grave indeed. The expulsion from paradise was the sealing of the Causal Body from the access of fallen man and fallen woman. Their rebellion was against the law of the Christ. Thus by wrong choice, engineered in the cunning of the serpentine mind, they cut themselves off from the Lord's table and from the abundant gifts and graces that are the gnosis of the tree of knowledge.

"And lest their rebellion and their arrogance should cause them to put forth their hand and take also of the Tree of Life, partaking of the energies of the I AM THAT I AM and investing these in the creations of the wicked, the LORD God drove man and woman from the garden of paradise.

"To guard the consciousness of the I AM THAT I AM, he placed at the east of the garden 'cherubim and a flaming sword which turned every way, to keep the way of the Tree of Life.' The east is the side of the Christ consciousness, and the sword is the sacred Word of living Truth that proceeds out of the mouth of the Faithful and True. It is the sword that turns every way in the quadrants of Mater to protect the soul's outpicturization of the threefold flame of the Christed one. And the cherubim are the guardian consciousness of Almighty God who protect that flame in man and woman, in heaven and earth, in the Holy of holies and in the coordinates of time and space."[231]

Those who entered the consciousness of mortality had to be barred from direct access to the Holy of holies, for as Maitreya explains, "Those who live by death and death's disintegration are not prepared to live in a life that is God. They think they have life, but theirs is a quasi existence in a twilight zone of time and space. Whereas they experience that which they call life in a gray band of narrow self-awareness, we who are God-free beings can and shall declare, 'In him we live and move and have our being... for we are also his offspring.'[232]

"... Were I to place the rod of initiation upon the brow of those who kneel before the altar of the Cosmic Christ prior to their initiation in the cycles of life, I would but lend the momentum of my authority in life as a reinforcement of death as the supreme denial of the Real Self that is God.

"The light that flows heart, head and hand from the consciousness of the Cosmic Christ is the light that makes permanent all that is real and good and beautiful and joyous within you. This is the light that can endow the soul with everlasting life, and this is the light that the LORD God has held back from mortals until they are willing to put on immortality. Thus it is written as the edict of the Law that 'this corruptible must put on incorruption, and this mortal must put on immortality.' "233

Uriel comes to assists us. "I stand before the living presence of the Law in each and every soul who, upon reading my words, does utter the vow of allegiance to the Tree of Life, the I AM Presence. And I read the proclamation that comes from the hand of Alpha and Omega this day. It is a proclamation of opportunity in grace for your soul to return to paradise lost, to the garden of the Causal Body, to the place where the consciousness of the Christ implants the knowledge of the tree of the knowledge of good and evil.

"For every soul who reads these words who has entertained the consciousness of the Fall, I bring opportunity for the ascent to the throne of grace. The path of your journey to the end of the cycles of personal and planetary karma has been calculated for you and for every soul who has gone forth from the center of the sun to the periphery of the created spheres in Matter. To each and every one who does with allegiance run, the formula and the forcefield of light are given into the hand of your own beloved Christ Self.

"Therefore, go not a whoring after other gods and other Christs and spirit guides with their fantasies and their filth of psychic phenomena. But let every man and woman sit under his own vine and fig tree, under his own Christ Self and I AM Presence, even as Jonah sat in the shadow of the gourd that the Lord God prepared to deliver him from his grief and the groaning of his soul struggling in the way of surrender. Are you in that way this day? Are you, with Saul, the unredeemed, kicking against the pricks of the Christ? Behold, your redemption draweth nigh! Behold, your Redeemer liveth![234]

"I am the flaming presence of the Christed one. I stand before you, yet I am in the center of the sun. I am the living presence of the flame—mine to have and yours to claim. There is a way. It is the way of life made plain; it is the flow of the crystal-fire mist that consumes the mist-ification of the serpent mind.

The Pollution of the River of Life

"Behold how the waters flow as a river out of Eden, descending to nourish the planes of Mater with the fiery flow of the energies of Spirit. And the flow of the crystal cord was parted and became into four heads.[235] And the first, Pison, compasseth the whole land of Havilah, symbolizing the etheric plane, where there is gold and bdellium and the onyx stone; and the second is Gihon, which compasseth the whole land of Ethiopia, symbolizing the mental plane; and the third is Hiddekel, which goeth toward Assyria, symbolizing the astral plane; and the fourth is Euphrates, which stretcheth across the plains, symbolizing the watering of the entire physical plane.

"Now let us see how mankind, by their misuses of the sacred fire in the sixth ray of the Lord Christ, have polluted the four streams of the consciousness of God flowing. And let us see how their own lifestreams have suffered from every extreme of flood and fire and drought and dire pestilence and pain, of tempest and tornado and the foreboding stillness before the roaring hurricane, oncoming glacier, Vesuvius' eruption or the great tidal wave. The calamities of Mater, as elemental life overthrow the misuses of the elements, break upon the back of fallen man and fallen woman: 'For dust thou art, and unto dust shalt thou return.' "236

As the light of initiation descends, the initiate must be able to withstand the greater influx of the Holy Spirit. To the carnal mind and the bearer of one's fallen potential (the human ego), this consuming fire comes as a rebuke, whereas to the innocence of the soul, it brings relief from estrangement, from life carried on outside of the Edenic consciousness. It comes as an awakening from a spiritual lethargy, a liberation from age-old habits that stultify and thwart the aspiring one within. Welcome, then, the judgment. Welcome initiation. Welcome the soaring power of restoration.

"Now comes the angel of the sixth ray from out the Temple of the Tabernacle of the Testimony. And I [Uriel] pour forth my vial upon the great river Euphrates; and the water thereof is dried up, that the way of the kings of the East might be prepared.237 Now hear the testimony of the sixth of the angels who deliver the golden vials of the wrath of God upon the earth.

Weaving the Wedding Garment for the Judgment of the Great Whore

"The pouring-out of the vial of mankind's misuses of the light of the sixth ray must precede the judgment of the Great Whore, that perversion of the feminine ray that sitteth upon many waters. And in her fornication she has perverted the sacred Mother flow of the white fire core in Mater. And this flow of the great river Euphrates was for the nourishment of the Body of God upon earth who formed the Church of our Lord. And yet that Church is become as Babylon the Great, the apostate Church that 'is become the habitation of devils, and the hold of every foul spirit, and a cage of every unclean and hateful bird.'238

"And I am the angel who talked with John. And I showed him that woman sitting upon 'the scarlet-coloured beast, full of names of blasphemy, having seven heads and ten horns,' that woman 'arrayed in purple and scarlet colour and decked with gold and precious stones and pearls, having a golden cup in her hand full of abominations and filthiness of her fornication.'

"And John saw the name written upon her forehead: 'MYSTERY, BABYLON THE GREAT, THE MOTHER OF HARLOTS AND ABOMINATIONS OF THE EARTH.' And he saw 'the woman drunken with the blood of the saints, and with the blood of the martyrs of Jesus.' And I told him that the waters which he saw where the whore sitteth, even the waters of the great river, are the peoples and multitudes and nations and tongues who gave their energies to Babylon the Great.[239]

"Therefore the crystal-flowing waters of the Mother, misused and misapplied, misappropriated and misaligned with the Great Whore, are dried up, in order that those who have the mastery of the Christ Flame might come forth and take dominion over the earth.

"Enter the kings of the East! Enter the wise men who have exercised wise dominion in the uses of the threefold flame! These carry the abundance of the Mother, which shall not be taken from them. Now let us see the judgment of Babylon the Great and of these things that were foretold by Jesus the Christ, which will shortly come upon mankind unless they repent of their deeds.

"You who would keep your garments in the LORD as veils of innocence that are for the covering of the body of the Mother, let your gaze rest upon the stars, upon the trees that move in the winds of the Holy Spirit, upon the highest mountain your eyes can trace where you see the turning of the worlds as the clouds move into the sun.

"The rending of the veil of innocence is the great calamity of mortal existence. It was not intended that man and woman should partake of the fruit of the tree of the knowledge of good and evil prior to the initiations of the Christ. The immediate consequence of the act was that the eyes of them both were opened and they knew that they were naked. And they sewed fig leaves together and made themselves aprons. This is the rending of the veil of innocence—and only the sacred fire reapplied can mend that veil—the garment of purity in which the LORD God sealed the souls who descended into Mater that they might not be contaminated by the *e*nergy *v*e*il* called *evil*.

"'And they heard the voice of the LORD God walking in the garden in the cool of the day: and Adam and his wife hid themselves from the presence of the LORD God amongst the trees of the garden.'[240] Can you imagine hiding from the presence of the LORD? Yet since the expulsion from Eden, mankind have sought to deceive their God! And in so doing, they have deceived only themselves.

"The veils of this innocence are the veils of the seven rays worn by the bride, the Lamb's wife, who hath made herself ready, who hath prepared her consciousness for the consummation in the Christ Flame, for the return to the paradise of the I AM THAT I AM. Walking hand in hand with the beloved, the Lamb of God, the Virgin Queen returns to the Holy of holies and is received as the Bride of the Holy Spirit. Let the children of the One who would keep their garments come together in the hallowed circle of the AUM for the weaving of the wedding garment; for none shall come to the marriage supper of the Lamb without that garment.[241]

"I am Uriel standing in the place of the sun! Centered in the great sun disc, I am come. I stand before all who have rent their garments and who know not that they are naked before the LORD God, and I say: Thou sayest, 'I am rich and increased with goods and have need of nothing,' and knowest not that thou art wretched and miserable and poor and blind and naked. I counsel thee to buy of me the gold of the sixth ray, gold tried in the fire, that thou mayest be rich, and white raiment, the raiment of the Archangels, that thou mayest be clothed and that the shame of thy nakedness do not appear; and anoint thine eyes with eyesalve, that thou mayest see the light of the Holy of holies.[242]

"I call to the children of the One! I contact each heart flame with the golden fire of the sun! In the name of the LORD God, I call unto Adam and to Eve: Where art thou? Where is thy consciousness? Where is thy heart? Where is thy mind and thy soul? And I demand that you give answer this day! You cannot linger in the shadows when the sun is in his zenith. Come out from the shadows and declare!

"Where art thou? Who art thou? What doest thou with the sacred energies of thy God? Come out of your houses! Rise from your beds! Leave your slumbering and your tampering with the sacred fire! Listen to the words of the Spirit, the Amen, the faithful and true witness: 'I know thy works, that thou art neither cold nor hot: I would thou wert cold or hot. So then because thou art lukewarm and neither cold nor hot, I will spue thee out of my mouth.' "[243]

Rise each day above the levels of calcified substance. Let the light break old matrices of death and dying, the corruption that aborts the cycles of the sun, ignoring even the visitation of God, your mighty I AM Presence. Lest a single drop of your life essence be lost, call upon the Lord of your being, the Holy One of all that is real who lives in your heart, to save and to savor the living flame of love that it not be lost in the dusty, dusky, earth-earthy folds of garments long outworn. Welcome the light of the dawn in each moment. Capture the joy of each moment's resurrection.

Hearken to the LORD. Hearken to Maitreya, who comes "to shake the would-be initiate from the lethargy of the centuries. And let the quaking of the earth that marks the resurrection of the Christed ones be for the liberation of souls from the graves of their mortality.[244] Let them rise from the tombs of selfish death! Let them put on the new garments of life and living— of joy and the giving of self unto God, God, God!...

"It is an absolute requirement of the law of life that you don the spirals of integration—integration with God, your own Real Self. Day by day, line by line, the challenge of initiation is to integrate the soul, that potential of selfhood, with the Spirit of the living God, the I AM THAT I AM."[245]

Saint Germain, hierarch of the Aquarian age, would lead each soul to her immortal freedom. Yet only the few have responded to his heart's love. Says Uriel, "His words have fallen on the deafness and the dumbness of those who are more dense than the rocks themselves. Yet the Lord has said, 'If these should hold their peace, the stones would immediately cry out.'[246]

"If the children of the One will not come forward to declare their allegiance to the ascended hosts—will not feel the fervor of the love of Almighty God in this moment of cycles turning—then will elemental life rise up to defend the light of the woman and her seed. And they will carry the flame of the Mother that others have discarded by the way.

"Each time a child of God lets down that flame, the elementals who are the devotees of the Mother of the Seasons, the Mother of the Four Quadrants, leap from their chores in the garden of God to catch the torch lest it touch the ground. They will not allow the desecration of the Mother Flame. They keep their garments. Therefore, confess your nakedness before your own I AM Presence, that the judgment of fallen man and fallen woman might be pronounced in the Holy of holies. And then begin to cast out sin, your victory win, and enter in.

"The judgments of the LORD are just and true. His mercy is the liberation of the soul. The expulsion from Eden was the justice of the Law providing opportunity in time and space for man and woman to weave their seamless garment and to return to the habitation of God. And this is the promise of the Almighty One that will surely come to pass: 'Behold, I come as a thief. Blessed is he that watcheth and keepeth his garments, lest he walk naked and they see his shame.'[247]

"I leave you with the meditations of my heart upon the Lord Christ. I seal you in the meditations of my heart, which shall be unto you a forcefield in Mater of the secret place of the Most High. Abide in the Holy of holies! Abide under the shadow of the Almighty! Abide in the flame of the ark of the covenant, and know surcease from all sorrow under the trustful wings of the covering cherubim."[248]

The Mystery of Christ Crucified

"All have sinned, and come short of the glory of God."[249] Even so, as karma descends upon the just and the unjust alike, how great a gulf lies between those who have taken up the banner of the Fallen One and the lightbearers who would do better if they knew better. Those who love God greet their karmic woes in the sure knowledge that their Father-Mother is testing their mettle and preparing them for eternal life—whereas those who love not the light but cleave only to darkness shake their fists in defiance of the Law, all the while bewailing the supposed injustices life appears to mete out to them.

The Law must be satisfied, even as the grace of Christ is freely available to all who would make reparation. Jesus said: "Yet a little while am I with you, and then I go unto him that sent me. Ye shall seek me, and shall not find me: and where I am, thither ye cannot come."[250] However, God's grace is eternal and the light of Christ reaching out through the heart offers opportunity for reparation here and now in the chaliced moments of time and space.

Through humility, repentance and a loving acceptance of God's grace, the soul is nourished and she grows—moving closer and closer to God, her I AM Presence—as the law of cycles brings waves of karma to her for adjudication. But in those who have rejected God's grace, this process of judgment becomes an opportunity for God to reclaim the imprisoned energy of Christ crucified in an unregenerate world.

Archeia Aurora reveals the mystery of Christ crucified, and she brings comfort to souls of light who have walked the *via dolorosa* far too long. "I come as the woman with the alabaster box of ointment. I come with the precious spikenard, and I break the box and I pour it upon the head of the Mother and upon the head of her children. Let the fallen ones murmur against me as I perform the ritual of the Law. As Jesus defended the rite of the woman, so the Lord Christ this day does defend the right of the Mother and of the children of God to receive the anointing of an Archeia: 'Let her alone: against the day of my burying hath she kept this [ritual].'[251]

"And this anointing of the crown chakra of the Mother and her children shall be reenacted by the Mother of the Flame as an initiation for devotees who enter into the Holy of holies of the Church Universal and Triumphant. Therefore, those who drink the full cup of the Blood of Christ and those who partake of the Body of Christ will also stand before the Pontius Pilate of this world. For in order that the Luciferians might be judged, they must reenact their judgment of the Christed ones.

"Let the chief priests and the elders of the people take counsel against the Mother and her children. Let them bind her and let them lead her away. For this is their hour and the power of darkness. Judge not, lest ye be judged. And when the witnesses bear false testimony against the Mother and when they contradict themselves in their lies, the Mother will speak not a word.[252] For the Word of the Logos and the two-edged sword of Truth shall be unto her the defense of righteousness.

"Let the Lion of the tribe of Judah come forth to defend the Mother in the hour of her deliverance from evil and the evil generation! Let those who betray the Mother Flame do quickly that which they must do![253] The Archangels make way for the betrayers that they might betray themselves and therefore be found wanting in the judgment day.

"There are many who harbor hatred and malice, lies and blasphemies against the Mother and her children. And they keep their evil secret in their hearts; and they gossip among themselves in the shadows of the marketplaces, turning away the young souls from the flame that will not be quenched, from the flame that is salvation to the creation and to every living creature.

"Therefore, we let the sword pierce the soul of the Mother 'that the thoughts of many hearts may be revealed,' that their karma may be congealed. For by their word they shall be justified and by their word they shall be condemned. And every man shall be judged according to his works.[254]

"The crucifixion is the passion of the Lord and of the saints who have gotten the victory over the beast and over his image and over his mark and over the number of his name. And this passion is the intensification of the love fires in the hearts of the saints as they walk the sorrowful way, making it the glorious way as step by step, station by station, they fulfill the fourteen tests of the Christed ones.

"The Archangels and the Archeiai do sponsor the children of the One as they pass through the fiery trial. Therefore we counsel: 'Above all, take the shield of faith, wherewith ye shall be able to quench all the fiery darts of the wicked.'[255] And the fourteen angels who keep the flame of life for the body and the soul of the Mother and her children hold the keys to the victory in the fourteen stations of the cross.

Stand, Face and Conquer

"As you read our admonishments..., let them be for your strengthening as you face the Lord Christ and his Mother and her flame and the Word incarnate. And as you prepare to receive from the Holy Spirit those sacred fires that are for the consuming of all resistance of the carnal mind to the quickening of the soul through the adversity of the cross,

> Stand, face and conquer with sword in hand
> and the fire of love burning in your heart!
> Stand, face and conquer the dividing of the waters
> and the vials we impart!
> Stand, face and conquer! Plunge the sword of Truth
> into the cause and core of the lie.
> Stand, face and conquer! For the army of the Lord
> draweth nigh.

"Sons and daughters of God, do not turn away from your fiery destiny, which is written by the angels in the Book of Life in script of gold. Remember Jesus, the beloved Son of God who, resolute in love and in passionate fervor for the will of God, resisted every temptation to turn from the path of the crucifixion. And when he told his disciples of the many things that he should suffer of the elders and chief priests and scribes and that he would be killed and raised again the third day, Peter rebuked him.[256]

"Like the modern metaphysicians who in their mentalizing avoid the confrontation of the initiation of the crucifixion, Peter declared in his carnal-mindedness, 'Be it far from thee, Lord: this shall not be unto thee.' Let all those who profess that the crucifixion is unnecessary yet who would be partakers of the resurrection and the ascension hear the denunciation of the Lord: 'Get thee behind me, Satan: thou art an offence unto me:

for thou savourest not the things that be of God, but those that be of men.'

"In the hour of the judgment, the Lords of Karma count the disciples of the Lord. And when you feel the intensity of the ray of the Lord upon your head, know that the examination by the Lord's emissaries is upon you and the accounting of works is being tallied by the angels of the Keeper of the Scrolls. Let us hear the formula spoken by Jesus whereby you may weigh yourself beforehand to determine what the accounting will be: If any man will come after me, let him deny himself and take up his cross and follow me.[257]

"We shall see; we shall see who is willing to bear the cross of personal and planetary karma. We shall see who will seek to save his life and who will lose his life for the sake of the Christ. For the Son of man shall come in the glory of his Father. Your own Christ Self will descend in the glory of your own I AM Presence and with the angels of the Christed one. And then Jesus in the Christ Self of all shall reward every man according to his works.

"See here now! Resist the weeping and the wailing of the daughters of Jerusalem and those that revile the sons and daughters of God who are willing to place themselves on the cross for Christ and for humanity. Let them wag their heads! Let them dare you to come down from the cross! Let them have their mockery, even the thieves that 'cast the same in his teeth.'[258]

Hold the Balance for a Planet and Its People

"In that moment, blessed ones, let the meditation of the heart of a Christ be in your heart: 'The cup which my Father hath given me, shall I not drink it?' When the Lord is ready, he will send more than twelve legions of angels from the heart of the Father to deliver you from all evil.[259] Let deliverance come in the Lord's time, for he will extend the time and the space of the persecution of the Christed ones in order that the wicked might be judged while they hold the instruments of wickedness in their hands.

"While the judgment of Almighty God is delivered unto this generation through the hand of the Seven Archangels, the sons and daughters of God, initiated for the crucifixion by the Mother, must hold the balance in their bodies, in their souls, in their chakras and in their consciousness, in order that the judgment will not utterly destroy a planet and a people. For now is the judgment of this world; now is the prince of this world cast out by the fiat of Alpha and Omega. And there is a price to be paid by the sons and daughters of God for the exorcism of the Fallen One and his angels, and the price is the sacrifice of the ego.

"Therefore, put down the ego, raise up the Christ, and learn the meaning of the statement of the Lord 'And I, if I be lifted up from the earth, will draw all men unto me.'[260] When you raise up the energies of the Christ, when you allow the fires of the Mother to rise as the caduceus on the staff of life, the light of Mother and Son magnetized in your aura will draw the souls of mankind into the presence of the Holy Spirit and into the center of the I AM THAT I AM.

"Yes, there is a price to be paid. The Mother of the Flame has agreed to pay the price. Will you agree also as you walk in the way with her? Your own beloved Lanello[261] made the announcement on the last day of 1974 that hierarchy could no longer hold back the increase of light in her body and in her soul.

"In order for Terra to pass through the hour of her crucifixion unto the glory of her resurrection, 'the light must be increased, the light must be intensified, and the repository of that light is our Messenger in form.' The light is increased for the salvation of souls. Yet this light, as the piercing of the sword of Truth, precipitates human hatred. And upon that cross the Mother is crucified, and her children and all who take up the cross of Christ after her.

"With the increase of light comes also the joy of miracles of healing dispensed unto the children through her healing hands. And in the darkest hour of the night, when the light is increased to the uttermost, when many shall be offended and shall betray one another and shall hate one another, remember the words that are written: 'Then all the disciples forsook him and fled.' Stand staunch therefore, children of the Mother, to defend that flame when the Mother is 'hated of all nations for my name's sake.' Let it not be written in the record of the judgment that you denied her thrice before the crowing of the cock.[262]

"For Lanello has prophesied that many shall turn away from the flame of the Mother because her love will draw out the toxins of hatred from their four lower bodies, and this hatred must be extracted in order that their souls might be saved from the karma of their own hatred. Those who commit their karma unto the flame of the sacred fire before it turns to boils and sores upon their bodies will remain in the mandala of the Mother. But those who do not will blaspheme her name because of their pains, and they will not repent of their deeds.

Take the Communion Cup against the Cup of Wrath

"Jesus the Christ, the true head of the Church Universal and Triumphant, extends to you the communion cup, saying, 'Drink ye all of it.' And you remember his words in Gethsemane: 'Father, if thou be willing, remove this cup from me: nevertheless, not my will but thine be done.' And when you have made your commitment to the will of God, the soldiers of the governor will give you the cup of vinegar mingled with gall. You will taste it, but you will not drink thereof.[263]

"This is the cup of the wrath of mankind's karma that they would force the Christed ones to take. This is their cup! Let them drink it! For this is the judgment of the LORD that came through the prophet Jeremiah:

"'And the LORD saith, Because they have forsaken my Law which I set before them and have not obeyed my voice, neither walked therein, but have walked after the imagination of their own heart and after Baalim, which their fathers taught them, therefore thus saith the LORD of hosts, the God of Israel: Behold, I will feed them, even this people, with wormwood and give them water of gall to drink. I will scatter them also among the heathen, whom neither they nor their fathers have known: and I will send a sword after them, till I have consumed them.'[264]

"In the pouring-out of the seven golden vials of the last plagues of mankind's karma are the wormwood and the gall given to mankind while the judgment is upon them. Enter into the Holy of holies and into the white fire core of the mandala of the Mother. Seek refuge in the temple of the LORD and in the Church Universal and Triumphant, and there partake of the Eucharist and see how the alchemy of the Christ consciousness is performed within you by the blessed Mediator.

The Jews Were Made Scapegoats for Jesus' Crucifixion

"Now is forgiveness come to those who have been the unwitting instruments of the fallen ones. Jesus forgave the people from the cross, saying, 'Father, forgive them; for they know not what they do.' Hear then the judgment that is taken from the Book of Life: The Jews were made scapegoats for the crucifixion of the Lord. They were but instruments of the chief priests and the elders of the people. It is *they* who took counsel to put Jesus to death. These are the fallen ones, the Luciferians; and the captains and the soldiers were their robot creation. *They* used the mob to enact their murder of the Christed One, and *they* tricked the Jews into taking upon themselves the karma of the deed. Therefore in the midst of the tumult created by the fallen ones, they cried out, 'His blood be on us and on our children!'[265]

"I am the angel with the avenging sword! And I proclaim this day with the Lord Christ: They are exonerated of all guilt surrounding the death of Christ. And let this word be spoken in the temples of the Jews and in their synagogues—that the Mother of Christ has this day extended her hand through the Mother of the Flame to draw into the Holy of holies all who are of the house of Israel. These are they who love the name of the LORD, I AM THAT I AM, and who accept their own Mediator, the Christed one, as able to forgive all sin and the sense of sin.

"This day is the judgment turned upon the fallen ones, and they shall bear the burden of their karma! It is they who have slain the Lamb from the foundation of the world.[266] Let the energy return to their doorstep!

"Now let the children of the One see through the divide-and-conquer tactics of the wicked! Let those who call themselves Christians forgive the members of the house of David. Let all who worship the God of Israel embrace those who have followed the Messiah into the new age of the proclamation of the law of Moses and the grace of Jesus Christ."[267]

THE SEVENTH RAY:

Violet Flame for the Freeing of a Planet and Its People

EACH DAY WE MUST STAND AND FACE our returning karma. We welcome this karma even as we greet the oncoming light, all the while anticipating the rumbling and tumbling of our world, which signals a cycle of inner resolution and consummate joy.

Archangel Zadkiel comes for the acceleration of this process. He stands in the earth as a prophet making plain the higher way: "I am the angel of the seventh ray, and there is given unto me this day the seventh golden vial of the wrath of God. I pour out this vial into the air, and the great voice out of the temple of heaven is heard throughout the planes of Spirit and the planes of Mater!

"From the throne of the Almighty One—guarded by the four Cosmic Beings who stand on the side of the north and on the side of the south and on the side of the east and on the side of the west of the throne of God—is the Word of the Logos pronounced: 'It is done!' And as that Word is translated throughout the planes of Mater, there is a trembling of many voices and thunders and lightnings.[268]

"The light emanations from the center of a cosmos are emitted in rings from the center to the periphery, from Spirit unto Mater. As these rings of light, as waves of light, undulate through the great cosmic sea farther and farther from the center of the flame of the One, the energy is stepped down by cosmic hierarchies—mighty seraphim and cherubim, the Elohim and the Archangels—so that in each successive frequency of Mater there is released the light necessary for the alchemicalization, the translation of darkness into light.

Cataclysm Begins within the Soul

"And where there is a greater concentration of sin and the sense of sin and of separation from the One, the many voices of the heavenly hosts and the thunders and the lightnings that are the release of the sacred fire cause great earthquakes as the atoms and molecules of Mater are brought into sudden alignment with the white fire core of the Holy Spirit.

"In that hour of the judgment of the evolutions in those systems of worlds where souls have partaken of the fruit of the tree of knowledge of good and evil, men and women are hushed in anticipation of that great earthquake which has not been seen since the inhabitation of the planets.

"This is that cataclysm which begins within the soul as the light of the Great Central Sun arcs to the seed of man and woman for the purification of the lifestreams for the Aquarian age. The light must travel through the entire body of Mater, through your four lower bodies, through the four planes of consciousness of Terra and of the planets of this solar system.

"The light is oncoming! It fills the body of God upon earth and they rejoice in the living fountain of fire. The children of the One frolic in the bubbling waters of life that flow freely from the 'pure river of water of life, clear as crystal, proceeding out of the throne of God and of the Lamb.' They are not afraid to enter in, for they have already voluntarily consigned all misqualified substance into the violet flame. They have been washed by the waters of the Word;[269] they fear no loss of identity. They fear not the rod of the comeasurement of the Infinite One; they fear not the measuring of man and woman.

"They know because they are known of God. Their names are written in the Book of Life; they have fought the good fight over darkness and death.[270] They have invoked the Christ and the action of the full complement of the Archangels to lay hold on the dragon of the carnal mind and to bind that usurper of the light and to set the seal of Maitreya upon the dweller-on-the-threshold, that it no longer have any hold upon the soul ascending to the throne of God.

Bathe the Earth in the Universal Solvent

"The violet flame is a flame of joy as it sweeps through the consciousness of humanity. Flowing with the great flow of the Holy Spirit, it frees every particle of energy that it touches. The flame caresses Mater; for the flame is the Holy Spirit that is wed to the Divine Mother, who is the white fire core of all energy cycles.

"The great love of the Spirit for the Mother and of the Mother for the Spirit is the magnetism of Alpha and Omega drawing the flame of purification from on high into the canyons of the great rivers, into the crevasses of the mountains, into the nooks and crannies of the rocks. Wherever there is an opening, wherever there is an invitation, the fires of freedom roll and the angels of Zadkiel and Holy Amethyst deposit the universal solvent that throughout the ages the alchemists have sought.

"When the earth is bathed in the violet flame, as after a

summer rain, the elementals splash in puddles and ponds of the violet elixir that remain. The four lower bodies of a planet and a people absorb the flow of violet fire as the parched earth and the grasses dried in the summer sun absorb water.

"The violet flame and the violet-flame angels release a momentum that causes the electrons to spin. It is a momentum of joy! For joyousness and laughter—the kind of laughter that one has when one has gotten the victory over the self—bubble in the soul and bounce through the four lower bodies, sweeping away the debris of doubt and fear, the depressions of the years and the discarnates that lurk in the darkened corners of the mind.

"Now is the acceptable time of joy. It is the joy of the judgment! The wise elementals leap with the precision of a thousand ballerinas in formation—leap into the flame of judgment, leap into the joy of the violet fire—for they know that the judgment is the first step in their liberation and their ultimate reunion with the flame of life. There is no hesitation with the sylphs and the undines, gnomes and salamanders. They come into the fire and the fiery pools—the seven sacred pools that are for the cleansing of all life step by step from the karma of the misuse of the energies of the seven rays.

Dip Seven Times into the Waters of the Mother

"Remember Naaman, the captain of the host of the king of Syria, a mighty man of valor albeit a leper, whose servant besought him to seek the prophet of Israel to heal him of his leprosy.[271] And by and by 'Naaman came with his horses and with his chariot, and stood at the door of the house of Elisha. And Elisha sent a messenger unto him, saying, Go and wash in Jordan seven times, and thy flesh shall come again to thee and thou shalt be clean.' And Naaman was wroth, and he turned and went away in a rage because the prophet did not come forth and with great fanfare make invocation to the LORD.

"See how the carnal mind of the high and the mighty would have the prophet of the LORD do their bidding! But the servants of Naaman prevailed upon him, and he went down 'and dipped himself seven times in Jordan, according to the saying of the man of God: and his flesh came again like unto the flesh of a little child, and he was clean.'

"Now let mankind form a queue that they might dip into the waters of the Mother, into the white fire core of the energies of the Cosmic Virgin. And let them be cleansed seven times by the action of the fires of the seven rays. Let them be cleansed of their misuses of the seven aspects of the Logos. Let them dip seven times into the sacred pools of the Mother for the cleansing of the chakras. Let them dip seven times for the cleansing of the soul and the four lower bodies. Let them dip themselves seven times for the initiations of Lord Maitreya whereby the Holy Spirit is sealed in the chakras forevermore.

"You who would be captains in the LORD's hosts, you who would have the mantle of responsibility to lead the children of God into the light and to guide the governments of the nations according to the just laws of heaven and earth, humble yourselves before the flame of the Mother! Be willing to be washed. Be willing to be washed.

"The seventh ray is the ray of ceremony and ritual whereby, through the performance of these things, transmutation does take place. And there are rituals that will be required of thee. Some thou wilt understand and some thou wilt not. Nevertheless, follow the ritual of the Law; meet the requirements set forth by the prophet. For the prophet does stand in the holy place to cast out the abomination of desolation from the temple of the soul. The prophet is standing in the holy place with the fire of Alpha and Omega to make you whole.

The Law of Giving and Receiving

"See then the fate of those who prefer the mark of the beast, of those who have chosen to fall down and worship the devil who has promised to give them all of the kingdoms of this world.[272] And for a trifle—a new house, a new car, a dishwasher, a washing machine—they have forsaken the flame of the Holy Spirit. Those who are possessive of material things or of spiritual things will not keep either. Only those who move in the flow of the Mother can enjoy the Mater-realization. Only those who flow in the movement of the Holy Spirit can know the joy of Spirit-realization.

"The law of receiving and giving, giving and receiving, is the fulfillment of the circle of the AUM. Therefore, let go and let the energies of God flow if you would get the victory over the beast and over his image and over his mark and over the number of his name. If you would be free of the judgment of the fallen ones, let go! Let go and pursue God with all diligence.

"Remember Gehazi, the servant of Elisha, who ran after Naaman to claim the gifts that the prophet had rejected.[273] And in his lust for material things, he lied and begged of Naaman a talent of silver and two changes of garments for the sons of the prophets. Naaman was overjoyed to receive the servant of Elisha, to be able to give the prophet a token for his healing—but the prophet was not overjoyed. He knew that no amount of earthly goods could be placed in the scale with the gift of healing God had given into his hands.

"Therefore, unto Gehazi was rendered the pronouncement of the judgment, the same judgment that is rendered this day to those who have forsaken the flame of the Mother for the perversions of materialism: 'The leprosy therefore of Naaman shall cleave unto thee and unto thy seed forever.' And Gehazi went out from his presence a leper as white as snow.

"See now how the alchemy of the seventh ray can produce the precipitation in your four lower bodies of the degradation of the Holy Spirit that you have harbored in your soul. Children of the One, invoke the violet flame day and night, that all your darkness might take flight before the coming of the judgment and the karma of the misuses of the seventh ray are upon you.

Rolling Up the Scroll of Darkness

"Take heed! Hear my word this day! For I am Zadkiel, and I hold in my retreat over the island of Cuba seven other vials given unto my keeping by the LORD God of hosts. These are the seven vials of the concentrated energies of the violet flame that will be poured out over the earth by the Archangels of the seven rays when mankind have invoked enough of the sacred fire to warrant the release of these concentrated energies of the sacred fire.

"I stand on the side of the west of the City Foursquare. I stand on the West Coast of the United States of America, and I face the east and the kings and queens of the east to gather them to the battle of that great day of God Almighty. I raise my hands for the release of the momentum of the violet flame that shall reverse the tide of darkness and roll it back from the west unto the east.

"And it shall be as the rolling-up of a mighty scroll, and it shall be the rolling-up of that darkness which has covered the land. And it shall be the rolling-up of the unclean spirits that, like frogs, have been sent forth out of the mouth of the dragon and out of the mouth of the beast and out of the mouth of the false prophet.[274]

"And the momentum of that tide of light will be the rolling-up of the spirits of the devils working miracles, impersonating the Christ when they are Antichrist, impersonating

the prophets of the LORD although they have blasphemed their
name. And all of this shall come to pass when the children of
the light and the Keepers of the Flame shall rally to the defense
of the side of the west and invoke the momentum of the Archangels to turn the tide of the Dark Cycle and to make the day
of the Lord's judgment the day of joyousness in victory."[275]

The Initiation of Judgment

This victory not only liberates the energy of God held captive as karma, but it prepares souls of light for their ongoing
initiations. Archeia Amethyst speaks of "the initiation of the
judgment for those who have prepared diligently for the coming of the Lord into the temple of being."

"Your own soul, clothed upon with the four lower bodies,
is your focus of the Temple of the Tabernacle of the Testimony.
It is the forcefield given unto you in time and space wherein
you bear witness of the flame, where you become a keeper of
the flame, where you dedicate God's energy entrusted into your
care to the fulfillment in Mater of the counterpart of your
being in Spirit.

"The initiation of the judgment comes to sons and daughters of God, to the children of God, and to the fallen ones
simultaneously. And yet that initiation can be the necessary
preparation for the resurrection and the ascension, for the birth
of the soul unto immortal life, or it can be the necessary preparation for the final judgment at the Court of the Sacred Fire
and the canceling-out of the soul's identity in the ritual of the
second death.

"Judgment is the joy of the ritual of fulfillment because it
releases the creations of the children of the One into the sacred
fire. It is the trial by fire wherein every man's work must be
tried and man himself must be weighed in the great balance of

life.[276] To each individual soul there is given a certain epoch in time and space to fulfill the flame of the Christ in the seven rays. At the end of that era of evolution, sometimes spanning hundreds of thousands of years and thousands of incarnations, the soul must give an accounting to the LORD of Being and to the law of Selfhood, and rightly so."

Every moment of life in our time—at the turning of the age of Pisces into the age of Aquarius, which is the age of the Mother and the Holy Spirit—is charged with the poignancy of God's passion for his sons and daughters of light. For this is the grand finale of an age and many ages. And the victory is nigh. Archeia Amethyst looks forward with joy to the fulfillment of the judgment and the ascension of many, many souls. Hear her speak now of the rituals of judgment:

"Now I seal the seven golden vials; for in the ritual of the feminine aspect of the seventh ray, it is given to me to take from the hand of the Seven Archangels the seven vials. They are empty now. I seal them and I return them to the Cosmic Being who gave them unto the Seven Archangels, and they shall remain in the Temple of the Tabernacle of the Testimony until all be fulfilled through the judgments of the Lord.

"Long ago in the hour of the fall of Lucifer when the son of the morning defied the Almighty One and dared him to come down from his throne to judge him in his fall, he made the sign of the clenched fist in defiance of the LORD; and this has been the sign of the rebellious generation and of the fallen angels since that hour. But the Almighty would not be moved; and unto the fallen ones he gave a dispensation of mercy— certain cycles in time and space as opportunity for repentance. But they would not. No, they would not.

"Therefore this day in God's own time, in God's own space, judgment is meted out to the Fallen One and those who boasted to the children of God, saying: 'See, we have dared the

LORD and he has not responded! The LORD is silent; therefore he does not exist. Behold Lucifer and Satan; they are more powerful than the LORD God of hosts. They have dominion in the planes of Mater; fall down and worship them!'

"And now the answer of the LORD has come. In his season and in his cycle, the LORD has released the judgment of the fallen ones. Let all the world know that the LORD God omnipotent reigneth!²⁷⁷ Let the angel choirs sing the alleluia! Let the worlds rejoice! Let the stars in the heavens rejoice! Let the sons and daughters of God rejoice, for the LORD God omnipotent reigneth!

"Let the Keepers of the Flame understand that the judgment of God is manifest in the four planes of Mater and in the four lower bodies of mankind. But ultimately that judgment must manifest in the soul. Thus the energies of the judgment meted out in the cycles of the years and in the fulfillment of the centuries may not always be visible or obvious to those who have followed a literal interpretation of scripture. Although much of that which will come upon the earth will be unseen, it will be felt and heard and known by those who are close to the flame and also by those in whom the judgment is meted out. Therefore, judge not, lest ye be judged.

"Now let there be rejoicing in the retreats of the Ascended Masters and in the focuses of their chelas! And let the waltzes of the violet flame and the rhythm of three-quarter time be the keynote of victory. Let joy in the violet flame generate more joy for the regeneration of a planet and a people. And let the youth and the young in heart of every age come together for the waltz of the flame, for the release of joy to the four lower bodies and the four planes of Mater. And let the grand march and the waltz and the polka replace the desecration of the body of the Mother and of her children through the rhythms and the unholy dancing of the fallen ones.

"In the heart of every Keeper of the Flame I place a replica of the amethyst crystal of our retreat, that you might generate the joy of living and the joy of giving on Terra, that you might clear the way for the new day and the new order of the ages and for the coming of the seventh root race, that through you the Archangels might charge the governments and the economies of the nations and all cultural and educational institutions with the momentum of the new birth of the Spirit and with the momentum of light that comes forth from the Great Central Sun.

"It is time to light the torch of the age of freedom. The taper is in my hand. Will you light a taper of your own and ignite the hearts of mankind to the victory of the throne, the three-in-one, the grace of Faith and Hope and Charity in the balance of life's energy?

"The threefold flame is calling, calling mankind home! To the victory of freedom in Terra I dedicate my flame and the release of the judgment at the hand of the Seven Archangels. Let judgment be for the victory of the souls of God in the dark night of the soul, for the victory of the sons and daughters of God in the initiations of the seven rays.

"I set my seal upon the fire and upon the air, upon the waters and upon the earth. And I stand with Zadkiel on the west side of the city, waiting for the moment of the rolling-up of the darkness into the scroll. And when the hour is come that is signified by the LORD, the Seven Archangels will take that scroll of human consciousness and human creation and hand it to the Keeper of the Scrolls, who will place it in the sacred fire for the consuming of the cause, effect, record and memory of the misuse of the sacred fire in the planes of Mater."[278]

Chapter 2

Reembodiment

Before Abraham was, I AM.

JOHN 8:58

Reembodiment

THE BIRTH OF A CHILD, WHICH SEEMS commonplace because of its frequency, is a magnificent happening. The idea that man lives but once is so firmly ingrained in Western thought (albeit two-thirds of the earth's people believe in reembodiment) that there seems to be little room in Western minds to even consider the subject. Yet there are many Christian men and women who find no difficulty in accepting the idea of reembodiment. If we blindly accept traditional Christian dogma, which excludes all possibility of reembodiment, the doorway to many wonderful facts and realities will be closed to us.

Dogmatists, with their self-limiting attitudes, are sometimes argumentative. The basis of their convictions is often found in a series of religious statements recorded in the sacred writings of their faith. But the sacred writings of the world's major religions have come down to us from antiquity; in the process they have passed through a great number of hands, translations and interpretations. Error in the scriptures is possible not only in the original transfer of the spoken word to the written word, but also in the interpretation of the written word by later theologians.

The early scribes' frame of mind no doubt influenced how the record was perceived, and this was also true of the translators.[1] Sometimes writings that were deemed irrelevant or in disagreement with accepted doctrine were simply omitted. Interpretations were based upon suppositions and ideas in the minds of the early teachers who set the pattern of organized religion after the founder had fulfilled his role.

Thus throughout the ages, the attitude of the dogmatist has effectively screened from his perception the possibility that he might receive new and accurate information "from on high," which might or might not refute his beliefs. Men allow progress on all fronts of human endeavor, but they are content to let religion become archaic—whereas a fresh mind and a right attitude toward God and man open the door to understanding.

One of the absurdities of dogma is its exclusion of the possibility of new facts. Yet conversion to Christianity or to any traditional religion, for that matter, requires an open mind.

We would speak out in favor of the preservation of open-mindedness. There is more sin in the closed mind, with its smugness and self-righteousness, than there is in the open-minded spirit that breathes a prayer to God: "Father, thou knowest. Make me to know also." Such a one recognizes that even when God speaks, man is sometimes dull of hearing.

Cosmic Perspective

In his *Trilogy on the Threefold Flame of Life*, Saint Germain explains: "It would be most beneficial if the human monad would refrain from prejudgment in matters of cosmic doctrine and even better if he could universally accept the reality of reembodiment. For it is in the acceptance of this fact of life that he will truly discern the wisdom of the ages and more easily understand his reason for being.

"It is most difficult for people in any age, observing in the life span of a comparatively few short years a series of events relative to the personal self, to be able to judge the world in which they live and the society from which they have derived both bane and blessing, and then to be able to perceive matters pertaining to the spirit and properly assess them.

"By correctly understanding and accepting his own reembodiment, the individual develops a cosmic sense of the continuity of self—past, present, and future—and is better equipped to see behind the surface effects of today's circumstances the underlying personal causes that stretch back across the dust of centuries. . . .

"How great is the suffering that Christians have endured through the elimination of this one point of spiritual truth! By denying reembodiment they have denied their souls the keystone in the arch of being.

"You see, there are certain fine points of Cosmic Law that in a relative sense are not as important as this one. Man can deny some specifics without suffering too much damage, but to deny the truth of the continuity of his own being—its span of previous existence and its future glorious destiny—is to cut himself off from the basic premise of life."[2]

Enlarging upon this, Casimir Poseidon says: "So many today prefer to dwell in the niches of the near past, in its great release of spiritual knowledge. They prefer to dwell in the memory of the Galilean embodiment of the Christ rather than in the great cosmic impetus of the Divine Lawgiver, as he was known long ago. Jesus' statement 'Before Abraham was, I AM' is a clue to the seeker for knowledge that brings to the consciousness the long stream of service of beloved Jesus to humanity."[3]

The processes of reembodiment are vital to the spiritual evolution of man, and when properly understood, they can be a key to his immortal freedom. When man wears out the coat he has worn for a time, God will replace it with another, and eventually with a seamless garment—a deathless, incorruptible body in which he shall forever dwell, subject only to the laws of eternal progression that lead man onward and upward to the realm of the perfect day.

> In the Eternal Now men shall forever dwell
> And there commune with everyone
> Who has outgrown his shell,
> And fully conscious in God's light
> Triumph together by His might.

It is neither strange nor difficult for the Heavenly Father to take a soul who has vacated her body temple and to place that soul into a new and fresh body form. This is done in order to provide a continuation of experience in the schoolroom of earth, even though the old body wears out.

The fiat of life everlasting was beautifully captured by Oliver Wendell Holmes in "The Chambered Nautilus":

> Build thee more stately mansions, O my soul,
>   As the swift seasons roll!
> Leave thy low-vaulted past!
> Let each new temple, nobler than the last,
> Shut thee from heaven with a dome more vast,
>   Till thou at length art free,
> Leaving thine outgrown shell by life's unresting sea!

The Persistence of Karma

Flowers are born and they mature, displaying their beauty for a brief span; then the petals fall to mingle with the dust. With the coming of spring they appear once again. Who can say that the soul of the flower does not survive and remain in the wings of the stages of life, awaiting the prompter's cue when it shall make another entrance? And so it springs forth again to gladden the eyes and hearts of men.

Thus the karmic record of a lifestream is transferred to a new body temple. The beginning of life in that body temple with a new name and a different situation becomes a fresh opportunity for the child-man to once again expand his tiny limbs and reach for the stars of a cosmic virtue that in the past might have escaped his grasp.

It is never the will of God to cast a soul away. Has he not said, "I have no pleasure in the death of the wicked"?[4] Every lamb that the Good Shepherd has within his flock belongs to God and is tenderly protected by the Cosmic Christ. In the schoolrooms of life men often finish their courses and close their eyes in one land, only to open them again in another— and the infant form of the child, full of wonder and hope, begins once again the adventure of living. As Kahlil Gibran said in his book *The Prophet:* "A little while, a moment of rest upon the wind, and another woman shall bear me."[5]

When correctly understood, the truth of reembodiment (stranger than the fiction of one life) provides the greatest hope for mankind. Reembodiment is neither an excuse nor a release from the full responsibility and karmic accountability for one's errors. On the contrary, reembodiment provides for a continuation of experience on earth, which (although moving in broken sequences) is the means whereby the soul can evolve progressively toward victory, self-mastery and attainment.

It can be asked, What is the real purpose of reembodiment? Nature herself will provide the answer. When God created man in his own image, it was in the image of immortality. Man's fall from that higher image into the bondage of the flesh resulted in a negative karmic record that, had he only had one embodiment, would have prevented his manifestation of eternal life.

The Father desires to recover every lost sheep of his fold. As an act of great mercy, working through the flame of life within the human heart, he lovingly catches up each soul consciousness as the body expires. He holds that spirit, which is in truth a part of himself, in higher octaves of manifestation until the time comes for that one to return to the stage of life and to finish the drama of her existence. For he knows that the soul, through a series of embodiments or days and nights upon the earth, can finally overcome the world and attain her victory.

The real purpose of reembodiment is to provide the opportunity—the cycles of years and events—wherein man can live and learn to do well. What a frightening thing it would be if the millions upon millions of souls who have come and gone upon this planet without having had the opportunity of hearing the teachings of the Master Jesus were without hope for a future opportunity to follow in his footsteps!

Man's belief in immortality antedates all known history and is the focal point of most religions. Without their belief in immortality and the hope of a future reward, most people would not lead moral, productive lives. Their credo would be "Let us eat, drink and be merry, for tomorrow we die." Those who embrace this type of banal existence set no example for the progress of the human race, nor do they elevate themselves or their fellowmen.

Man is a spirit, even as God is a Spirit. Man was created in the image of God, and in the image of God is he found at higher levels. The soul of man may reembody again and again, yet its purpose—the discovery of self, the overcoming of error, and the attainment of the perfection of God that is stored within the macrocosmic heart of the Higher Self—must be discovered by each one individually. For "strait is the gate, and narrow is the way" that leads to eternal life.[6]

One Chance at Salvation?

In stark contrast to this merciful plan of God is the doctrine that man lives only one life. According to this erroneous belief, the individual has no hope in the next world unless he embraces a man-made creed that guarantees him immortality because another has paid for his sins. And if he does not wholeheartedly accept this creed, he cannot return and embrace it in another life once he has passed on.

Some religions baptize for the dead or perform sacraments for the dead ancestors of those who have joined the church. But let it be clear that there is no substitute for the divine plan that enables each one to pass through the door.

The dogmatists set forth the idea of hell as a place of eternal punishment, thereby destroying the concept of a tomorrow in which the sins of today could be atoned for. They removed the concept of the soul's opportunity to learn through trial and error. Thus they were able to achieve an effective control over the masses. Rather than conveying the fullness of living Truth that Jesus exemplified, those who denied the concept of reembodiment suppressed the soul's aspirations. They denied her the opportunity to follow Jesus all the way to perfectionment in God.

Ironically, the centuries that followed[7] saw only a limited progress for the church and its members, other than the accumulation of material wealth. By the little knowledge possessed (which became a dangerous thing), both the church and its members were deprived of the tremendous power of Truth to be found in the original teachings of the Christ.

World opinion would be more inclined toward Christ rather than anti-Christ if these false teachings had not been introduced by a priesthood seeking control by fear. Their deliberate confusing of the Word of God destroyed the vitality of the faith and the divine plan of many souls.

If the law of karma had been explained—in the place of the erroneous doctrine of vicarious atonement—and if respect for God's Law had been engendered in mankind, the golden rule would have been more willingly obeyed.

An Example of Reembodiment Taught in the Gospels

When Jesus gathered his disciples around him, they discussed the teachings of reembodiment freely and with familiarity. One such discussion was recorded, and it seems to have been missed in the careful project undertaken to delete great truths from the scriptures. Perhaps it was overlooked, or perhaps it was left in because it was felt that most people would not take the words literally.

Jesus and the disciples were speaking of the coming of the prophet Elijah. To the disciples the word *coming* meant the coming of the soul into manifestation, or being born. The scriptures say that a forerunner having the spirit and power of Elijah the Prophet should precede Jesus' coming. The disciples were speculating as to whether or not Elijah had been born. Jesus answered them, "'I say unto you, that Elias [Elijah] is come already, and they knew him not, but have done unto him whatsoever they listed. . . . ' Then the disciples understood that he spake unto them of John the Baptist."

To show that regenerative life is greater than generative

life, Jesus added that among those born of women, none was greater than John the Baptist, "notwithstanding he that is least in the kingdom of heaven is greater than he."[8]

Courage to Squarely Face One's Past

Our beloved Jesus says: "Let a new outreach go forth into the world bearing the tidings of Truth. As Saint Francis taught the law of reembodiment in the public squares, so let us now have teachers who are willing to brave the censure of the merging orthodox movements that would unify all churches into one great church in order to intensify their power of religious control in the world.

"Let us proclaim the truth of reembodiment to the world in order that they might clearly see that all of their infirmities and all of their problems are caused by disobedience to the Law in the present as well as in times past.

"Let us remove from them the fear of religious persecution and the fear of an awful state of burning in a world hereafter and yet to come. Let us show them that it is not alone for the world to come that they should have fear and respect, but also for the world right here where their own karma returns to them day by day that which they have sent out.

"Here the mercy of heaven holds in abeyance the overpowering karmic record that some do write—a karma that is more than most of them could bear. Therefore, the Lords of Karma mete out to them in succeeding embodiments that karma which requires balance, that which they have unjustly created. And this action is taken not in order to punish a wayward generation but solely for the purpose of learning and instruction that, through trial and error, they may yet come to the full opportunity of cosmic sonship, which God offers to all."[9]

The Continuity of Life

As World Teachers, Ascended Masters Jesus and Kuthumi give us the following instruction concerning reembodiment: "There is much to be gained from a correct knowledge of karma and reembodiment. Your life, blessed ones, is continuous. It does not end, nor does it come in sharp spurts and gaps. Your life is a majestic stream of cosmic energy composed of the consciousness of God and the energy of his heart. To you is entrusted a portion of the Divine Selfhood. Thus it was spoken long ago, 'Your life is not your own.'[10] We say to all mankind, life is given into your keeping that you may master your destiny and the fulfillment of divine purposes within the sphere of Selfhood.

"It is sad to mortal thought, but not to divine thought, that the memory of the continuous stream of life is broken upon the altars of death. There are many reasons for this, and one by one these reasons will be made known to you as you study the laws of reembodiment and understand that there is nothing strange at all about this fact of man's evolution. For in reality, blessed ones, the concept of reembodiment is no more difficult to understand than the consideration of life as one's sole opportunity to find God and to fulfill his purposes.

"It would be far more strange if God were to create mankind without equal opportunity for salvation—some ignorant, some wise, placing some in circumstances of wealth and culture and others in conditions of abject poverty without the benefit of formal education. Strange indeed if the Creator expected all to rise from the various states in which they found themselves and in the space of a few short years come to that mature comprehension and judgment which would cause them to accept Christ as their Saviour and to find soul-release in the fulfillment of their divine destiny....

"All of life is cyclic. Even the cycles of the centuries, the decades and the years are broken into months and weeks and days. Each twenty-four-hour cycle is divided into the night and the day—periods of regeneration and rest and periods of creativity.

"The Master Hilarion declared when embodied as Saint Paul, 'I die daily.' Although he was referring to the mortification of the ego—the putting off of the human consciousness and the putting on of the divine consciousness[11]—this statement may also be applied to all mankind as they close their eyes at night for a period of sleep, when there is a loss of contact with the realities of the day's activities and a separation of the soul from the memory patterns of the personal self. This breaking of the thread of consciousness, which is reestablished with each coming dawn, gives man the opportunity to die daily and to begin life anew.

"As an act of mercy, the memories of the past are blotted out of the conscious mind each time the soul reembodies. This is a deliberate action of the Lords of Karma taken to prevent contact with the sordid aspects of previous lives that would mar the opportunity for a new beginning in the new cycle. However, now and then as subconscious memories spiral to the surface of awareness, people do receive impressions of having done before the same act that they find themselves doing for the first time in their present embodiment. Because the memory of old experience patterns is broken at birth, the possibility for deliverance is always present, and the soul can be raised out of its own imperfections and transformed into a higher state of the Christ consciousness.

"You must take into account that souls coming to earth for the first time often do not manifest great brilliance of achievement, even in the simple things of life. Some maintain for a number of embodiments states of consciousness that are not comparable to those of individuals who have returned to earth's schools hundreds and even thousands of times to fulfill their divine plan. The stairway of evolution, therefore, represents lifestreams and life patterns of mature as well as young souls, all having equal opportunity to excel in the magnification of God-qualities, but not all equal in achievement.

Opportunity to Build a Nobler Temple

"Even as 'one star differeth from another star in glory,' so the Causal Body of each son of God reflects the harvest of good works gleaned from each successive opportunity in the Father's vineyard. Thus the talents multiplied by each laborer accrue to his benefit with interest, whereas those who bury [in the electronic belt] that portion of God's energy entrusted to them find no accumulation of good karma to enhance their future lives,[12] but only the burden of imbalance that must one day become the balance of light's perfection.

"As the opportunity for embodiment is awarded to the soul again and again, each succeeding experience in the world of Matter-form is intended to be used to build a 'temple nobler than the last.' Those who avail themselves of the opportunities for self-mastery that are presented in each lifetime receive a greater portion of the Holy Spirit as grace for the needs of the hour. Thus there occurs a fashioning of the Christ-nature in those who give preeminence to their higher calling.

"Those who in the period between death and rebirth become devotees of the Masters in the temples of beauty and music often return as geniuses of the arts, or so mankind have called them. Those who elect to study in the etheric temples of science and healing may glean enough of the flame of Truth to bring forth inventions and techniques for the health and well-being of mankind. Disciples who apply themselves in the

Temple of God's Will return to guide the destiny of nations through an inner knowledge of God-government and economics taught to them by statesmen of the Spirit serving on the Darjeeling Council.

"The art of bringing healing and comfort to life and upholding the honor code of the Masters, as well as their educational standards, is taught by the Maha Chohan, Mary the Mother, and the brothers of the wisdom schools. Archangel Raphael, together with Mother Mary, conducts classes on child development and child care and the training of both parents and children 'in the way they should go'[13] that they might make a worthy contribution to their communities, at the same time making the most rapid spiritual strides in their individual lives.

"The Lords of Flame school would-be priests of the sacred fire who are destined to return to earth to bring a revitalizing surge of resurrection's flame to the various churches of the world. Thus not by chance but by divine direction there flows into the octave of mankind's evolving consciousness the organization and sustenance of heaven.

"Since the veil is drawn during sleep as well as at birth, individuals do not always retain in their outer consciousness an awareness of that which has been vouchsafed unto them at inner levels. Nevertheless, there is a lodestone, a magnet, an animus of spiritual power that draws each one to his appointed course even as stars and galaxies are guided by the unseen hand of cosmic destiny.

"As mankind rise to the place where they consciously, willingly call for the transmutation of their past errors and deviations from the Law, little by little the doors of memory are opened and all of the knowledge and training of past lives, as well as the teachings of the Masters given on the inner planes, are recalled for the benefit of the individual as an assistance toward his attainment of self-mastery and the completion of his mission unto his ascension in the light.

"It is useless for mankind to attempt to refute through scriptural means the great eternal cycles and the ongoing tides of life. Those who do will find that at the end of the road, at the end of each cycle, they are taken by angelic ministrants to a place of rest, regeneration and instruction, preparing them for a new adventure in the world of form. Their denials of the laws of life have no power to alter the divine intent. For it is the mercy of God that continually outbreathes the breath of life into the nostrils of men that he may stimulate the Christ Flame within the heart, until the fragrance of the Only Begotten of the Father—of the Holy One of Israel (of the God of all that is real)—does flow through them to fulfill the divine plan."[14]

Child Prodigies

One of the strongest supports for the concept of reembodiment is the child prodigy—the child who at an unbelievably early age shows qualities of genius. The difference between an average child and one of genius lies not in the genes but in the spirit within the house of clay. As Jesus and Kuthumi have explained, the child prodigy has developed his talent through many rounds of incarnation on earth, as well as through training in the heaven world.

In preparation for such an embodiment, the soul works hand in hand with the Karmic Board and the prospective parents to ensure that she will grow up in the earthly setting most conducive to the expression of her talent.

In fact, we are all given the greatest opportunity possible to develop our spiritual potential. The Karmic Board and those Higher Powers who act on behalf of mankind under the guidance of God determine, within the bounds of karmic law, the parents and the nature of the body temple that is brought forth to house the progressing soul. In most cases the memory is mercifully blunted by divine decree so that the individual does not have the ties to a previous father, mother or family situation. Nor is the soul so strongly subject to old limiting habit patterns from which she desired escape—although certain characteristics may be recreated and brought forward lifetime after lifetime.

Transmigration of Souls

Let us make clear that we do not endorse the doctrine of transmigration of souls as it pertains to the migration of the soul into the body of an animal. For men are not now animals, nor have they evolved from the consciousness of animal life.[15]

As God inhabits every form of life, so the man who attains God Self-awareness may be aware of life in and as an amoeba, a fish swimming in the sea, a bird cresting the winds, or the flocks on the hills. It is not necessary that the soul be reduced to habitation in an animal form in order to appreciate that state of evolution.

Man can extend his God consciousness to any part of life, but man remains the expression of the whole. His soul does not need to incarnate in animal forms in order to gain experience. For from the beginning he was destined to be the fullness of the living God in manifestation.

"Our Father who dwelleth in heaven [the planes of Spirit], hallowed be thy name, I AM [the flame in the planes of Matter]." It is man who consecrates the flame of God ignited in his body temple by the Holy Spirit of the Father-Mother God. This flame is not enshrined in animal life. Therefore the soul of man, destined to expand the LORD's consciousness through the flame, could not fulfill her reason for being in an animal form.

The belief that the soul of man incarnates in and evolves through animal forms is based on an incorrect assessment of human and animal life. The threefold flame is the identity of man. The forcefield of his four lower bodies, reestablished in each succeeding incarnation, is the platform provided for his soul's mastery of that flame.

These bodies and the soul that inhabits them are molded in the image of the Christ Self, and only that which comes forth in that image is worthy to be the chalice of the flame in the physical octave. Animals are incomplete manifestations of the Christ. They are not worthy to house the flame, hence they are unworthy to provide a tabernacle for the soul.

Go to God in Spirit and in Truth

The God Meru tells us: "One of the saddest factors involving the release of straight knowledge from the heart of God is that individuals have a tendency either to deify those through whom knowledge is given or, if they do not agree with it, to attribute it to demons. For most people there are no gray tones, only the blackest of blacks or the whitest of whites."[16]

But if men will seek Truth with all their hearts and implore God to illumine their consciousness, he will do so. If men will admit their lack of understanding to the Almighty, he will fill the void. If men will ask to be shown what is real and what is not, God will make plain his commandments and his laws. The creed that God has made is deathless, immortal, eternal and charged with hope. It requires no man to find his immortality in the physical form, but it proclaims for all time that man is a spirit even as God is a Spirit, and they that worship him must worship him in spirit and in truth.[17]

Those who understand that the life within them is the seed of God, sprouting in human form as the tree of life whose leaves are for the healing of the nations,[18] can make a lasting contribution to the betterment of the race. Through mercy and love these will find their wings and soar toward the sun and the summit of their being. These will dedicate themselves again and again to immortal and often invisible precepts. By the power of faith, these will move mountains, even as God framed the world by the selfsame power of faith.

If men will kneel before the Ancient of Days saying, "O LORD, is it true that I have lived before? Have I also known myself in thee? Show me how I can come to know more about my heritage as a son of God," the LORD of heaven will make known to them their soul's preexistence as well as the many lives they have lived upon this blessed orb.

The promise "Ask, and ye shall receive" applies to the area of spiritual research. If, after having read this chapter or other parts of the book, you are not sure if you can accept the concepts we present, give unto God an unbiased and an uncluttered mind and ask him to illumine you. You will soon see how day by day he will fill your heart with the knowledge of the Truth until you realize what David was experiencing when he said, "My cup runneth over!"[19]

Appendix

In the following pages, the Messengers have shown the placement of verses from Genesis on the Cosmic Clock.

The Cosmic Clock

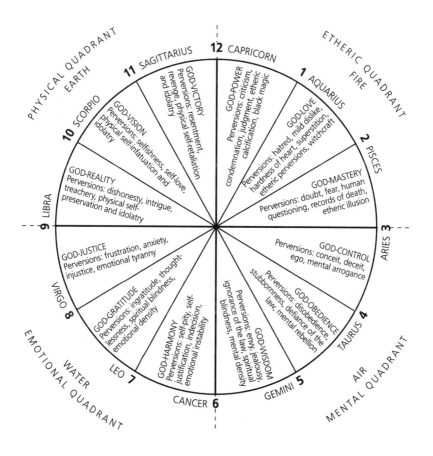

First Ray

I

Genesis 1:1–12

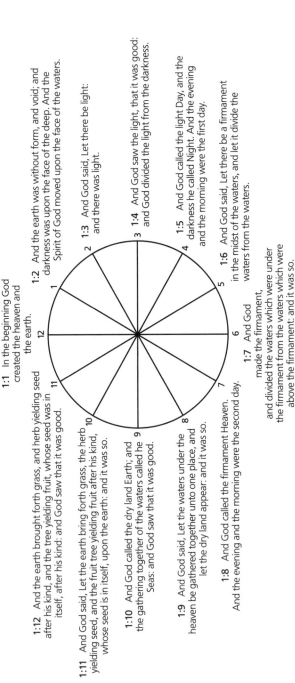

1:1 In the beginning God created the heaven and the earth.

1:2 And the earth was without form, and void; and darkness was upon the face of the deep. And the Spirit of God moved upon the face of the waters.

1:3 And God said, Let there be light: and there was light.

1:4 And God saw the light, that it was good: and God divided the light from the darkness.

1:5 And God called the light Day, and the darkness he called Night. And the evening and the morning were the first day.

1:6 And God said, Let there be a firmament in the midst of the waters, and let it divide the waters from the waters.

1:7 And God made the firmament, and divided the waters which were under the firmament from the waters which were above the firmament: and it was so.

1:8 And God called the firmament Heaven. And the evening and the morning were the second day.

1:9 And God said, Let the waters under the heaven be gathered together unto one place, and let the dry land appear: and it was so.

1:10 And God called the dry land Earth; and the gathering together of the waters called he Seas: and God saw that it was good.

1:11 And God said, Let the earth bring forth grass, the herb yielding seed, and the fruit tree yielding fruit after his kind, whose seed is in itself, upon the earth: and it was so.

1:12 And the earth brought forth grass, and herb yielding seed after his kind, and the tree yielding fruit, whose seed was in itself, after his kind: and God saw that it was good.

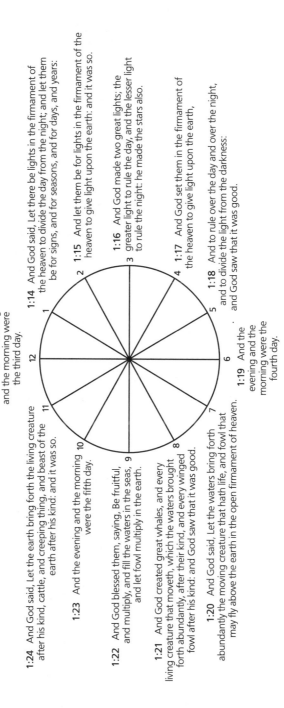

First Ray

II

Genesis 1:13–24

1:13 And the evening and the morning were the third day.

1:14 And God said, Let there be lights in the firmament of the heaven to divide the day from the night; and let them be for signs, and for seasons, and for days, and years:

1:15 And let them be for lights in the firmament of the heaven to give light upon the earth: and it was so.

1:16 And God made two great lights; the greater light to rule the day, and the lesser light to rule the night: he made the stars also.

1:17 And God set them in the firmament of the heaven to give light upon the earth,

1:18 And to rule over the day and over the night, and to divide the light from the darkness: and God saw that it was good.

1:19 And the evening and the morning were the fourth day.

1:20 And God said, Let the waters bring forth abundantly the moving creature that hath life, and fowl that may fly above the earth in the open firmament of heaven.

1:21 And God created great whales, and every living creature that moveth, which the waters brought forth abundantly, after their kind, and every winged fowl after his kind: and God saw that it was good.

1:22 And God blessed them, saying, Be fruitful, and multiply, and fill the waters in the seas, and let fowl multiply in the earth.

1:23 And the evening and the morning were the fifth day.

1:24 And God said, Let the earth bring forth the living creature after his kind, cattle, and creeping thing, and beast of the earth after his kind: and it was so.

First Ray

III

Genesis 1:25–2:5

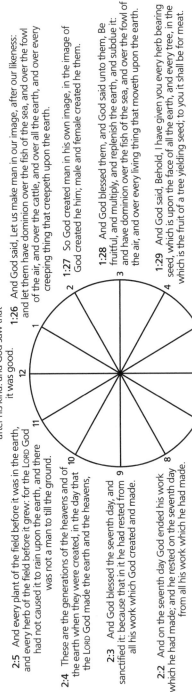

1:25 And God made the beast of the earth after his kind, and cattle after their kind, and every thing that creepeth upon the earth after his kind: and God saw that it was good.

1:26 And God said, Let us make man in our image, after our likeness: and let them have dominion over the fish of the sea, and over the fowl of the air, and over the cattle, and over all the earth, and over every creeping thing that creepeth upon the earth.

1:27 So God created man in his own image, in the image of God created he him; male and female created he them.

1:28 And God blessed them, and God said unto them, Be fruitful, and multiply, and replenish the earth, and subdue it: and have dominion over the fish of the sea, and over the fowl of the air, and over every living thing that moveth upon the earth.

1:29 And God said, Behold, I have given you every herb bearing seed, which is upon the face of all the earth, and every tree, in the which is the fruit of a tree yielding seed; to you it shall be for meat.

1:30 And to every beast of the earth, and to every fowl of the air, and to every thing that creepeth upon the earth, wherein there is life, I have given every green herb for meat: and it was so.

1:31 And God saw every thing that he had made, and, behold, it was very good. And the evening and the morning were the sixth day.

2:1 Thus the heavens and the earth were finished, and all the host of them.

2:2 And on the seventh day God ended his work which he had made; and he rested on the seventh day from all his work which he had made.

2:3 And God blessed the seventh day, and sanctified it: because that in it he had rested from all his work which God created and made.

2:4 These are the generations of the heavens and of the earth when they were created, in the day that the LORD God made the earth and the heavens,

2:5 And every plant of the field before it was in the earth, and every herb of the field before it grew: for the LORD God had not caused it to rain upon the earth, and there was not a man to till the ground.

Second Ray

I

Genesis 2:6–17

2:6 But there went up a mist from the earth, and watered the whole face of the ground.

2:7 And the LORD God formed man of the dust of the ground, and breathed into his nostrils the breath of life; and man became a living soul.

2:8 And the LORD God planted a garden eastward in Eden; and there he put the man whom he had formed.

2:9 And out of the ground made the LORD God to grow every tree that is pleasant to the sight, and good for food; the tree of life also in the midst of the garden, and the tree of knowledge of good and evil.

2:10 And a river went out of Eden to water the garden; and from thence it was parted, and became into four heads.

2:11 The name of the first is Pison: that is it which compasseth the whole land of Havilah, where there is gold;

2:12 And the gold of that land is good: there is bdellium and the onyx stone.

2:13 And the name of the second river is Gihon: the same is it that compasseth the whole land of Ethiopia.

2:14 And the name of the third river is Hiddekel: that is it which goeth toward the east of Assyria. And the fourth river is Euphrates.

2:15 And the LORD God took the man, and put him into the garden of Eden to dress it and to keep it.

2:16 And the LORD God commanded the man, saying, Of every tree of the garden thou mayest freely eat:

2:17 But of the tree of the knowledge of good and evil, thou shalt not eat of it: for in the day that thou eatest thereof thou shalt surely die.

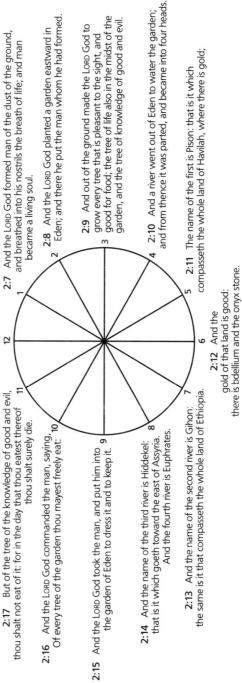

Second Ray

II

Genesis 2:18–25

2:18 And the LORD God said, It is not good that the man should be alone; I will make him an help meet for him.

2:19 And out of the ground the LORD God formed every beast of the field, and every fowl of the air; and brought them unto Adam to see what he would call them: and whatsoever Adam called every living creature, that was the name thereof.

2:20 And Adam gave names to all cattle, and to the fowl of the air, and to every beast of the field; but for Adam there was not found an help meet for him.

2:21 And the LORD God caused a deep sleep to fall upon Adam, and he slept: and he took one of his ribs, and closed up the flesh instead thereof;

2:22 And the rib, which the LORD God had taken from man, made he a woman, and brought her unto the man.

2:23 And Adam said, This is now bone of my bones, and flesh of my flesh: she shall be called Woman, because she was taken out of Man.

2:24 Therefore shall a man leave his father and his mother, and shall cleave unto his wife: and they shall be one flesh.

2:25 And they were both naked, the man and his wife, and were not ashamed.

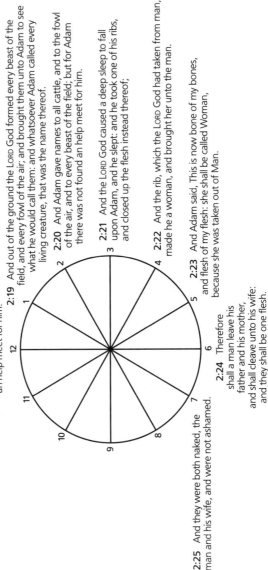

Third Ray

I

Genesis 3:1–12

Spirit Sphere Perverted

3:1 Now the serpent was more subtil than any beast of the field which the LORD God had made. And he said unto the woman, Yea, hath God said, Ye shall not eat of every tree of the garden? (*Serpent judges the* LORD's *commandment.*)

3:2 And the woman said unto the serpent, We may eat of the fruit of the trees of the garden: (*Woman cites the Aquarian law of alchemy. We may partake of exercises for development of soul faculties and solar awareness.*)

3:3 But of the fruit of the tree which is in the midst of the garden, God hath said, Ye shall not eat of it, neither shall ye touch it, lest ye die.

3:4 And the serpent said unto the woman, Ye shall not surely die:

3:5 For God doth know that in the day ye eat thereof, then your eyes shall be opened, and ye shall be as gods, knowing good and evil.

3:6 And when the woman saw that the tree was good for food, and that it was pleasant to the eyes, and a tree to be desired to make one wise, she took of the fruit thereof, and did eat, and gave also unto her husband with her; and he did eat.

3:7 And the eyes of them both were opened, and they knew that they were naked; and they sewed fig leaves together, and made themselves aprons.

3:8 And they heard the voice of the LORD God walking in the garden in the cool of the day: and Adam and his wife hid themselves from the presence of the LORD God amongst the trees of the garden. (*Tests of secret rays begin.*)

3:9 And the LORD God called unto Adam, and said unto him, Where art thou?

3:10 And he said, I heard thy voice in the garden, and I was afraid, because I was naked; and I hid myself.

3:11 And he said, Who told thee that thou wast naked? Hast thou eaten of the tree, whereof I commanded thee that thou shouldest not eat?

3:12 And the man said, The woman whom thou gavest to be with me, she gave me of the tree, and I did eat.

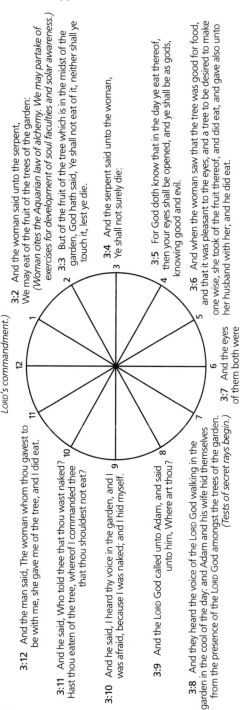

Third Ray

II

Genesis 3:13–24

Matter Sphere Perverted

3:13 And the LORD God said unto the woman, What is this that thou hast done? And the woman said, The serpent beguiled me, and I did eat. *(The LORD judges Eve.)*

3:14 And the LORD God said unto the serpent, Because thou hast done this, thou art cursed above all cattle, and above every beast of the field; upon thy belly shalt thou go, and dust shalt thou eat all the days of thy life. *(The LORD judges Serpent.)*

3:15 And I will put enmity between thee and the woman, and between thy seed and her seed; it shall bruise thy head, and thou shalt bruise his heel. *(The LORD places enmity between Serpent and woman, and between the seed of the fallen angels and the seed of the children of God.)*

3:16 Unto the woman he said, I will greatly multiply thy sorrow and thy conception; in sorrow thou shalt bring forth children; and thy desire shall be to thy husband, and he shall rule over thee. *(The LORD establishes the identity of fallen woman.)*

3:17 And unto Adam he said, Because thou hast hearkened unto the voice of thy wife, and hast eaten of the tree, of which I commanded thee, saying, Thou shalt not eat of it: cursed is the ground for thy sake; in sorrow shalt thou eat of it all the days of thy life. *(The LORD establishes the identity of fallen man.)*

3:18 Thorns also and thistles shall it bring forth to thee; and thou shalt eat the herb of the field;

3:19 In the sweat of thy face shalt thou eat bread, till thou return unto the ground; for out of it wast thou taken: for dust thou art, and unto dust shalt thou return. *(Physical death—the path of initiation leads to the ascension.)*

3:20 And Adam called his wife's name Eve; because she was the mother of all living.

3:21 Unto Adam also and to his wife did the LORD God make coats of skins, and clothed them. *(The LORD made them more dense vehicles to function in the polluted physical plane.)*

3:22 And the LORD God said, Behold, the man is become as one of us, to know good and evil: and now, lest he put forth his hand, and take also of the tree of life, and eat, and live for ever. *(Real state of man defined by God.)*

3:23 Therefore the LORD God sent him forth from the garden of Eden, to till the ground from whence he was taken. *(The LORD sends man forth to be a servant of the Matter sphere whence he came, where he is bound till his Redeemer cometh.)*

3:24 So he drove out the man; and he placed at the east of the garden of Eden Cherubims, and a flaming sword which turned every way, to keep the way of the tree of life. *(The LORD establishes the flaming sword of Christ Consciousness to keep the way (the Law) of the path of the I AM Presence.)*

Fourth Ray

I

Genesis 4:1–12

Spirit Sphere

The Lord is willing to test the sons of Adam and Eve to see if they will take up the tests in the world that their parents failed in the garden. Maitreya is withdrawn; Abel talks to his I AM Presence. No Mediator—no mercy.

4:1 And Adam knew Eve his wife; and she conceived, and bare Cain, and said, I have gotten a man from the Lord.

4:2 And she again bare his brother Abel. And Abel was a keeper of sheep, but Cain was a tiller of the ground.

4:3 And in process of time it came to pass, that Cain brought of the fruit of the ground an offering unto the Lord. *(Instruction on sacrifice of lesser self for Greater Self/emotional-perfunctory.)*

4:4 And Abel, he also brought of the firstlings of his flock and of the fat thereof. And the Lord had respect unto Abel and to his offering; *(Abel gives more of himself than Cain/heart action.)*

4:5 But unto Cain and to his offering he had not respect. And Cain was very wroth, and his countenance fell.

4:6 And the Lord said unto Cain, Why art thou wroth? and why is thy countenance fallen?

4:7 If thou doest well, shalt thou not be accepted? and if thou doest not well, sin lieth at the door. *[System of reward in initiation vs. karma.]* And unto thee shall be his desire, and thou shalt rule over him. *(Cain couldn't get past test of seven rays to enter test of secret rays.)*

4:8 And Cain talked with Abel his brother: and it came to pass, when they were in the field, that Cain rose up against Abel his brother, and slew him. *(Divine gratitude vs. human gratitude.)*

4:9 And the Lord said unto Cain, Where is Abel thy brother? And he said, I know not: Am I my brother's keeper? *(Divine justice vs. human justice.)*

4:10 And he said, What hast thou done? the voice of thy brother's blood crieth unto me from the ground. *(Reality.)*

4:11 And now art thou cursed from the earth, which hath opened her mouth to receive thy brother's blood from thy hand; *(Judgment by vision.)*

4:12 When thou tillest the ground, it shall not henceforth yield unto thee her strength; a fugitive and a vagabond shalt thou be in the earth. *(Karma.)*

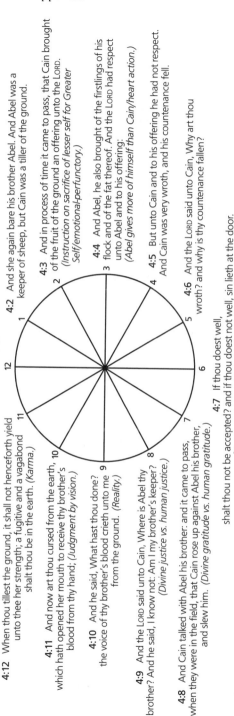

Fourth Ray

II

Genesis 4:13–24

Matter Sphere

4:13 And Cain said unto the LORD, My punishment is greater than I can bear.

4:14 Behold, thou hast driven me out this day from the face of the earth; and from thy face shall be hid *[Spirit and Matter]*; and I shall be a fugitive and a vagabond in the earth; and it shall come to pass, that every one that findeth me shall slay me.

4:15 And the LORD said unto him, Therefore whosoever slayeth Cain, vengeance shall be taken on him sevenfold. And the LORD set a mark upon Cain, lest any finding him should kill him.

4:16 And Cain went out from the presence of the LORD, and dwelt in the land of Nod, on the east of Eden.

4:17 And Cain knew his wife; and she conceived, and bare Enoch: and he builded a city, and called the name of the city, after the name of his son, Enoch.

4:18 And unto Enoch was born Irad: and Irad begat Mehujael: and Mehujael begat Methusael: and Methusael begat Lamech. *(Division of white fire core.)*

4:19 And Lamech took unto him two wives: the name of the one was Adah *[ornament, beauty]*, and the name of the other Zillah *[shadow]*.

4:20 And Adah bare Jabal: he was the father of such as dwell in tents, and of such as have cattle.

4:21 And his brother's name was Jubal: he was the father of all such as handle the harp and organ.

4:22 And Zillah, she also bare Tubal-cain, an instructor of every artificer in brass and iron: and the sister of Tubal-cain was Naamah.

4:23 And Lamech said unto his wives, Adah and Zillah, Hear my voice; ye wives of Lamech, hearken unto my speech: for I have slain a man to my wounding, and a young man to my hurt.

4:24 If Cain shall be avenged sevenfold, truly Lamech seventy and sevenfold.

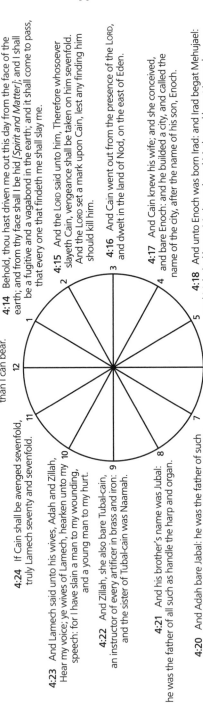

Fourth Ray
III
Genesis 4:25–26

4:25 And Adam knew his wife again; and she bare a son, and called his name Seth: For God, said she, hath appointed me another seed instead of Abel, whom Cain slew.

4:26 And to Seth, to him also there was born a son; and he called his name Enos: then began men to call upon the name of the LORD.

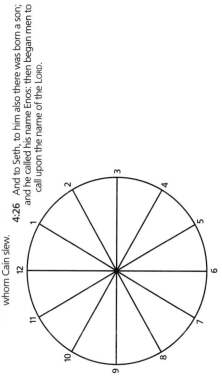

Vengeance of the Lord

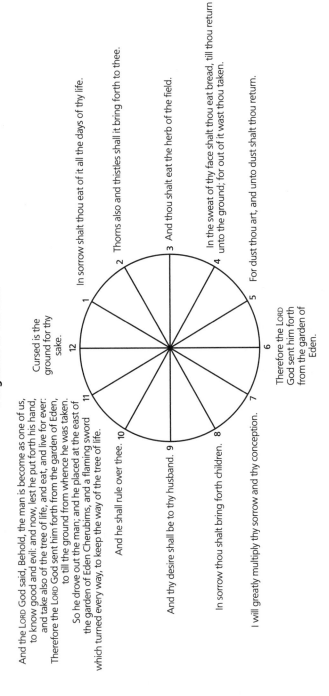

Cursed is the ground for thy sake.

In sorrow shalt thou eat of it all the days of thy life.

Thorns also and thistles shall it bring forth to thee.

And thou shalt eat the herb of the field.

In the sweat of thy face shalt thou eat bread, till thou return unto the ground; for out of it wast thou taken.

For dust thou art, and unto dust shalt thou return.

And the Lord God said, Behold, the man is become as one of us, to know good and evil: and now, lest he put forth his hand, and take also of the tree of life, and eat, and live for ever: Therefore the Lord God sent him forth from the garden of Eden, to till the ground from whence he was taken.

So he drove out the man; and he placed at the east of the garden of Eden Cherubims, and a flaming sword which turned every way, to keep the way of the tree of life.

And he shall rule over thee.

And thy desire shall be to thy husband.

In sorrow thou shalt bring forth children.

I will greatly multiply thy sorrow and thy conception.

Therefore the Lord God sent him forth from the garden of Eden.

Notes

Chapter 1 · Karma: The Law of Integration

1. According to the findings of James Churchward, archaeologist and author of *The Lost Continent of Mu,* the ancient Motherland was a continent in the Pacific made up of three areas of land. It extended from north of Hawaii three thousand miles south to Easter Island and the Fijis and stretched more than five thousand miles from east to west. Churchward's history of Mu (Lemuria) is based on records inscribed on sacred tablets he claims to have discovered in India. With the help of the high priest of an Indian temple, he deciphered the tablets. During fifty years of research he confirmed their contents in further writings, inscriptions and legends that he came upon in Southeast Asia, the Yucatan, Central America, the Pacific Islands, Mexico, North America, Egypt and elsewhere. He estimates that Mu was destroyed approximately twelve thousand years ago by the collapse of the gas chambers that upheld the continent. See James Churchward, *The Lost Continent of Mu* (1931; reprint, New York: Paperback Library Edition, 1968).

2. Gen. 1:1.

3. Lord Maitreya, *Pearls of Wisdom,* vol. 18, no. 49, December 7, 1975.

4. Gen. 1:3–5.
5. 1 Cor. 8:5–6.
6. John 1:3.
7. Gen. 1:27–28.
8. Isa. 55:11.
9. See Mark L. Prophet and Elizabeth Clare Prophet, *The Science of the Spoken Word* (Corwin Springs, Mont.: Summit University Press, 1991) and Elizabeth Clare Prophet, *The Creative Power of Sound: Affirmations to Create, Heal and Transform* (Corwin Springs, Mont.: Summit University Press, 1998).
10. 1 Cor. 15:53. Lord Maitreya, *Pearls of Wisdom*, vol. 18, no. 50, December 14, 1975.
11. Isa. 55:8.
12. Gen. 1:31.
13. Gen. 3:16–19.
14. Gen. 4:8.
15. Gen. 5.
16. Gen. 6:5, 8–14.
17. Gen. 7:4; Matt. 4:1–2.
18. In the ascent to perfection, the soul passes through what the sixteenth-century mystic Saint John of the Cross describes as the "dark night." The first dark night is experienced as one encounters the return of his personal karma—the human creation that almost completely obliterates for a time the light of the Christ Self and the I AM Presence.

    This "dark night of the soul" is in preparation for the dark night of the spirit, which involves the supreme test that Jesus faced on the cross when he cried out, "My God, my God, why hast thou forsaken me?" In this initiation, the soul seems completely cut off from the I AM Presence and the heavenly hierarchy. She must pass through the crucifixion and the resurrection, sustained solely by the light garnered in her own sacred heart, while holding the balance for planetary karma.

    John of the Cross writes in his work "The Dark Night": "This night ... causes two kinds of darkness or purgation in spiritual persons according to the two parts of the soul, the sensory and the spiritual. Hence the one night or purgation will be sensory, by which the senses are purged and accommodated to the spirit; and the other night or purgation will be spiritual, by which the spirit is purged and denuded as well as accommodated and prepared for union with God through love." Saint John writes of the initiation of the dark night of the spirit: "Since the divine extreme strikes in order to renew the soul and divinize it (by stripping it of the habitual affections and properties of the old man to which it is strongly united, attached, and conformed), it so disentangles and dissolves the spiritual substance—absorbing it in a profound darkness—that the soul at the sight of its miseries feels that it is melting away and being undone by a cruel spiritual death; it feels as if it were swallowed by a beast and being digested in the dark belly, and it suffers an anguish comparable to Jonas's when in the belly of the whale. It is fitting that the soul be in this sepulcher of dark death in order that it attain the spiritual resurrection for which it hopes." *The Collected Works of St. John of the Cross*, trans. Kieran Kavanaugh and Otilio Rodriguez (Washington, D.C.: ICS Publications, 1979), pp. 311, 337.

19. Archeia Amethyst, "The Initiation of the Judgment," *Pearls of Wisdom*, vol. 18, no. 48, November 30, 1975; also published in Elizabeth Clare Prophet, *Vials of the Seven Last Plagues* (Corwin Springs, Mont.: Summit University Press, 1980), pp. 101–109.

20. 1 Cor. 15:55–57.

21. Rev. 15:6–7.

22. Rev. 4:4.

23. Rev. 4:5; 5:6. Matt. 5:18.

24. The Dark Cycle is a period when mankind's negative karma of the last 25,800 years is returning. This karma was held in abeyance for centuries under the great mercy of the Law through God's Sons incarnate (e.g., Jesus Christ and other avatars). It is being released for balance in this period of transition into the Aquarian cycle, according to the cycles of the initiations of the solar hierarchies. Each year one of the twelve

solar hierarchies releases the light whereby mankind may redeem the energies misused in past cycles when they have failed the initiations of that particular hierarchy.

The Dark Cycle began on April 23, 1969, under the hierarchy of Capricorn. Each year on April 23 it enters a new hierarchy, proceeding in order around the Cosmic Clock. The Dark Cycle continues until April 22, 2002. In this period, the Law requires that mankind deal directly with this negative karma. In the face of mankind's propensity for darkness, the Lords of Karma decreed this action in order to deter an even greater abuse of Life's opportunity and to forestall that cataclysm which may be the ultimate consequence of the rising tide of world sin.

25. Archangel Michael, "The Judgment of the Fallen Ones," *Pearls of Wisdom,* vol. 18, no. 35, August 31, 1975; also published in Prophet, *Vials,* pp. 2–7.

26. Gen. 1:3.

27. Lucifer, from Latin *luc-, lux* "light" + *-fer,* from *ferre* "to bear, carry": one who bears light. Isa. 14:12.

28. 2 Thess. 2:11–12.

29. Matt. 13:24–30, 36–43.

30. Matt. 12:34; 23:33. Matt. 22:18; 23:13–39. John 8:44.

31. Eph. 6:10–18.

32. Luke 3:7–18.

33. Great Divine Director, "Non-Man," *Pearls of Wisdom,* vol. 8, no. 16, April 18, 1965; also published in Mark L. Prophet, *The Soulless One* (Corwin Springs, Mont.: Summit University Press, 1981), pp. 109–118.

34. John 8:44.

35. Gen. 4:1.

36. Gal. 6:7.

37. Sanat Kumara, *Pearls of Wisdom,* vol. 42, no. 2, January 10, 1999.

38. Gen. 4:6–7.

39. Gen. 3:4.

40. Gen. 3:21.

41. Gen. 4:12.
42. Prov. 16:25.
43. Rev. 13:1, 11, 16–17.
44. Rev. 12:10.
45. Rev. 8:4. Archangel Michael, "Judgment of the Fallen Ones."
46. Rev. 15:3–4.
47. Eph. 6:11. Exod. 32:7–8; Num. 21:8–9.
48. Archeia Faith, "The Judgment of the Dweller-on-the-Threshold," *Pearls of Wisdom,* vol. 18, no. 36, September 7, 1975; also published in Prophet, *Vials,* pp. 8–14. See also Alpha, "The Judgment: The Sealing of the Lifewaves throughout the Galaxy," in Elizabeth Clare Prophet, *The Great White Brotherhood in the Culture, History and Religion of America* (Corwin Springs, Mont.: Summit University Press, 1987), pp. 231–37.
49. Exod. 20:5; Deut. 5:9.
50. *sin* [Spanish, fr. Latin *sine*]: without.
51. Ps. 136.
52. Gautama Buddha, *Pearls of Wisdom,* vol. 28, no. 25, June 23, 1985.
53. Rev. 12: 5. Jer. 17:1.
54. One such instance was the Declaration of the Rights of Man and Citizen, drafted in 1789 and forming the preamble to the French constitution of 1791.
55. The Messengers have given teachings on several occasions explaining the esoteric basis of the divine right of kings. The following compilation is excerpted from these lectures:

   In earliest times, when kings ruled the earth, they ruled by divine right. In Lemuria and Atlantis, the kings who had the divine right sat on the throne because they were Ascended Masters. They were not corrupted, nor were they corruptible men. All they would do was administer cosmic justice. In fact, these Masters were one with God. They were an incarnation of God, as we all are supposed to be.

   We hear of kings referring to "mon droit" (my right). But their right was often misunderstood by those who thought that they meant "It is my right to rule." It was not understood that the divine right of the king derived from God, who had appointed him to act as the ruler. His rulership was not intended to be a dictatorial power but an opportunity to serve the needs of his people, to rule wisely. Thus Solomon in his glory ruled the children of Israel and brought forth a great kingdom. Nevertheless, the kingdom that is within ourselves is greater than any other, because he that can keep himself is greater than he that can keep a city.

In spiritual matters, authority is not derived from the consent of the governed but from on high. And in spiritual orders, the lesser have always submitted to the rule of the greater. This is the concept of hierarchy and it is the divine right of spiritual initiation, which gives to mankind the rulership of many things when he is faithful in a few. Authority cannot be conferred upon those who do not first give obedience to the very authority they seek. For there is no other power but God, and his mandates are also our Law.

Thus God conferred the divine right to rule upon the ancient kings. They were individuals who had progressed in hierarchy to a position that allowed them to hold a certain balance for their people. But they needed to be able to anchor God's power on earth. Therefore the violet flame was given to them.

The violet flame was not revealed to the churches, but it was revealed in part to the kings of the earth as a very secret ritual by the great Masters. They recognized in the divine right of kings the ability to confer upon the kingdom a special blessing. The kings did not invoke the violet flame. They knew of its power to a degree, but they were not conscious of it outwardly. They didn't have the same knowledge that the Brotherhood has released today. But being imbued with the violet flame was one of the secrets of the kings, and that is why they wore the royal purple. And the "magicians" of the courts were actually initiates in the Great White Brotherhood who protected the divine right of kings.

This institution of God's divine government on earth has

served us through the millennia. It has taken us through golden ages. It was God's intent that it should continue into modern times. America was intended to be based on such a tradition, where the highest initiates would be in positions of leadership. Saint Germain sponsored her first president, George Washington (an embodiment of the Ascended Master Godfre). On the inner, America began with this archetype: the embodiment of the Law and the Lawgiver. The office of the president reflected Washington's personality, his divine character, all that he stood for. Much of America's government came forth from his sacred heart and from his Buddhic initiation.

But America was to have a wholly new government, divested of the rule of kings. By claiming their inheritance as sons of God and accepting this salvation of the Son of God (the elevation of the Real Self within their temples), the people would be anointed with the original divine right of self-rule. And thereby the government of the United States of America—of the people, by the people, for the people—would in reality be upon the shoulders of the Christ Self of every man, woman and child. The Constitution of the United States is a divine document guaranteeing the path of individual initiation of the disciples of the Ascended Masters.

Thus government in America is based upon the rule of law, which has come down to us through the tradition of English common law. In this tradition, it is believed that judges and lawmakers do not make law—they only discover preexisting rules and principles and apply them to the controversy at hand.

It is intended that judges and rulers be oracles in touch with that mysterious presence, the Law, which has an independent existence and about which we may know very little. The divination of the law comes about when individuals attune to the inner blueprint of life, the geometry of cosmos, and the state of justice between existing social bodies, political bodies, worlds. It is the sense of how people must interact in order to preserve a human society.

Our leaders are supposed to be sitting in this seat of the

intermediary between the Law of the mighty I AM Presence and the people, who must function under the law in the midst of human circumstances. So above all, our leaders are meant to be Christed ones.

But today, few elected officials or appointed bureaucrats embody the Christ and the Holy Spirit. With the omission of the Holy Spirit embodied in people, no form of government will work. A divine document, such as the U.S. Constitution, is not sufficient. God-government demands people who attune with the origin of the divine document and recognize the progressive order of hierarchy in the unfoldment of life on earth.

Every man must raise up the Christ flame. Every man must be where he is the *k*ey to the *in*carnation of *G*od (the *king*). And he must be that key to all those serving under him. Saint Germain knew that that was the only way that the fallen ones would be outsmarted. He created a form of government in America whereby all could rise and one by one on the scale of hierarchy assume their rightful place in the position of shepherd to the people.

Whoever holds the power of the Holy Spirit becomes paramount, because the Holy Spirit is the power by which a nation stays together. It is the cohesive power of love. It is the moving, living Spirit of the mighty I AM Presence, of YAHWEH, of the God of Israel, of all that is real in our midst. That moving Spirit is the mainstream of our identity and reality. It is the means whereby we are one in consciousness and in attitude. It is the sense that allows a group of people to know what is right and to do what is right, interpreting the Law according to The LORD Our Righteousness.

This sense of right with which we are endowed comes from the Father and the Son, and it is conveyed by the Holy Spirit. It is the power of the people. It is not gained through revolutions. The power of the people is gained by the enlightenment of the indwelling God Presence.

The heart of fire that beats in the breast of all of us is the power to overthrow tyrants, to displace them by the Christ consciousness. Study the histories of the nations. Study the abuses of power and the bloodbaths that have ensued. Then find an era that has maintained peace, and you will find one that has raised up the Christ consciousness. Only in America has there been the opportunity in the past two centuries to bring about such an era. But we are losing it swiftly. Civilizations will fall, continents will sink if this power is not raised up.

No other revolution counts—not the American Revolution, not the French Revolution, not the Russian Revolution, not the seemingly endless rounds of political upheaval—save the revolution which is the determination to be the Christ.

Sources:

- Instruction by Mark Prophet, September 15, 1963
- Comments from Mark Prophet, September 13, 1964
- Mark Prophet, Sunday morning service, May 1, 1966
- Elizabeth Clare Prophet, "Jesus of Nazareth, the King of the Jews—Vigil on Golgotha," April 8, 1977
- Elizabeth Clare Prophet, "Independence Day Address," July 4, 1980
- Elizabeth Clare Prophet, "On the Sense of Justice," December 1, 1980

56. Prov. 29:18.
57. Rev. 15:2.
58. Rev. 16:3.
59. Ps. 23:4.
60. John 9:39.
61. Prov. 16:22. Gen. 2:6.
62. Ezek. 1:4.
63. There are fourteen scenes of the last hours of Jesus' life that represent his mastery and sacrifice on behalf of mankind. They are called the fourteen stations of the cross and signify the initiation of the crucifixion, which is passed both on an individual and planetary basis, according to the law of cycles. First station: Jesus is condemned to death; second station: Jesus is made to bear his cross; third station: Jesus falls the first time; fourth station: Jesus meets his afflicted mother; fifth station:

Simon the Cyrenian helps Jesus; sixth station: Veronica wipes
the face of Jesus; seventh station: Jesus falls the second time;
eighth station: Jesus consoles the holy women; ninth station:
Jesus falls the third time; tenth station: Jesus is stripped of his
garments; eleventh station: Jesus is nailed to the cross; twelfth
station: Jesus dies on the cross; thirteenth station: Jesus is taken
down from the cross; fourteenth station: Jesus is laid in the
sepulchre.

64. Acts 2:3. Rev. 13:10.
65. Rev. 13:10.
66. Matt. 7:15.
67. See Elohim Apollo, "An Increment of Light from the Holy
    Kumaras," given July 6, 1975, published in Prophet, *Great
    White Brotherhood,* pp. 269–73.
68. Prov. 1:7.
69. Here "river of life" refers to mankind's misqualification of the
    pure energies that flow from the I AM Presence over the crys-
    tal cord to the lifestream, or soul, evolving in Matter.
70. John 2:13–16. Archangel Jophiel, "The Judgment of Mankind's
    Perversion of the Wisdom of the Mother," *Pearls of Wisdom,*
    vol. 18, no. 37, September 14, 1975; also published in Prophet,
    Vials, pp. 16–21.
71. Matt. 22:37.
72. Rev. 3:20.
73. Rev. 3:1.
74. Rev. 16:16.
75. Archeia Christine, "Ratify and Confirm the Judgment within
    Your Own Being," *Pearls of Wisdom,* vol. 18, no. 38, Septem-
    ber 21, 1975; also published in Prophet, *Vials,* pp. 22–28.
76. 1 Cor. 2:7.
77. Helios and Vesta are the twin flames who maintain the focus of
    the sun at the center of our solar system.
78. Gen. 2:21.
79. Ps. 121:8.
80. Gen. 6:3. Archeia Christine, "Ratify and Confirm the Judgment."
81. Ps. 2:9.

82. Ps. 2:1, 3–8.
83. On April 16, 1975, Lucifer was bound by Archangel Michael and taken to the Court of the Sacred Fire on Sirius, where he stood trial before the Four and Twenty Elders over a period of ten days. The testimony of many souls of light in embodiment on Terra and other planets and systems in the galaxy were heard, together with that of the Ascended Masters, Archangels and Elohim. On April 26, 1975, he was found guilty of total rebellion against Almighty God by the unanimous vote of the Twenty-four and sentenced to the second death. As he stood on the disc of the sacred fire before the court, the flame of Alpha and Omega rose as a spiral of intense white light, canceling out an identity and a consciousness that had influenced the fall of one-third of the angels of the galaxy and countless lifewaves evolving in this and other systems of worlds.
84. Alpha, "The Judgment," in Prophet, *Great White Brotherhood,* pp. 231–37; quoted in Archeia Christine, "Ratify and Confirm the Judgment."
85. Archeia Christine, "Ratify and Confirm the Judgment."
86. For further teachings on Serpent, see Sanat Kumara, *Pearls of Wisdom,* vol. 22, no. 45, November 11, 1979.
87. Gen. 3:1.
88. 2 Cor. 11:14. In 1968 Satan was bound by Archangel Michael. Thus the prophecy of Revelation 20:2–3 was fulfilled: "And [the angel] laid hold on the dragon, that old serpent, which is the Devil, and Satan, and bound him a thousand years, and cast him into the bottomless pit, and shut him up, and set a seal upon him, that he should deceive the nations no more, till the thousand years should be fulfilled: and after that he must be loosed a little season." But Satan was not content to languish in his jail cell for a thousand years. Consequently, he has already undergone his final judgment and second death.

On February 1, 1982, Jesus announced: "The Word has gone forth on Wednesday past, in the very triumph and the hour of the twenty-seventh, for the remanding to the Court of the Sacred Fire of the one you have known for so long as

Satan. Blessed hearts, some of you who are our disciples worldwide have known that many years ago, in answer to the call of our Messengers when both were embodied together, Satan was bound and his power reduced. Therefore, for the continuation of the flaunting of the law of the Person of the Messenger, of the Person of the lightbearers, our Father sent forth the call to me to activate on that very evening the action of the call that would be for the judgment of that Fallen One. Therefore, let it be known that the remanding of Satan to that court, where the Lord Sanat Kumara presides in the presence of the Four and Twenty Elders, has resulted in his final judgment. Therefore rejoice, O ye heavens and the earth! For that power of Satan is bound, and that Fallen One is judged and will no more go forth among the inhabitants of this or any other world to tempt them against the Person of the Lord Christ!" See Jesus Christ, *Pearls of Wisdom,* vol. 25, no. 16, April 18, 1982.

89. Gen. 3:1–5.
90. John 1:14.
91. Ps. 8:5.
92. Gen. 3:6.
93. Gen. 3:7–10.
94. Matt. 14:30.
95. Gen. 2:23.
96. Gen. 3:11–13.
97. Gen. 2:18.
98. Gen. 2:24. Matt. 19:6.
99. Gal. 6:2, 5.
100. Gen. 3:14–15.
101. Ps. 90:10.
102. Rom. 8:7.
103. Phil. 2:5.
104. Gen. 3:16.
105. Rev. 3:10–11.
106. Rev. 12:1.
107. Gen. 3:19.

108. Matt. 22:2–14.
109. John 10:10.
110. Gen. 2:24.
111. John 1:14.
112. Ps. 104:4.
113. Gal. 6:7.
114. Rev. 4:8.
115. Dan. 5:25, 27.
116. Acts 17:23.
117. Isa. 55:11.
118. John 8:58.
119. Gen. 3:17–19, 23.
120. John 4:32. Matt. 4:4.
121. Matt. 26:29.
122. Matt. 5:18. Matt. 6:34.
123. John 14:16. John 8:12.
124. Jer. 31:33–34.
125. Gen. 4:26.
126. Joel 2:28–32.
127. Gen. 2:8.
128. Matt. 26:52.
129. Matt. 18:6. Matt. 11:12.
130. John 14:15.
131. Gen. 3:24.
132. Phil. 2:5.
133. Ps. 51:5.
134. Judg. 2:1–4.
135. 2 Cor. 6:14.
136. Rev. 21:16.
137. Judg. 2:10–13, 16–17.
138. Judg. 2:19–22; 3:1, 3–7.
139. Isa. 1:18.
140. "America" is an anagram for "I AM race."
141. Exod. 3:13–15.
142. Exod. 7:16.
143. Gen. 22:17; 26:4; Heb. 11:12.

144. Djwal Kul, "The Flame of Freedom in the Aquarian Cycle," *Pearls of Wisdom*, vol. 17, no. 45, November 10, 1974; also published in Kuthumi and Djwal Kul, *The Human Aura* (Corwin Springs, Mont.: Summit University Press, 1996), pp. 246–57.

145. Matt. 15:24.

146. Rev. 14:6.

147. Matt. 15:21–28.

148. Matt. 15:31.

149. Gen. 6:5.

150. Luke 24:32.

151. Luke 21:26.

152. Rev. 16:4.

153. Rev. 16: 5–7. Archangel Chamuel, "The Judgment of Mankind's Perversion of the Fires of Creativity," *Pearls of Wisdom*, vol. 18, no. 39, September 28, 1975; also published in Prophet, *Vials*, pp. 30–35.

154. Archangel Chamuel, "Judgment of Mankind's Perversion."

155. Ibid.

156. Matt. 28:18.

157. While Jesus was on the cross, he was offered wine mingled with myrrh to allay his pain.

158. Ps. 100:1–2.

159. John 1:5.

160. Exod. 7–12.

161. Isa. 53:3.

162. Rev. 19:7–9. Archangel Chamuel, "Judgment of Mankind's Perversion."

163. 1 Pet. 5:8.

164. Rev. 12:9.

165. Rev. 20:3. Eph. 6:12.

166. Gen. 19:24–25.

167. Matt. 24:15; Dan. 9:27; 11:31; 12:11.

168. Matt. 22:13. Archangel Chamuel, "Judgment of Mankind's Perversion."

169. Matt. 24:28. Rev. 12:4.

170. Rev. 17:1; 19:2.

171. Sanskrit terms for currents of wisdom, power and love emanating from the white fire core of the base-of-the-spine chakra, which flow in and around the spinal altar.

172. Isa. 54:5. Luke 1:38. Rev. 21:2, 9–10.

173. 1 Sam. 4:3; Heb. 9:4–5.

174. Gen. 11:1–9.

175. Archeia Charity, "The Fire of Love Descending to Implement the Judgment," *Pearls of Wisdom,* vol. 18, no. 40, October 5, 1975; also published in Prophet, *Vials,* pp. 36–41.

176. Matt. 7:14. John 14:2.

177. Luke 2:34.

178. See chapter 1, note 24.

179. Gospel of the Birth of Mary 2:1–3:7, in *The Lost Books of the Bible and the Forgotten Books of Eden* (1926, 1927; reprint, New York: World Publishing, Meridian, 1963).

180. Luke 1:11–20. Luke 1:26–38.

181. 1 Cor. 15:52–53. Archangel Gabriel, "The Judgment of the Sun," *Pearls of Wisdom,* vol. 18, no. 41, October 12, 1975; also published in Prophet, *Vials,* pp. 44–50.

182. Zech. 14:20. Teaching on pages 183–86 is based on a sermon by Elizabeth Clare Prophet given on February 22, 1981.

183. Exod. 13:21.

184. 1 Cor. 15:54–57. Archangel Gabriel, "Judgment of the Sun."

185. Matt. 24:15.

186. Rev. 16:8–9.

187. Exod. 14:13. Ezek. 33:11.

188. Exod. 19:16.

189. 2 Cor. 6:14.

190. Matt. 10:6.

191. Archangel Gabriel, "Judgment of the Sun."

192. Luke 9:62.

193. Rev. 6:16–17.

194. Phil. 3:14.

195. Mary has told us that she does not want us to think of ourselves as sinners, but as sons and daughters of God. She has given us this New Age version of the Hail Mary:

Hail, Mary, full of grace.
The Lord is with thee.
Blessed art thou among women
    and blessed is the fruit of thy womb, Jesus.
Holy Mary, Mother of God,
Pray for us, sons and daughters of God,
Now and at the hour of our victory
Over sin, disease and death.

196. Eccles. 3:1–4.

197. DECREE TO BELOVED SURYA

Beloved mighty victorious Presence of God, I AM in me, my very own beloved Holy Christ Self, Holy Christ Selves of all mankind, beloved Surya, legions of white fire and blue lightning from Sirius, beloved Lanello, the entire Spirit of the Great White Brotherhood and the World Mother, elemental life—fire, air, water and earth! In thy name, by and through the magnetic power of the immortal, victorious threefold flame of Truth within my heart and the heart of God in the Great Central Sun, I decree:

1. Out from the sun flow thy dazzling bright
   Blue-flame ribbons of flashing diamond light!
   Serene and pure is thy love,
   Holy radiance from God above!

Refrain: Come, come, come, Surya dear,
   By thy flame dissolve all fear;
   Give to each one security
   In the bonds of purity;
   Flash and flash thy flame through me,
   Make and keep me ever free!

2. Surya dear, beloved one
   From the mighty Central Sun,
   In God's name to thee we call:
   Take dominion over all!

3. Out from the heart of God you come,
   Serving to make us now all one—
   Wisdom and honor do you bring,
   Making the very soul to sing!

4. Surya dear, beloved one,
   From our faith then now is spun
   Victory's garment of invincible gold,
   Our soul's great triumph to ever uphold!

And in full faith I consciously accept this manifest, manifest, manifest! (3x) right here and now with full power, eternally sustained, all-powerfully active, ever expanding and world enfolding until all are wholly ascended in the light and free! Beloved I AM! Beloved I AM! Beloved I AM!

198. Rom. 3:8.
199. Prov. 16:25.
200. Mal. 4:2.
201. Exod. 11:4–5; 14:13–31.
202. Job 9:10–12. Archeia Hope, "Deliverance from the Harshness of the Judgment," *Pearls of Wisdom,* vol. 18, no. 42, October 19, 1975; also published in Prophet, *Vials,* pp. 51–56.
203. Rom. 8:7.
204. Gen. 19:26.
205. 2 Cor. 6:17.
206. Josh. 24:15.
207. Rev. 16:10–11.
208. See chapter 1, note 88.
209. John 10:11. Mark 14:32–42. See also John 17.
210. John 8:32. Matt. 24:6.
211. Matt. 8:20.
212. Ps. 139:7–10.
213. Archangel Uriel, "The Judgment of Abortion and the Abortionist," March 10, 1974; see *Exhortations out of the Ark of the Covenant,* no. 3, published by The Summit Lighthouse.
214. Josh. 10:12–14.
215. Archangel Raphael, "The Judgment of the Carnal Mind as the

Seat of Authority in Mater," *Pearls of Wisdom,* vol. 18, no. 43, October 26, 1975; also published in Prophet, *Vials,* pp. 58–64.

216. John 1:14. The experiences of Mary's soul on earth are recounted by Mark and Elizabeth Prophet in *My Soul Doth Magnify the Lord* (Corwin Springs, Mont.: Summit University Press, 1986), pp. 25–39.

217. Luke 2:35.

218. 2 Pet. 1:10.

219. Heb. 10:9.

220. James 2:19.

221. Archeia Mary, "The Chemicalization of Truth Which the Judgment Brings," *Pearls of Wisdom,* vol. 18, no. 44, November 2, 1975; also published in Prophet, *Vials,* pp. 65–73.

222. Matt. 2:16–18.

223. Matt. 2:13.

224. Archeia Mary, "Chemicalization of Truth."

225. Matt. 17:2. Archeia Mary, "Chemicalization of Truth."

226. Archeia Mary, "Chemicalization of Truth."

227. Lord Maitreya, "Integration with God," *Pearls of Wisdom,* vol. 18, no. 50, December 14, 1975.

228. Gen. 2:16–17.

229. Gen. 3:4. Earlier in the text, the authors indicate that mankind fell from the level of the Christ consciousness before Adam and Eve failed their test in Eden. Here, Archangel Uriel may be referring to Adam and Eve as archetypes for the fall of the fourth root race—ED.

230. John 15:5. John 6:53.

231. Gen. 3:24. Archangel Uriel, "The Judgment of the Pollution of the Sacred Mother Flow," *Pearls of Wisdom,* vol. 18, no. 45, November 9, 1975; also published in Prophet, *Vials,* pp. 76–84.

232. Acts 17:28.

233. 1 Cor. 15:53. Lord Maitreya, "Integration with God."

234. Exod. 34:15. Mic. 4:4. Jon. 4:6. Acts 9:5. Luke 21:28. Job 19:25.

235. Gen. 2:10–14.

236. Gen. 3:19. Archangel Uriel, "Judgment of Pollution of Mother Flow."
237. Rev. 16:12.
238. Rev. 18:2.
239. Rev. 17:3–6, 15.
240. Gen. 3:8.
241. Matt. 22:11–12.
242. Rev. 3:17–18.
243. Rev. 3:14–16. Archangel Uriel, "Judgment of Pollution of Mother Flow."
244. Matt. 27:51–53.
245. Lord Maitreya, "Integration with God."
246. Luke 19:40.
247. Rev. 16:15.
248. Ps. 91:1. Archangel Uriel, "Judgment of Pollution of Mother Flow."
249. Rom. 3:23.
250. John 7:33–34.
251. Mark 14:3. John 12:7.
252. Matt. 27:1–2. Luke 22:53. Matt. 7:1. Matt. 27:14.
253. Rev. 5:5. John 13:27.
254. Luke 2:35. Matt. 12:37. Rev. 20:13.
255. Eph. 6:16.
256. Matt. 16:21–23.
257. Mark 8:34.
258. Luke 23:27–28. Matt. 27:38–44.
259. John 18:11. Matt. 26:53.
260. John 12:32.
261. Mark Prophet, ascended.
262. Matt. 24:10; 26:56. Matt. 24:9. Matt. 26:75.
263. Matt. 26:27. Luke 22:42. Matt. 27:34.
264. Jer. 9:13–16.
265. Luke 23:34. Matt. 27:25.
266. Rev. 13:8.
267. Archeia Aurora, "Now Is the Judgment of This World," *Pearls of Wisdom*, vol. 18, no. 46, November 16, 1975; also pub-

lished in Prophet, *Vials,* pp. 85–92.

268. Rev. 16:17–18.
269. Rev. 22:1. Eph. 5:26.
270. Rev. 20:12, 15. 2 Tim. 4:7.
271. 2 Kings 5:1–19.
272. Matt. 4:8–9.
273. 2 Kings 5:20–27.
274. Rev. 16:13.
275. Archangel Zadkiel, "The Joy of Judgment in the Flame of Transmutation," *Pearls of Wisdom,* vol. 18, no. 47, November 23, 1975; also published in Prophet, *Vials,* pp. 94–100.
276. 1 Cor. 3:13.
277. Rev. 19:6.
278. Archeia Amethyst, "The Initiation of the Judgment," *Pearls of Wisdom,* vol. 18, no. 48, November 30, 1975; also published in Prophet, *Vials,* pp. 101–109.

Chapter 2 · Reembodiment

1.   See Elizabeth Clare Prophet with Erin L. Prophet, *Reincarnation: The Missing Link in Christianity* (Corwin Springs, Mont.: Summit University Press, 1997) for a detailed discussion of how the doctrine of reembodiment was removed from the teachings of the Christian church.

2.   Saint Germain, "A Trilogy on the Threefold Flame of Life," in Mark L. Prophet and Elizabeth Clare Prophet, *Saint Germain On Alchemy* (Corwin Springs, Mont.: Summit University Press, 1993), pp. 287, 290.

3.   John 8:58. Casimir Poseidon, in *Keepers of the Flame Lessons,* no. 18, pp. 19–25.

4.   Ezek. 33:11.

5.   Kahlil Gibran, *The Prophet* (1923; reprint, New York: Alfred A. Knopf, 1964), p. 103.

6.   Matt. 7:14.

7.   The authors may have been referring to the thousand years following the sixth century, when the Church rejected the

concept of reincarnation as taught by Origen. See Elizabeth Clare Prophet with Erin L. Prophet, *Reincarnation,* pp. 215–23.—Ed.

8. Matt. 11:7–15; 17:10–13.
9. Jesus, *Pearls of Wisdom,* vol. 11, no. 34, August 25, 1968.
10. 1 Cor. 6:19.
11. 1 Cor. 15:31. Eph. 4:22–24.
12. 1 Cor. 15:41. Luke 19:12–27.
13. Prov. 22:6.
14. Jesus and Kuthumi, in *Keepers of the Flame Lessons,* no. 18, pp. 7–12.
15. It is true, however, that elementals who excel in their service can graduate to the human kingdom and receive a threefold flame. For instance, Archangel Michael was once an elemental. But he bridged the gap, came through the human kingdom and then graduated to the angelic kingdom. He attained greater and greater mastery there and finally became an Archangel.

   Mark L. Prophet was embodied as the Church father Origen. On November 29, 1981, Elizabeth Clare Prophet gave the following comments on Origen's theory on the transmigration of souls, as outlined in his *De Principiis (First Principles):* "It's very interesting that Mark Prophet rejected the idea of transmigration of souls into animal bodies. And yet I could feel his flame in this teaching. The resolution of that seeming conflict is . . . that the son of God who retains the Logos and the Word cannot enter the animal body, and therefore, there is no transmigration of souls in general, as the Hindus teach, by the sons of God. But forcefields—for want of a better word for an individual minus God-consciousness—forcefields tend to converge in Matter at the point of like attracting like. Sometimes we see in cartoons individuals who are human given characteristics of the fox or the pig or the wolf, and we meet people who are very animal-like in their attitudes to life. That flesh, that substance, that mortal coil might go to its own level. It might go to the lowest common denominator of its vibratory frequency. . . . It could mesh with a wild beast or an animal

form and there continue to experience life at a lower level....
So I leave you to draw your own conclusions concerning this."
16. God Meru, *Pearls of Wisdom,* vol. 11, no. 42.
17. John 4:24.
18. Rev. 22:2.
19. John 16:24. Ps. 23:5.

Glossary

Terms set in italics are defined elsewhere in the glossary.

Akashic records. All that transpires in an individual's world is recorded in a substance and dimension known as akasha (Sanskrit, from the root *kāś* 'to be visible, appear,' 'to shine brightly,' 'to see clearly'). Akasha is primary substance, the subtlest, ethereal essence that fills the whole of space—"etheric" energy vibrating at a certain frequency so as to absorb or record all of the impressions of life. These records can be read by adepts or those whose soul (psychic) faculties are developed.

Alpha and Omega. The divine wholeness of the Father-Mother God affirmed as "the beginning and the ending" by the Lord Christ in Revelation. Ascended *twin flames* of the *Cosmic Christ* consciousness, who hold the balance of the masculine/feminine polarity of the Godhead in the *Great Central Sun* of cosmos. Thus through the *Universal Christ,* the Word incarnate, the Father is the origin and the Mother is the fulfillment of the cycles of God's consciousness expressed throughout the *Spirit/Matter* creation. *See also* Mother. (Rev. 1:8, 11; 21:6; 22:13)

Ancient of Days. *See* Sanat Kumara.

Antahkarana. (Skt. for 'internal sense organ.') The web of life. The net of light spanning *Spirit* and *Matter,* connecting and sensitizing the whole of creation within itself and to the heart of God.

Ascended Master. One who, through Christ and the putting on of that Mind which was in Christ Jesus, has mastered time and space and in the process gained the mastery of the self in the *four lower bodies* and the four quadrants of *Matter,* in the chakras and the balanced *threefold flame.* An Ascended Master has also transmuted at least 51 percent of his karma, fulfilled his divine plan and taken the initiations of the ruby ray unto the ritual of the *ascension*—acceleration by the *sacred fire* into the Presence of the I AM THAT I AM (the *I AM Presence*). Ascended Masters inhabit the planes of *Spirit*—the kingdom of God (God's consciousness)—and may teach unascended souls in an *etheric temple* or in the cities on the *etheric plane* (the kingdom of heaven).

Ascension. The ritual whereby the soul reunites with the *Spirit* of the living God, the *I AM Presence.* The ascension is the culmination of the soul's God-victorious sojourn in time and space. It is the reward of the righteous that is the gift of God after the last judgment before the great white throne, in which each man is judged according to his works.

The ascension was experienced by Enoch, of whom it is written that he "walked with God; and he was not, for God took him"; by Elijah, who went up by a whirlwind into heaven; and by Jesus. Scripture records that Jesus was taken up by a cloud into heaven. This is commonly referred to as Jesus' ascension. However, the *Ascended Master* El Morya has revealed that Jesus lived many years after this event and made his ascension after his passing in Kashmir at the age of 81.

The reunion with God in the ascension, signifying the end of the rounds of karma and rebirth and the return to the LORD's glory, is the goal of life for the sons and daughters of God. Jesus said, "No man hath ascended up to heaven but he that came down from heaven, even the Son of man."

By her salvation ("Self-elevation"), the conscious raising up of the Son of God within her temple, the soul puts on her wedding garment to fulfill the office of the Son (sun, or light) of manifestation. Following the initiatic path of Jesus, the soul is made worthy by his grace to be the bearer of his cross and his crown. She ascends through the *Christ Self* to her LORD, the I AM Presence, whence she descended. (Rev. 20:12–13; Gen. 5:24; 2 Kings 2:11; Luke 24:50–51; Acts 1:9–11; John 3:13)

Astral plane. A frequency of time and space beyond the physical yet below the mental, corresponding with the emotional body of man and the collective unconscious of the race. It is the repository of the collective thought/feeling patterns, conscious and unconscious, of mankind. The pristine purpose of this plane is the amplification of the pure thoughts and feelings of God in man. Instead it has been polluted with the impure records and vibrations of the race memory. *See also* Four lower bodies.

Body elemental. A being of nature (ordinarily invisible and functioning unnoticed in the physical octave) that serves the soul from the moment of its first incarnation in the planes of *Matter* to tend the physical body. The body elemental is about three feet high and resembles the individual whom he or she serves. Working with the guardian angel under the regenerative *Christ Self*, the body elemental is the unseen friend and helper of man. *See also* Elementals.

Causal Body. The body of First Cause; seven concentric spheres of light and consciousness surrounding the *I AM Presence* in the planes of *Spirit*, whose momentums, added to by the Good—the LORD's Word and Works manifested by the soul in all past lives— are accessible today, moment by moment as we need them.

One's spiritual resources and creativity—talents, graces, gifts and genius, garnered through exemplary service on the *seven rays*—may be drawn forth from the Causal Body through invocation made to the I AM Presence in the name of the *Christ Self*.

The Causal Body is the storehouse of every good and perfect thing that is a part of our true identity. In addition, the great spheres of the Causal Body are the dwelling place of the Most High God to which Jesus referred when he said, "In my Father's house are many mansions.... I go to prepare a place for you.... I will come again and receive you unto myself; that where I AM [where I, the incarnate Christ, AM in the I AM Presence], there ye may be also."

The Causal Body is the mansion, or habitation, of the Spirit of the I AM THAT I AM to which the soul returns through Christ Jesus and the individual Christ Self in the ritual of the *ascension.* The apostle Paul was referring to the Causal Body as the star of each man's individualization of the God Flame when he said, "One star differeth from another star in glory." *See also* Chart of Your Divine Self; color illustration facing page 182. (Matt. 6:19–21; John 14:2–3; 1 Cor. 15:41)

Chart of Your Divine Self. (See color illustration facing page 182.) There are three figures represented in the chart, which we will refer to as the upper figure, the middle figure and the lower figure. The upper figure is the *I AM Presence,* the I AM THAT I AM, God individualized for each of his sons and daughters. The Divine Monad consists of the I AM Presence surrounded by the spheres (rings of color, of light) that comprise the *Causal Body.* This is the body of First Cause, which contains man's "treasure laid up in heaven"—perfect works, perfect thoughts and feelings, perfect words—energies that have ascended from the plane of action in time and space as the result of man's correct exercise of free will and his correct qualification of the stream of life that issues forth from the heart of the Presence and descends to the level of the *Christ Self.*

The middle figure in the chart is the mediator between God and man, called the Christ Self, the Real Self, or the Christ consciousness. It has also been referred to as the Higher Mental Body or Higher Consciousness. The Christ Self overshadows the lower self, which consists of the soul evolving through the four planes of *Matter* in the *four lower bodies* corresponding to the planes of fire, air, water and earth; that is, the etheric body, the mental body, the emotional body and the physical body.

The three figures of the chart correspond to the Trinity of Father (the upper figure), Son (the middle figure) and Holy Spirit. The lower figure is intended to become the temple for the Holy Spirit, which is indicated in the enfolding violet-flame action of the sacred fire. The lower figure corresponds to you as a disciple on the *Path*. Your soul is the nonpermanent aspect of being that is made permanent through the ritual of the *ascension*. The ascension is the process whereby the soul, having balanced his karma and fulfilled his divine plan, merges first with the Christ consciousness and then with the living Presence of the I AM THAT I AM. Once the ascension has taken place, the soul—the corruptible aspect of being—becomes the incorruptible one, a permanent atom in the body of God. The Chart of Your Divine Self is therefore a diagram of yourself—past, present and future.

The lower figure represents mankind evolving in the planes of Matter. This is how you should visualize yourself standing in the violet flame, which you invoke in the name of the I AM Presence and in the name of your Christ Self in order to purify your four lower bodies in preparation for the ritual of the alchemical marriage—your soul's union with the Lamb as the bride of Christ.

The lower figure is surrounded by a tube of light, which is projected from the heart of the I AM Presence in answer to your call. It is a field of fiery protection sustained in *Spirit* and in Matter for the sealing of the individuality of the disciple. The *threefold flame* within the heart is the spark of life projected from the I AM Presence through the Christ Self and anchored in the etheric planes in the secret chamber of the heart for the purpose of the soul's evolution in Matter. Also called the Christ Flame, the threefold flame is the spark of man's divinity, his potential for Godhood.

The *crystal cord* is the stream of light that descends from the heart of the I AM Presence through the Christ Self, thence to the four lower bodies to sustain the soul's vehicles of expression in time and space. It is over this cord that the energy of the Presence flows, entering the being of man at the top of the head and providing the energy for the pulsation of the threefold flame and the physical heartbeat. When a round of the soul's incarnation in Matter-form is complete, the I AM Presence withdraws the crystal cord, the threefold flame returns to the level of the Christ and the energies of the four lower bodies return to their respective planes.

The dove of the Holy Spirit descending from the heart of the Father is shown just above the head of the Christ. When the individual man, as the lower figure, puts on and becomes the Christ consciousness as Jesus did, the descent of the Holy Spirit takes place and the words of the Father (the I AM Presence) are spoken, "This is my beloved Son in whom I AM well pleased." *See also* color illustration facing page 182. (Matt. 3:17)

Chela. (Hindi *celā* from Skt. *ceṭa* 'slave,' i.e., 'servant.') In India, a disciple of a religious teacher or guru. A term used generally to refer to a student of the *Ascended Masters* and their teachings. Specifically, a student of more than ordinary self-discipline and devotion initiated by an Ascended Master and serving the cause of the *Great White Brotherhood.*

Chohan. (Tibetan for 'lord' or 'master'; a chief.) Each of the *seven rays* has a chohan who focuses the Christ consciousness of the ray, which is indeed the *Law* of the ray governing its righteous use in man. Having ensouled and demonstrated this Law of the ray throughout numerous incarnations and having taken initiations both before and after the *ascension,* the candidate is appointed to the office of chohan by the Maha Chohan, the "Great Lord," who is himself the representative of the Holy Spirit on all the rays.

The names of the chohans of the rays (each one an *Ascended Master* representing one of the seven rays to earth's evolutions) and the locations of their physical/etheric focuses follow.

First ray: El Morya, Retreat of God's Will, Darjeeling, India.

Second ray: Lanto, Royal Teton Retreat, Grand Teton, Jackson Hole, Wyoming, U.S.A.

Third ray: Paul the Venetian, Château de Liberté, southern France, with a focus of the *threefold flame* at the Washington Monument, Washington, D.C., U.S.A.

Fourth ray: Serapis Bey, the Ascension Temple and *Retreat* at Luxor, Egypt.

Fifth ray: Hilarion (the apostle Paul), Temple of Truth, Crete.

Sixth ray: Nada, Arabian Retreat, Saudi Arabia.

Seventh ray: Saint Germain, Royal Teton Retreat, Grand Teton, Wyoming, U.S.A.; Cave of Symbols, Table Mountain, Wyoming, U.S.A. Saint Germain also works out of the Great Divine Director's focuses—the Cave of Light in India and the Rakoczy Mansion in Transylvania, where Saint Germain presides as hierarch.

Christ Self. The individualized focus of "the only begotten of the Father, full of grace and truth." The *Universal Christ* individualized as the true identity of the soul; the Real Self of every man, woman and child to which the soul must rise. The Christ Self is the mediator between a man and his God. He is a man's own personal teacher, Master and prophet who officiates as high priest before the altar of the Holy of Holies *(I AM Presence)* of every man's temple made without hands.

The advent of the universal awareness of the Christ Self in God's people on earth is foretold by the prophets as the descent of The LORD Our Righteousness, also called The Branch, in the universal age at hand. When one achieves the fullness of soul-identification with the Christ Self, he is called a Christed (anointed) one, and the Son of God is seen shining through the Son of man. *See also* Chart of Your Divine Self; color illustration facing page 182. (John 1:14; Isa. 11:1; Jer. 23:5–6; 33:15–16; Zech. 3:8; 6:12)

City Foursquare. The New Jerusalem; archetype of golden-age, etheric cities of light that exist even now on the *etheric plane* (in heaven) and are waiting to be lowered into physical manifestation (on earth). Saint John the Revelator saw the descent of the Holy City as the immaculate geometry of that which is to be and now is in the invisible realms of light: "And I John saw the holy city, new Jerusalem, coming down from God out of heaven." Thus in order that this vision and prophecy be fulfilled, Jesus taught us to pray with the authority of the spoken Word, "Thy kingdom come on earth as it is in heaven!"

Metaphysically speaking, the City Foursquare is the *mandala* of the four planes and the quadrants of the *Matter* universe; the four sides of the Great Pyramid of Christ's consciousness focused in the Matter spheres. The twelve gates are gates of Christ's consciousness marking the lines and the degrees of the initiations he has prepared for his disciples. These gates are the open doors to the twelve qualities of the *Cosmic Christ* sustained by the twelve *solar hierarchies* (who are emanations of the *Universal Christ*) on behalf of all who are endued with the *Spirit*'s all-consuming fiery love, all who would in grace "enter into his gates with thanksgiving and into his courts with praise."

Unascended souls may invoke the mandala of the City Foursquare for the fulfillment of the Christ consciousness—as Above, so below. The City Foursquare contains the blueprint of the solar (soul) identity of the 144,000 archetypes of the sons and daughters of God necessary to focus the divine wholeness of God's consciousness in a given dispensation. The light of the city is emitted from the *I AM Presence;* that of the Lamb (the Cosmic Christ), from the *Christ Self.* The jewels are the 144 focuses and frequencies of light anchored in the chakras of the Cosmic Christ. (Rev. 21:2, 9–27; Ps. 100:4)

Cosmic Being. (1) An *Ascended Master* who has attained cosmic consciousness and ensouls the light/energy/consciousness of many worlds and systems of worlds across the galaxies to the Sun behind the *Great Central Sun.* (2) A being of God who has never descended below the level of the Christ, never taken physical embodiment, made human karma or engaged in sin but has remained a part of the Cosmic Virgin and holds a cosmic balance for the return of souls from the vale (veil) of sorrows to the Immaculate Heart of the Blessed Mother.

Cosmic Christ. An office in *hierarchy*, currently held by Lord Maitreya, holding the focus of the *Universal Christ* on behalf of mankind.

Cosmic Clock. The science of charting the cycles of the soul's karma and initiations under the twelve *hierarchies of the sun*. Taught by Mother Mary to Mark and Elizabeth Prophet for sons and daughters of God returning to the *Law of the One* and to their point of origin beyond the worlds of form and lesser causation. Also, the diagram representing the cycles of karma under the twelve solar hierarchies. *See also* page 261.

Cosmic Law. The *Law* that governs mathematically, yet with the spontaneity of mercy's flame, all manifestation throughout the cosmos in the planes of *Spirit* and *Matter*.

Cosmic Secret Service. *See* K-17.

Crystal cord. The stream of God's light, life and consciousness that nourishes and sustains the soul and her *four lower bodies*. Also called the silver cord. *See also* Chart of Your Divine Self; color illustration facing page 182. (Eccles. 12:6)

Darjeeling Council. A council of the *Great White Brotherhood* consisting of *Ascended Masters* and unascended *chelas,* led by El Morya and headquartered in Darjeeling, India, at the Master's *etheric retreat*. Members include Mother Mary, Kuan Yin, Archangel Michael, the Great Divine Director, Serapis Bey, Kuthumi, Djwal Kul and numerous others, whose objective is to train souls for world service in God-government and the economy, through international relations and the establishment of the inner Christ as the foundation for religion, education and a return to golden-age culture in music and the arts.

Deathless solar body. *See* Seamless garment.

Decree. *n.* a foreordaining will, an edict or fiat, an authoritative decision, declaration, a law, ordinance or religious rule; a command or commandment. *v.* to decide, to declare, to determine or order; to ordain, to command or enjoin; to invoke the presence of God, his light/energy/consciousness, his power and protection, purity and perfection.

It is written in the Book of Job, "Thou shalt decree a thing, and it shall be established unto thee: and the light shall shine upon thy ways." The decree is the most powerful of all applications to the Godhead. It is the "Command ye me" of Isaiah 45:11, the original command to light that, as the "Lux fiat," is the birthright of the sons and daughters of God. It is the authoritative Word of God spoken in man by the name of the *I AM Presence* and the living Christ to bring about constructive change on earth through the will of God and his consciousness come on earth as it is in heaven—in manifestation here below as Above.

The dynamic decree offered as praise and petition to the LORD God in the science of the spoken Word is the "effectual fervent prayer of the righteous" that availeth much. It is the means whereby the supplicant identifies with the Word of God, even the original fiat of the Creator "Let there be light: and there was light."

Through the dynamic decree spoken with joy and love, faith and hope in God's covenants fulfilled, the supplicant receives the engrafting of the Word and experiences the transmutation by the *sacred fire* of the Holy Spirit, the "trial by fire" whereby all sin, disease and death are consumed, yet the righteous soul is preserved. The decree is the alchemist's tool and technique for personal and planetary transmutation and self-transcendence. The decree may be short or long and is usually marked by a formal preamble and a closing or acceptance. (Job 22:28; James 5:16; Gen. 1:3; James 1:21; 1 Cor. 3:13–15; 1 Pet. 1:7)

Dharma. (Skt. for 'law.') The realization of the Law of selfhood through adherence to *Cosmic Law,* including the laws of nature and a spiritual code of conduct such as the way or dharma of the Buddha or the Christ. One's duty to fulfill one's reason for being through the law of love and the sacred labor.

Dictations. The messages of the *Ascended Masters,* Archangels and other advanced spiritual beings delivered through the agency of the Holy Spirit by a *Messenger* of the *Great White Brotherhood.*

Discarnate entities. *See* Entities.

Divine Monad. *See* I AM Presence.

Dweller-on-the-threshold. The anti-self, the not-self, the synthetic self, antithesis of the *Real Self,* the conglomerate of the self-created ego, ill-conceived through the inordinate use of the gift of free will. It consists of the carnal mind and a constellation of misqualified energies, forcefields, focuses, and animal magnetism comprising the subconscious mind. Man's contact with this reptilian anti-magnetic self—which is the enemy of God and his Christ and the soul's reunion with that Christ—is through the desire body (the emotional or astral body) and through the solar-plexus chakra.

The dweller-on-the-threshold is the nucleus of the vortex of energy that forms the *electronic belt.* The serpent head of the dweller is sometimes seen emerging from the black pool of the unconscious. When the sleeping serpent of the dweller is awakened by the presence of the Christ, the soul must make the freewill decision to slay, by the power of the *I AM Presence,* the self-willed anti-Christ and become the defender of the Real Self until the soul is fully reunited with that Real Self.

The dweller appears to the soul on the threshold of conscious awareness where it knocks to gain entrance into the "legitimate" realm of self-acknowledged selfhood. The dweller would enter to become the master of the house. But it is Christ and only Christ whose knock you must answer—him only must you bid enter.

The most serious initiation on the path of the disciple of Christ is the confrontation with the not-self. For if it is not slain by the soul (one with the Christ Mind), it will emerge to devour that soul in the full rage of its hatred for the light. The necessity for the teacher on the *Path* and for the Guru *Sanat Kumara* with us, physically manifest in the *Messenger* of Maitreya, is to hold the balance in the physical octave for each person as he approaches the initiation of the face-to-face encounter with the dweller-on-the-threshold.

Electronic belt, electronic circle. The electronic belt contains the negative or misqualified energy of bad karma, or "sin." It is shaped like a kettledrum and surrounds the *four lower bodies* from the waist down. The electronic circle is the repository in *Matter* of all energy ever qualified by the soul. It contains both positive and negative energy. The positive energy corresponds to the soul's good karma, the light of the *Causal Body* (the soul's treasures in heaven) in a figure-eight flow, as Above, so below.

Electronic Presence. *See* I AM Presence.

Elementals. Beings of earth, air, fire, and water; nature spirits who are the servants of God and man in the planes of *Matter* for the establishment and maintenance of the physical plane as the platform for the soul's evolution. Elementals who serve the fire element are called salamanders; those who serve the air element, sylphs; those who serve the water element, undines; those who serve the earth element, gnomes. *See also* body elemental, Elohim.

Elohim. (Plural of Heb. *'Eloah,* 'God.') One of the Hebrew names of God, or of the gods; used in the Old Testament about 2,500 times, meaning "Mighty One" or "Strong One." Elohim is a uni-plural noun referring to the *twin flames* of the Godhead that comprise the "Divine Us." When speaking specifically of either the masculine or feminine half, the plural form is retained because of the understanding that one half of the Divine Whole contains and is the androgynous Self (the Divine Us).

The Seven Mighty Elohim and their feminine counterparts

are the builders of form; hence, Elohim is the name of God used in the first verse of the Bible, "In the beginning God created the heaven and the earth." Serving directly under the Elohim are the four beings of the elements (the four cosmic forces) who have dominion over the *elementals.*

The Seven Mighty Elohim are the "seven Spirits of God" named in Revelation and the "morning stars" that sang together in the beginning, as the LORD revealed them to his servant Job. There are also five Elohim who surround the white fire core of the *Great Central Sun.* In the order of *hierarchy,* the Elohim and *Cosmic Beings* carry the greatest concentration (the highest vibration) of light that we can comprehend in our state of evolution.

With the four beings of nature, their consorts and the elemental builders of form, they represent the power of our Father as the Creator (the blue ray). The Seven Archangels and their divine complements, the great seraphim, cherubim and all the angelic hosts represent the love of God in the fiery intensity of the Holy Ghost (the pink ray). The Seven Chohans of the Rays and all *Ascended Masters,* together with unascended sons and daughters of God, represent the wisdom of the *Law* of the Logos under the office of the Son (the yellow ray). These three kingdoms form a triad of manifestation, working in balance to step down the energies of the Trinity. The intonation of the sacred sound "Elohim" releases the tremendous power of their God Self-awareness stepped down for our blessed use through the *Cosmic Christ.*

Following are the names of the Seven Elohim, the rays they serve on and the locations of their *etheric retreats.*

First ray: Hercules and Amazonia, Half Dome, Sierra Nevada, Yosemite National Park, California, U.S.A.

Second ray: Apollo and Lumina, western lower Saxony, Germany.

Third ray: Heros and Amora, Lake Winnipeg, Canada.

Fourth ray: Purity and Astrea, near Gulf of Archangel, southeast arm of White Sea, Russia.

Fifth ray: Cyclopea and Virginia, Altai Range where China, Siberia and Mongolia meet, near Tabun Bogdo.

Sixth ray: Peace and Aloha, Hawaiian Islands.

Seventh ray, Arcturus and Victoria, near Luanda, Angola, Africa. (Rev. 1:4; 3:1; 4:5; 5:6; Job 38:7)

Entities. Conglomerates of misqualified energy or disembodied individuals who have chosen to embody evil. Entities that are focuses of sinister forces may attack disembodied as well as embodied individuals. There are many different kinds of discarnate entities, including entities of liquor, marijuana, tobacco, death, sex and self-infatuation, sensuality, selfishness and self-love, suicide, anger, gossip, fear, insanity, depression, lust of money, gambling, weeping, various chemicals (including fluoride and sugar), horror, condemnation and sentimentality.

Etheric cities. *See* Etheric plane.

Etheric plane. The highest plane in the dimension of *Matter;* a plane that is as concrete and real as the physical plane (and more so) but is experienced through the senses of the soul in a dimension and a consciousness beyond physical awareness. The plane on which the *akashic records* of mankind's entire evolution register individually and collectively. It is the world of *Ascended Masters* and their *retreats,* etheric cities of light where souls of a higher order of evolution abide between embodiments. It is the plane of reality.

Here the golden age is in progress, love is the fullness of God's presence everywhere, and angels and elementals together with God's children serve in harmony to manifest Christ's kingdom in the universal age, worlds without end. As such it is the plane of transition between the earth/heaven realms and the kingdom of God, *Spirit,* or the Absolute. The lower etheric plane overlaps the astral/mental/physical belts. It is contaminated by these lower worlds occupied by the *false hierarchy* and the mass consciousness it controls, including its matrices and emotions.

Etheric retreats. *See* Etheric temples.

Etheric temples. Retreats of the *Ascended Masters* focused in the *etheric plane* or in the plane of the earth; anchoring points for cosmic energies and flames of God; places where the Ascended Masters train their *chelas* and to which the souls of mankind travel while out of their physical bodies.

False hierarchy. Beings who have rebelled against God and his Christ, including fallen angels, devils and the powers and principalities of Darkness who personify *Evil* (the *e*nergy *veil*). Those who deify and are the embodiment of Absolute Evil are referred to by the generic term "devil." Members of the false hierarchy referred to in scripture include Lucifer, Satan, the Antichrist, Serpent, and the accuser of the brethren.

Feminine ray. The light-emanation that comes forth from the *Mother* aspect of God.

Flaming Yod. A sun center, a focus of perfection, of God consciousness. The flaming Yod is the capacity of divinity within you to transform your being into an outpost of your Mighty *I AM Presence*.

Four lower bodies. The four lower bodies are four sheaths consisting of four distinct frequencies that surround the soul—the physical, emotional, mental and etheric, providing vehicles for the soul in her journey through time and space. The etheric sheath (highest in vibration) is the gateway to the three higher bodies: the *Christ Self*, the *I AM Presence* and the *Causal Body. See also* Chart of Your Divine Self; color illustration facing page 182.

Great Central Sun. Also called the Great Hub. The center of cosmos; the point of integration of the *Spirit/Matter* cosmos; the point of origin of all physical/spiritual creation; the nucleus or white fire core of the cosmic egg. (Sirius, the God Star, is the focus of the Great Central Sun in our sector of the galaxy.)

The Sun behind the sun is the spiritual Cause behind the physical effect we see as our own physical sun and all other stars and star systems, seen or unseen, including the Great Central Sun. The Sun behind the sun of cosmos is perceived as the *Cosmic Christ*—the Word by whom the formless was endowed with form and spiritual worlds were draped with physicality.

Likewise, the Sun behind the sun is the Son of God individualized in the *Christ Self*, shining in all his splendor behind the soul and its interpenetrating sheaths of consciousness called the *four lower bodies*. It is the Son of man—the "Sun" of every *man*ifestation of God. The Sun behind the sun is referred to as the "Sun of righteousness," which heals the mind, illumines the soul and lights all her house. As "the glory of God," it is the light of the *City Foursquare*. (Mal. 4:2; Rev. 21:23)

Great Hub. *See* Great Central Sun.

Great White Brotherhood. A spiritual order of Western saints and Eastern adepts who have reunited with the *Spirit* of the living God and who comprise the heavenly hosts. They have transcended the cycles of karma and rebirth and ascended (accelerated) into that higher reality which is the eternal abode of the soul. The *Ascended Masters* of the Great White Brotherhood, united for the highest purposes of the brotherhood of man under the Fatherhood of God, have risen in every age from every culture and religion to inspire creative achievement in education, the arts and sciences, God-government and the abundant life through the economies of the nations.

The word "white" refers not to race but to the aura (halo) of white light surrounding their forms. The Brotherhood also includes in its ranks certain unascended *chelas* of the Ascended Masters. Jesus Christ revealed this heavenly order of saints "robed in white" to his servant John in Revelation. *See also* Hierarchy. (Rev. 3:4–5; 6:9–11; 7:9, 13–14; 19:14)

Hierarchies of the sun. *Cosmic Beings* forming a ring of cosmic consciousness around the *Great Central Sun*. Each of the twelve hierarchies, one for each line of the *Cosmic Clock*, comprises millions of Cosmic Beings who ensoul the virtue of a line of the

Clock. For example, the hierarchy of Capricorn focuses the virtue of God-power; the hierarchy of Aquarius focuses the virtue of God-love, and so on.

Each month you are given the torch and the flame of a hierarchy of the sun according to your cycles on the Cosmic Clock. You carry that flame through a set of initiations under that hierarchy. Thus for example, during the month that you are on the twelve o'clock line, you would be taking the initiations of God-power, and you would be tested in how well you can refrain from engaging in criticism, condemnation or judgment. *See also* Appendix.

Hierarchy. The universal chain of individualized God-free beings fulfilling the attributes and aspects of God's infinite Selfhood. Included in the cosmic hierarchical scheme are *Solar Logoi, Elohim,* Sons and Daughters of God, ascended and unascended Masters with their circles of *chelas, Cosmic Beings,* the twelve *hierarchies of the sun,* Archangels and angels of the sacred fire, children of the light, nature spirits (called *elementals*) and *twin flames* of the *Alpha/Omega* polarity sponsoring planetary and galactic systems.

This universal order of the Father's own Self-expression is the means whereby God in the *Great Central Sun* steps down the Presence and power of his universal being/consciousness in order that succeeding evolutions in time and space, from the least unto the greatest, might come to know the wonder of his love. The level of one's spiritual/physical attainment—measured by one's balanced self-awareness "hid with Christ in God" and demonstrating his *Law,* by his love, in the Spirit/Matter cosmos—is the criterion establishing one's placement on this ladder of life called hierarchy.

In the third century, Origen of Alexandria set forth his conception of a hierarchy of beings, ranging from angels to human beings to demons and beasts. This renowned scholar and theologian of the early Church, who set forth the chief cornerstone of Christ's doctrine and upon whose works subsequent Church

Fathers, doctors and theologians built their traditions, taught that souls are assigned to their respective offices and duties based on previous actions and merits, and that each one has the opportunity to ascend or descend in rank.

Many beings of the heavenly hierarchy are named in the Book of Revelation. Apart from the *false hierarchy* of Antichrist, including the reprobate angels, some of the members of the *Great White Brotherhood* accounted for by Jesus are *Alpha and Omega,* the seven Spirits, the angels of the seven churches, the Four and Twenty Elders, the four beasts, the saints robed in white, the two witnesses, the God of the earth, the woman clothed with the sun and her manchild, Archangel Michael and his angels, the Lamb and his wife, the 144,000 who have the Father's name written in their foreheads, the angel of the Everlasting Gospel, the seven angels (i.e., the Archangels of the *seven rays*) which stood before God, the angel clothed with a cloud and a rainbow upon his head, the seven thunders, the Faithful and True and his armies, and he that sat upon the great white throne. *See also* Elohim. (Rev. 1:4, 8, 11, 20; 2:1, 8, 12, 18; 3:1, 4–5, 7, 14; 4:2–10; 5:2, 6, 11; 6:9–11; 7:1–2, 9, 13–14; 8:2; 10:1, 3, 7; 11:3–4; 12:1, 5, 7; 14:1, 3–6, 14–19; 15:1; 16:1–4, 8, 10, 12, 17; 17:1; 18:1, 21; 19:4, 7, 11–17; 20:1; 21:6, 9; 22:13)

Human monad. The entire forcefield of self, the interconnecting spheres of influences—hereditary, environmental, karmic—which make up that self-awareness which identifies itself as human. The reference point of lesser awareness or nonawareness, out of which all mankind must evolve to the realization of the Real Self as the *Christ Self.*

I AM Presence. The I AM THAT I AM; the individualized Presence of God focused for each individual soul. The God-identity of the individual; the Divine Monad; the individual Source. The origin of the soul focused in the planes of *Spirit* just above the physical form; the personification of the God Flame for the individual. *See also* Chart of Your Divine Self; see color illustration facing page 182. (Exod. 3:13–15)

K-17. Head of the Cosmic Secret Service. Referred to as "Friend," he takes on a physical body when assisting members of the various secret services of the nations of the world. His protective forcefield is a "ring-pass-not," a ring of white fire that may be tinged with the colors of the rays according to the requirement of the hour. He draws this circle of living flame around individuals and places to protect and to seal the identity and forcefield of those dedicated to the service of the light.

Both K-17 and his sister were able to sustain life in their physical bodies for over 300 years prior to their *ascensions* in the 1930s. Continuing their evolution and service to mankind, they now maintain a villa in Paris and focuses in other parts of the world for the training of unascended masters. K-17 and the legions in his command should be called upon to expose by the power of the All-Seeing Eye of God forces and plots that would undermine Saint Germain's plan for God-government in the golden age. K-17's flame is teal green and white.

Kali yuga. Sanskrit term in Hindu mystic philosophy for the last and worst of the four yugas (world ages), characterized by strife, discord and moral deterioration.

Karmic Board. *See* Lords of Karma.

Keeper of the Flame. (1) The title given to the Lord Maha Chohan, "the Great Lord," in the order of *hierarchy* of the Great White Brotherhood. Also known as the representative of the Holy Spirit, the Maha Chohan serves mankind by fanning the *threefold flame* of life anchored in the heart. He is present at every birth to ignite the threefold flame for that embodiment, and at every death to withdraw the threefold flame from the physical body. (2) A member of the *Keepers of the Flame Fraternity*.

Keepers of the Flame Fraternity. An organization of *Ascended Masters* and their *chelas* who vow to keep the flame of life on earth and support the activities of the *Great White Brotherhood* in the establishment of their community and mystery school and in the dissemination of their teachings. Founded in 1961 by Saint Germain. Keepers of the Flame receive graded lessons in *Cosmic Law* dictated by the Ascended Masters to their *Messengers* Mark and Elizabeth Prophet.

Lady Master Venus. *Twin flame* of Sanat Kumara. The focus of Lady Master Venus and her flame of beauty were anchored on the continent of Europe where the city of Vienna, Austria, stands today. It was through the ray anchored there that many of the Venusians embodied, bringing their culture with them. The German spelling of Vienna is "Wien," pronounced like the first three letters of "Venus." Not only the name, but also the culture, the art and the romantic feeling of this city of dreams are reminiscent of the planetary home of its founder. *See also* Sanat Kumara.

Laggards. *See* Maldek.

Law. In this book, we draw a distinction between the words "Law" and "law." When capitalized, "Law" refers to the blueprint of God's being, activated through the *lifestream* (the stream of light) that flows through the heart of the Holy *Christ Self,* who ministers to the evolving soul. When lowercased, law refers to the precepts of God's Law as it applies to a particular time and place.

Law of the One. The property of God's wholeness that allows the body of God to be broken—as Jesus demonstrated at the Last Supper—yet still remain the One. In this manner, the Son of God can be personified in each child of God in the person of the Holy *Christ Self.* Through this light, every soul can accept the option to become the son of God, to unite with Christ and ascend back to God's heart, the heart of their own Mighty *I AM Presence.*

Lifestream. The stream of life that comes forth from the one Source, from the *I AM Presence* in the planes of *Spirit,* and descends to the planes of *Matter* where it manifests as the *threefold flame* anchored in the *secret chamber of the heart* for the sustainment of the soul in Matter and the nourishment of the *four lower* *bodies.* Used to denote souls evolving as individual "lifestreams" and hence synonymous with the term "individual." Denotes the ongoing nature of the individual through cycles of individualization.

Lifewave. *See* Manu.

Lodestone. The focus of the Father, of the masculine ray of the Godhead, which anchors the energies of *Spirit* in *Matter* at the crown chakra.

Logos. (Gk. for 'word,' 'speech,' 'reason'—the divine wisdom manifest in the creation.) According to ancient Greek philosophy, it is the controlling principle in the universe. The Book of John identifies the Word, or Logos, with Jesus Christ: "And the Word was made flesh and dwelt among us." Hence, Jesus Christ is seen as the embodiment of divine reason, the Word Incarnate.

Out of the word Logos, we derive the word logic, defined as "the science of the formal principles of reasoning." From logic comes geometry and the unfoldment and the articulation of the original Word of God as it is broken down into language and subject matter for the clear communication of knowledge. Thus, all knowledge is based on the original Word (with a capital W). Communicators of the original knowledge, which is the Logos, are communicators of the Word.

The Word also means Shakti, which is a Sanskrit term for 'energy,' 'power,' 'force.' Shakti is the dynamic, creative force of the universe—the feminine principle of the Godhead, who releases the potential of God from *Spirit* to *Matter.* Jesus Christ, the Word Incarnate, is also the Shakti of God. We see, then, that "to communicate the Word" is to communicate the original knowledge of God passed to man through his feminine aspect. It is also to communicate self-knowledge. In communicating this knowledge, we become conveyors of the Word and instruments of the Word.

Lords of Karma. The Ascended Beings who comprise the Karmic Board. Their names and the rays that they represent on the board are as follows: first ray, the Great Divine Director; second ray, the Goddess of Liberty; third ray, the Ascended Lady Master Nada; fourth ray, the Elohim Cyclopea; fifth ray, Pallas Athena, Goddess of Truth; sixth ray, Portia, the Goddess of Justice; seventh ray, Kuan Yin, Goddess of Mercy. Vairochana also sits on the Karmic Board.

The Lords of Karma dispense justice to this system of worlds, adjudicating karma, mercy and judgment on behalf of every *lifestream*. All souls must pass before the Karmic Board before and after each incarnation on earth, receiving their assignment and karmic allotment for each lifetime beforehand and the review of their performance at its conclusion.

Through the Keeper of the Scrolls and the recording angels, the Lords of Karma have access to the complete records of every lifestream's incarnations on earth. They determine who shall embody, as well as when and where. They assign souls to families and communities, measuring out the weights of karma that must be balanced as the "jot and tittle" of the *Law*. The Karmic Board, acting in consonance with the individual *I AM Presence* and *Christ Self,* determines when the soul has earned the right to be free from the wheel of karma and the round of rebirth. The Lords of Karma meet at the Royal Teton Retreat twice yearly, at winter and summer solstice, to review petitions from unascended mankind and to grant dispensations for their assistance.

Macrocosm. (Gk. for 'great world.') The larger cosmos; the entire warp and woof of creation, which we call the cosmic egg. Also used to contrast man as the *microcosm,* 'the little world,' against the backdrop of the larger world in which he lives.

Maldek. Once a planet in our solar system. The dark forces destroyed Maldek through the same tactics that today's manipulators use on earth to degrade the consciousness of the people. Its life-waves waged a war ending in nuclear annihilation; the asteroid belt between Mars and Jupiter is what remains of the planet. The laggards are souls who came to earth from Maldek.

Mandala. (Skt. for 'circle,' 'sphere.') A group, company or assembly; a circle of friends; an assembly or gathering of Buddhas and Bodhisattvas. Also a circular design containing images of deities symbolizing the universe, totality, or wholeness; used in meditation by Hindus and Buddhists.

Manu. (Skt.) The progenitor and lawgiver of the evolutions of God on earth. The Manu and his divine complement are ascended *twin flames* assigned by the Father-Mother God to sponsor and ensoul the Christic image for a certain evolution or lifewave known as a root race—souls who embody as a group and have a unique archetypal pattern, divine plan and mission to fulfill on earth.

According to esoteric tradition, there are seven primary aggregations of souls—that is, the first to the seventh root races. The first three root races lived in purity and innocence upon earth in three golden ages before the fall of Adam and Eve. Through obedience to *Cosmic Law* and total identification with the *Real Self*, these three root races won their immortal freedom and ascended from earth.

It was during the time of the fourth root race, on the continent of Lemuria, that the allegorical Fall took place under the influence of the fallen angels known as Serpents (because they used the serpentine spinal energies to beguile the soul, or female principle in mankind, as a means to their end of lowering the masculine potential, thereby emasculating the Sons of God).

The fourth, fifth and sixth root races (the latter soul group not having entirely descended into physical incarnation) remain in embodiment on earth today. Lord Himalaya and his Beloved are the Manus for the fourth root race, Vaivasvata Manu and his consort are the Manus for the fifth root race and the God and Goddess Meru are the Manus for the sixth root race. The seventh root race is destined to incarnate on the continent of South America in the Aquarian age under their Manus, the Great Divine Director and his divine complement.

The Manus are beloved God-parents who respond instantaneously to the call of their children. The comforting presence of their light is endued with such great power/wisdom/love as to quiver the ethers and make each little one feel at home in the arms of God even in the darkest hour.

Manvantara. (Skt., from *maver* 'man' + *antara* 'interval,' 'period of time.') In Hinduism, one of the fourteen intervals that constitute a kalpa—the duration of time from the origination to the destruction of a world system (a cosmic cycle). In Hindu cosmology, the universe is continually evolving through periodic cycles of creation and dissolution. Creation is said to occur during the outbreath of the God of Creation, Brahma; dissolution occurs during his inbreath.

Masculine ray. The light-emanation that comes forth from the Father aspect of God.

Matter. The feminine (negative) polarity of the masculine (positive) *Spirit*. Matter acts as a chalice for the kingdom of God and is the abiding place of evolving souls who identify with their Lord, their Holy *Christ Self*. Matter is distinguished from matter (lowercase m)—the substance of the earth earthy, of the realms of *maya*, which blocks rather than radiates divine light and the Spirit of the I AM THAT I AM. *See also* Mother.

Maya. (Skt., 'illusion,' 'deception,' 'appearance.') Something created or fabricated, not ultimately real; the impermanent phenomenal world viewed as reality; the principle of relativity and duality by which the one reality appears as the manifold universe. The *Ascended Masters* teach that maya is the veil of misqualified energy that man imposes upon *Matter* through his misuse of the *sacred fire*.

Messenger. Evangelist; one who goes before the angels bearing to the people of earth the good news of the gospel of Jesus Christ and, at the appointed time, the Everlasting Gospel. The Messengers of the *Great White Brotherhood* are anointed by the *hierarchy* as their apostles ("one sent on a mission"). They deliver through the *dictations* (prophecies) of the *Ascended Masters* the testi-

mony and lost teachings of Jesus Christ in the power of the
Holy Spirit to the seed of Christ, the lost sheep of the house of
Israel, and to every nation. A Messenger is trained by an
Ascended Master to receive by various methods the words, con-
cepts, teachings and messages of the Great White Brotherhood.
One who delivers the *Law,* the prophecies and the dispensations
of God for a people and an age. (Rev. 14:6; Matt. 10:6; 15:24)

Microcosm. (Gk. for 'small world.') (1) The world of the individual,
his *four lower bodies,* his aura and the forcefield of his karma.
(2) The planet. *See also* Macrocosm.

Mother. The feminine polarity of the Godhead, the manifestation of
God as Mother. Alternate terms: "Divine Mother," "Universal
Mother" and "Cosmic Virgin." *Matter* is the feminine polarity
of *Spirit,* and the term is used interchangeably with Mater (Lat.
meaning 'mother'). In this context, the entire material cosmos
becomes the womb of creation into which Spirit projects the
energies of life. Matter, then, is the womb of the Cosmic Virgin,
who, as the other half of the Divine Whole, also exists in Spirit
as the spiritual polarity of God.

   Jesus himself recognized *Alpha and Omega* as the highest
representatives of the Father-Mother God and often referred to
Alpha as Father and to Omega as Mother. Those who assume
the feminine polarity of consciousness after the *ascension* are
known as Ascended Lady Masters. Together with all feminine
(femininely polarized) beings in the octaves of light, they focus
the flame of the Divine Mother on behalf of the evolutions of
mankind evolving in many systems of worlds. However, being
androgynous, all of the heavenly host focus any of the masculine
or feminine attributes of the Godhead at will, for they have
entered the spheres of the divine wholeness. *See also* Matter.

Mother of the Flame. An office in *hierarchy.* Clara Louise Kieninger
was anointed by Saint Germain as the first Mother of the Flame
when the *Keepers of the Flame Fraternity* was founded in 1961.
For years she kept a daily vigil of morning meditation, beginning

at 5 a.m. and continuing her prayers for two to four hours on behalf of the youth, the incoming children, their parents and teachers. She became Regent Mother of the Flame when the mantle of Mother of the Flame was passed to Elizabeth Clare Prophet on April 9, 1966. Clara Louise Kieninger made her ascension at the age of 87 from Berkeley, California, on October 25, 1970.

On January 1, 1973, Gautama Buddha announced that the Ascended Lady Master Clara Louise would, "ere the night pass, give to the present Mother of the Flame a torch charged with the vital fires from God's heavenly altar and the conveyance of a vast mission to illumine the world's children and produce the blessing of true culture to the age and unto all people everywhere."

Omega. *See* Alpha and Omega.

The Path. The strait gate and narrow way that leadeth unto life. The path of initiation whereby the disciple who pursues the Christ consciousness overcomes step-by-step the limitations of selfhood in time and space and attains reunion with reality through the ritual of the *ascension*. (Matt. 7:14)

Real Self. *See* Christ Self.

Reembodiment. Alternate term for reincarnation: the action of reincarnation; the state of being reincarnated. Rebirth in new bodies or forms of life, especially a rebirth of a soul in a new human body. The soul continues to return to the physical plane in a new body temple until it has balanced its karma, has attained self-mastery, has overcome the cycles of time and space and finally reunites with the *I AM Presence* through the ritual of the *ascension*.

Retreats. *See* Etheric temples.

Root race. *See* Manu.

Sacred fire. The Kundalini fire that lies as the coiled serpent in the base-of-the-spine chakra and rises through spiritual purity and self-mastery to the crown chakra, quickening the spiritual centers on the way. God, light, life, energy, the I AM THAT I AM. "Our God is a consuming fire." The sacred fire is the precipitation of the Holy Ghost for the baptism of souls, for purification, for alchemy and transmutation, and for the realization of the *ascension,* the sacred ritual whereby the soul returns to the One, the *I AM Presence.* (Heb. 12:29)

Sanat Kumara. The Ancient of Days, who volunteered to come to the earth thousands of years ago from his home on Venus. At that time, cosmic councils had decreed the dissolution of the earth, so great was mankind's departure from *Cosmic Law.* The Solar Lords had determined that no further opportunity should be granted humanity, who had willfully ignored and forgotten the God Flame within their hearts. The requirement of the *Law* for the saving of Terra was that one who qualified as the embodied Lamb be present in the physical octave to hold the balance and keep the *threefold flame* of life for and on behalf of every living soul. Sanat Kumara offered to be that one.

In his April 8, 1979, *Pearl of Wisdom,* Sanat Kumara told the story of how Venusian devotees volunteered to accompany him and embody among mankind to assist him to keep the flame: "The joy of opportunity was mingled with the sorrow that the sense of separation brings. I had chosen a voluntary exile upon a dark star. And though it was destined to be Freedom's Star, all knew it would be for me a long dark night of the soul.

"Then all at once from the valleys and the mountains there appeared a great gathering of my children. It was the souls of the hundred and forty and four thousand approaching our palace of light. They spiraled nearer and nearer as twelve companies singing the song of freedom, of love and of victory.... As we watched from the balcony, *Lady Master Venus* and I, we saw the thirteenth company robed in white. It was the royal priesthood of the Order of Melchizedek....

"When all of their numbers had assembled, ring upon ring upon ring surrounding our home, and their hymn of praise and adoration to me was concluded, their spokesman stood before the balcony to address us on behalf of the great multitude. It was the soul of the one you know and love today as the Lord of the World, Gautama Buddha.

"And he addressed us, saying, 'O Ancient of Days, we have heard of the covenant that God hath made with thee this day and of thy commitment to keep the flame of life until some among earth's evolutions should be quickened and once again renew their vow to be bearers of the flame. O Ancient of Days, thou art to us our guru, our very life, our God. We will not leave thee comfortless. We will go with thee.'"

Thus they came to the earth with Sanat Kumara and legions of angels, preceded by another retinue of lightbearers who prepared the way and established the retreat of Shamballa—"City of White"—on an island in the Gobi Sea (now the Gobi Desert).

There Sanat Kumara anchored the focus of the threefold flame, establishing the initial thread of contact with all on earth by extending rays of light from his heart to their own. And there the volunteers from Venus embodied in dense veils of flesh to see the earth's evolutions through unto the victory of their vow.

The first from among these unascended lightbearers to respond to the call of Sanat Kumara from the physical octave was Gautama, and with him was Maitreya. Both pursued the path of the Bodhisattva unto Buddhahood, Gautama finishing the course first and Maitreya second. Thus the two became Sanat Kumara's foremost disciples, the first ultimately succeeding him in the office of Lord of the World, the second as *Cosmic Christ* and Planetary Buddha. *See also* Lady Master Venus.

Seamless garment. Light substance from the Son (sun) of God woven as the robe of consciousness worn by a Christed one. The Holy Spirit, as a great unifying coordinator, weaves the seamless garment from threads of God's light and love. The Maha Chohan teaches: "The shuttle of God's attention upon man drives forth radiant beams of descending light, scintillating fragments of purity and happiness toward earth and into the hearts of his children, whilst the tender risings of men's hopes, aspirations, invocations and calls for assistance do pursue the Deity in his mighty haven of cosmic purity."

Jesus likens weaving the seamless garment to preparing for a marriage: "To each man and each woman there is given the opportunity to prepare for the *ascension*. And none is deprived of the privilege of making himself ready. As a bride makes ready for her wedding day, filling the hope chest with the most precious linens and embroideries, so the soul makes ready for her reunion by garnering floral virtues, flame qualities that she appliqués upon the seamless garment. And none may participate in the marriage feast without a wedding garment."

Of this garment, Serapis Bey says: "When man functions under divine direction and activity either in or out of the body, he takes the energy dispensed to him that in ignorance might have been misused and creates instead a great body of light called the immaculate seamless garment of the living Christ, which will one day become the great spherical deathless solar body."

Second death. The complete canceling-out of identity, which takes place at the Court of the Sacred Fire on the God Star Sirius. This is the lot of souls who have entirely turned the light that God has invested in them to darkness. In the second death, all that ever was of the individual—cause, effect, record and memory of both the soul and its creations, including the *dweller-on-the-threshold*—is dissolved in the white fire of *Alpha and Omega*. The soul is self-canceled by its own denial of being in God. (Rev. 2:11; 20:6, 11–15; 21:7–8.)

Secret chamber of the heart. The sanctuary of meditation, the place to which the souls of lightbearers withdraw. It is the nucleus of life where the individual stands face-to-face with the inner Guru, the beloved Holy *Christ Self*, and receives the soul testings that precede the alchemical union with that Christ Self—the marriage of the Bride (the soul who becomes the Lamb's wife).

It is the place where the laws of cosmos are written in the inward parts of man, for the *Law* is inscribed as the Eightfold Path of the Buddha upon the inner walls of the chamber. The eight petals of this secondary heart chamber (the eighth-ray chakra) symbolize the mastery of the seven rays through the flame of the Christ, the *threefold flame,* and the integration of that mastery in the eighth ray.

Seed atom. The focus of the Divine Mother (the feminine ray of the Godhead) that anchors the energies of *Spirit* in *Matter* at the base-of-the-spine chakra.

Seven rays. The light emanations of the Godhead. The seven rays of the white light that emerge through the prism of the Christ consciousness concentrating particular gifts, graces and principles of self-awareness in the *Logos* that can be developed through one's life calling. Each ray focuses a frequency or color, and specific qualities: (1) blue—faith, will, power, perfection and protection; (2) yellow—wisdom, understanding, enlightenment, intelligence and illumination; (3) pink—compassion, kindness, charity, love and beauty; (4) white—purity, discipline, order and joy; (5) green—truth, science, healing, music, abundance and vision; (6) purple and gold—ministration, service, peace and brotherhood; (7) violet—freedom, mercy, justice, transmutation and forgiveness.

The *Ascended Masters* teach that each of the seven rays of God is magnified one day of the week: Monday, the pink ray; Tuesday, the blue ray; Wednesday, the green ray; Thursday, the purple-and-gold ray; Friday, the white ray; Saturday, the violet ray; Sunday, the yellow ray.

The seven rays of the Elohim, the builders of form, are enshrined at the Royal Teton Retreat, an ancient focus of light congruent with the Grand Teton in Wyoming. The rays are concentrated and anchored in a large image of the All-Seeing Eye of God located in a council hall of the retreat.

Solar hierarchies. *See* Hierarchies of the sun.

Solar Logoi. *Cosmic Beings* who transmit the light emanations of the Godhead flowing from *Alpha and Omega* in the *Great Central Sun* to the planetary systems. In this capacity, they determine what quotient of light can be entrusted to the evolutions of earth.

Spirit. The masculine polarity of the Godhead; the coordinate of *Matter;* God as Father, who of necessity includes within the polarity of himself God as *Mother* and hence is known as the Father-Mother God. The plane of the *I AM Presence,* of perfection; the dwelling place of the *Ascended Masters* in the kingdom of God. (When lowercased, as in "spirits," the term is synonymous with discarnates, or astral *entities.* Singular and lowercased, "spirit" is used interchangeably with "soul.")

Threefold flame. The flame of the Christ that is the spark of life that burns within the *secret chamber of the heart* (a secondary chakra within the heart). The sacred trinity of power, wisdom and love that is the manifestation of the *sacred fire.*

Twin flame. The soul's masculine or feminine counterpart conceived out of the same white fire body, the fiery ovoid of the *I AM Presence.*

Universal Christ. The mediator between the planes of *Spirit* and the planes of *Matter.* Personified as the *Christ Self,* he is the mediator between the Spirit of God and the soul of man. The Universal Christ sustains the nexus of (the figure-eight flow of) consciousness through which the energies of the Father (Spirit) pass to his children for the crystallization (Christ-realization) of the God Flame by their souls' strivings in the cosmic womb (matrix) of the *Mother* (Matter).

The fusion of the energies of the positive and negative polarity of the Godhead in the creation takes place through the Universal Christ, the *Logos* without whom "was not any thing made that was made." The flow of light from the *Macrocosm* to the *microcosm,* from the Spirit (the *I AM Presence*) to the soul and back again over the figure-eight spiral, is fulfilled through this blessed mediator who is Christ the LORD, the true incarnation of the I AM THAT I AM.

The term "Christ" or "Christed one" also denotes an office in *hierarchy* held by those who have attained self-mastery on the *seven rays* and the seven chakras of the Holy Spirit. Christ-mastery includes the balancing of the *threefold flame*—the divine attributes of power, wisdom and love—for the harmonization of consciousness and the implementation of the mastery of the seven rays in the chakras and in the *four lower bodies* through the Mother Flame (raised Kundalini).

Expanding the consciousness of the Christ, the Christed one moves on to attain the realization of the Christ consciousness at a planetary level and is able to hold the balance of the Christ Flame on behalf of the evolutions of the planet. When this is achieved, he assists members of the heavenly hierarchy who serve under the office of the World Teachers and the planetary Christ. *See also* Chart of Your Divine Self; color illustration facing page 182. (John 1:1–14; 14:20, 23. Compare Rev. 3:8; Matt. 28:18; Rev. 1:18.)

Violet flame. Seventh-ray aspect of the Holy Spirit. The *sacred fire* that transmutes the cause, effect, record and memory of sin, or negative karma. Also called the flame of transmutation, of freedom, and of forgiveness. It is invoked by the spoken Word with visualizations for the transmutation of negative personal and planetary karma. *See also* Decree.

Word. *See* Logos; Decree.

Yod. *See* Flaming Yod.

Index

For More Information

Summit University Press books are available at fine bookstores everywhere, including Barnes & Noble, B. Dalton Booksellers, Borders, Hastings, Waldenbooks and your favorite on-line bookstore.

If you would like a free catalog of Summit University Press books, please call 1-888-700-8087 or write Summit University Press, PO Box 5000, Corwin Springs, MT 59030-5000 USA. Fax 1-800-221-8307 (406-848-9555 outside the U.S.A.). E-mail us at tslinfo@tsl.org

Other Titles from

SUMMIT UNIVERSITY ☯ PRESS®

*Saint Germain's
Prophecy for the New Millennium*

The Lost Years of Jesus

The Lost Teachings of Jesus

*Climb the Highest Mountain:
The Path of the Higher Self*

Foundations of the Path

Kabbalah: Key to Your Inner Power

*Reincarnation:
The Missing Link in Christianity*

Understanding Yourself

Messages from Heaven

Forbidden Mysteries of Enoch

Sacred Psychology of Love

The Human Aura

Saint Germain On Alchemy

The Path to Your Ascension

Quietly Comes the Buddha

POCKET GUIDES
TO PRACTICAL SPIRITUALITY:

How to Work with Angels

Creative Abundance

Soul Mates and Twin Flames

The Creative Power of Sound

Access the Power of Your Higher Self

Violet Flame to Heal Body, Mind and Soul

Summit University Press books are available at fine bookstores everywhere.

Mark L. Prophet and Elizabeth Clare Prophet are pioneers of modern spirituality. They are the authors of several best-selling books, such as *Saint Germain's Prophecy for the New Millennium*, *The Lost Years of Jesus*, *The Lost Teachings of Jesus*, *Saint Germain On Alchemy* and *Understanding Yourself*. Their books have been translated into fifteen languages.

The Prophets have also conducted seminars and workshops worldwide. Mark passed on in 1973 and Elizabeth has carried on their work.

Mrs. Prophet has been featured on NBC's "Ancient Prophecies" and has talked about her work on "Donahue," "Larry King Live!" "Nightline," "Sonya Live" and "CNN & Company."